SEARCHING FOR EVERARDO

SEARCHING

FOR

EVERARDO

A Story of Love, War,
and the CIA in Guatemala

Jennifer K. Harbury

WARNER BOOKS

A Time Warner Company

AUTHOR'S NOTE: In some instances I have changed the names and identifying details of persons and places, in order to protect my friends and all those who bravely helped me despite the risks.

Copyright ©1997 by The Everardo Foundation
All rights reserved.

(w) Warner Books, Inc., 1271 Avenue of the Americas, New York, NY 10020

Printed in the United States of America

Library of Congress Cataloging-in-Publication Data
Harbury, Jennifer
    Searching for Everado : a story of love, war, and the CIA in
Guatemala / Jennifer K. Harbury.
       p.   cm.
    ISBN 0-446-52036-5
    1. Everado, 1957–   . 2. Guerrillas—Guatemala—Biography.
3. Mayas—Guatemala—Biography.   4. Guatemala—Politics and
government—1985–   5. Government, Resistance to—Guatemala.
6. Harbury, Jennifer.   7. Women human rights workers—United States—
Biography.   8. Women human rights workers—Guatemala—Biography.
9. Americans—Guatemala—Biography.   I. Title.
F1466.7.E84H3   1997
972.8105'3'0922—dc20
    [b]   96-42028
                                                              CIP

Book design: H. Roberts

This book is dedicated to you, Everardo.
We, the living, will never forget.

Acknowledgments

Happily, there have been so many people who have befriended and supported me throughout these long and difficult four years that I could not possibly name them all here. You know who you are and I send you my thanks and *abrazos*, you who came to sit with me during the long hunger strikes, you who picked up the telephone and called Congress and the White House day after day, you who sent me funds and cards and gifts and love. You opened my eyes and I will remember, always. Without you, neither I nor this book would exist.

I wish to send my special thanks to Jose and America, Pat and Dianna and Alice, the Assisi community, and my family. My Texas gang always gets a special hug. To Mike Wallace and Representative Torricelli I send my great respect and gratitude. To Emma and the *compañeros* and *compañeras*, I send my deepest love and thanks for keeping me alive.

Glossary

Compañero (or *compañera*): literally "friend" or "companion"; in Guatemala it is used to refer to members of the resistance forces, or URNG

Compa: abbreviated form of the word *compañero* or *compañera*

Dirigente: leader

Comandancia: commanders of the URNG

Frente: a large military unit of the resistance forces; ORPA forces, for example, now have two frentes, Luis Ixmata and Javier Tambriz, both named for fallen leaders

Voz Popular: literally "Popular Voice" or "Voice of the People"; the shortwave radio program broadcast by the ORPA forces from the Tajumulco Volcano since 1987

XX: symbols used to refer to the unidentified dead, almost always the victims of death-squad killings

SEARCHING FOR EVERARDO

Las Cabañas Military Base
Guatemala, July 1995

THE FIREFLIES ARE AT PLAY AGAIN, LIGHTING UP THE DARKENED fields in front of us like some exquisite witchcraft. I have not seen so many since I was very small, and their wild trajectories make the stars above seem cold and static. I crawl out from under my lightweight blanket and sit on a stretch of tangled grass to watch, lighting a cigarette and letting the silence steady me. It has been a brutal day, full of army rage, flashing cameras, and an ever-burning sun. The students lie sound asleep next to me, wrapped in their plastic covers against the intermittent evening rains, their faces young yet old, resolute, and terribly vulnerable. A few yards away is the army base, marked by a circle of luxuriant trees and a thin, glittering strand of barbed wire. In the shadows, it looks like a giant bouquet of prehistoric flowers tied together with a sparkling ribbon. A frightened young soldier sits at the front gate, hunched over his machine gun, watching us. He has been told that we are evil and deserve to be dead but that nothing must happen to us or there will be trouble, especially for him. He sits in silence, resisting the urge to speak to us, to ask us questions. He has long ago learned never to look for explanations.

He knows we have come for the dead, and this unnerves him. Just behind him and the trees and the preposterous green foliage lie the unmarked graves, crowded together in the narrow ledge leading to the river. The villagers have told us where to find them, but I knew already, long since, like all the others. We have been out there before, so many times, only to be driven away by the colonel, but not before we walked across that terrible strip of land. It is covered with long wild grasses that look like unkempt human hair, and the earth is uneven and ravaged by ominous mounds and depressions. The air seems too heavy to breathe and it echoes with the unmistakable silence of the dead. To walk across it breaks my heart, Everardo, for they tell me that you lie destroyed in one of those shallow graves beneath my feet.

I light another cigarette, letting it glow between my fingers without bringing it to my lips. They say there are two thousand people buried back there, all victims of the army's murderous rampage. Could it be true? I think so. A villager, thin and frightened, came by early this morning to share a small bunch of ripe bananas and a furtive conversation with us. He told us of hearing the terrible screams in the night, sometimes even during the daylight hours. Once he was passing on his way to the fields when a cry of agony rooted him to the spot. He listened in horror, unable to help and yet unable to leave. Finally a soldier came out of the gateway, angry and menacing. "Do you want to get going?" he asked. "Or do you want to stay here forever too?" The man left, of course, but he never forgot. Another villager has brought us a map, neatly lettered in his unschooled hand and color-coded for clarity. I have tucked it away, wrapped in sheer blue plastic, in my pack. They have been coming to us for days now, the villagers. Stealthy and frightened, they have been watching the army for fifteen years, remembering carefully, waiting for someone to come for the dead.

I lean forward and brush the drying mud from the yellow paper crosses we have laid out in a row. So far it is all that we can do, for the army will not permit us to open the graves or even enter the base. Our court orders are useless here, and the official prosecutor who has tried to help us is under death threats, along with his son. We can only sit here now, on our long vigil with our paper crosses, giving homage as best as we can to those who lie in that broken strip of earth.

In the silence, I try to stare past the shroud of sparkling fireflies, past the machine gunner and the circlet of trees. Are you out there, Everardo? You have been missing for so long, vanished for three years now. Have I finally found you here? You are still so real to me, it is hard to believe that you are dead and broken, lying motionless in some shallow grave. This is not what I fought for, not what I hoped for, all this time. I don't want to believe it. Yet I do believe it, no matter how hard my heart resists, for it has the ring of truth. You would never let me hide from the truth.

We are not far from where you were born and raised, Everardo. That village lies just up the road a ways, in a blur of wild greenery and steep slopes. The volcanoes where you fought for so many years encircle us like a bracelet. I can see the peaks clearly in the dark, sharp and beautiful against the blue-black sky. Up there at the top is where we first spoke to each other, where you so shyly danced with me for the first time, where I fell in love with you even though you didn't yet love me in return, or even quite trust me. I didn't mind, and you understood and were so kind about it that I loved you all the more. I never expected to see you again, but I did and I am glad. Despite everything that has happened, you were worth it all.

We are not very far from where you were tortured and chained for so long, Everardo. That army base lies just a few miles away from here. We passed it on the road driving in for the vigil. Did you die here as well? Did you have a chance to glimpse your beloved greenery and mountains one last time after your long captivity? Or did they drag you here dead in a burlap bag and bury you like a magnificent broken bird that they could never fully comprehend or value? Either way, I know you met your death with that silent stoicism, wistful for the life you never had but ready to be free at last. I know you.

I light a final cigarette and, once again, let it burn slowly in my fingers while I stare into the darkness. I can sense you back there, moving about with your catlike gait in your green uniform and small neatly laced boots. You say nothing to me, but then you never were much in favor of talk. You see words, at best, as an inelegant way of transmitting thoughts to those with inferior communication techniques. When I close my eyes I feel you close by, watching over me.

I want to rip open that strip of earth behind the base and tear your bones from the mud where they tossed you like so much refuse. I want to take you from their hands, free you, but I don't know if it will ever be possible. I will try. I am here for you, Everardo, out here with your trees and your mountains and your wild fireflies. I am here for you.

The Past

AT FIRST BLUSH WE WERE AN UNLIKELY PAIR, WEREN'T WE, EVERardo? Even you and I would have to admit that, although after a while our relationship seemed so natural we felt as if we had been born and raised together. With time we would remember our differences only when we saw them reflected in the startled glances of strangers as we walked hand in hand down the City streets together. Those stares would become a private joke for the two of us to savor, for we understood well enough what the others were seeing, or rather, thought they were seeing. They were looking at you, Everardo, with your perfect Mayan features and fierce black eyes, as you glided across the pavement with that lithe mountain walk of yours. Then they saw me at your side, a bit taller, a middle-aged, middle-class gringa with the disoriented look of a tourist just off the bus. No wonder we turned heads, Everardo, no wonder. And yet those quizzical glances never bothered us a bit, for we had long since learned that in the only ways that really mattered we were utterly alike.

Of course, the path that led me to you was hardly a direct or probable one, let alone planned or predicted. Our childhoods could not have been more different, nor for that matter could most of our adult lives. I grew up in the fifties in a quiet Connecticut suburb, the white prep school daughter of a Yale professor. The Holocaust was a very recent reality, with Anne Frank's diary at the top of every summer reading list. Nuclear war hung grimly over our heads like the proverbial sword of Damocles, and our cellar had a room well stocked with canned food, water, and batteries just in case. At school we had air-raid drills, as if during the meltdown of a nuclear blast, there would be some real hope of surviving and walking quietly home to find one's parents. It was the era of desegregation too, and I grew up listening to heated debates about busing, equality, Freedom Summer, and Martin Luther King, Jr. I was twelve years old when President John F. Kennedy was shot dead in Dallas, Texas.

At home I was sheltered, and yet I was not. I had everything I needed—food and clothes, love and security. The age of feminism was still far away, but even my grandmothers had finished college, one in Kentucky and one in Holland. Graduate school and a career of some sort were simply taken for granted as part of my future. All I had to do was study, and study hard, and the rest was a given. Beauty, social status, and money were low indeed on the totem pole of values. The women in my family were strong, bright, mulishly stubborn, and fiercely nonconformist. They expected nothing less from me, and my father, happily married to one of them himself, was not opposed.

The ivory tower I grew up in was certainly protective, yet not immune from the harshness of everyday life. My sister Kathy, a year older than myself, was born so tiny and premature that there was almost no chance for her survival. True to form, she put up a battle and came home in triumph after three months in the hospital. The struggle had left its mark though, for she was quite deaf, a detail both she and my mother considered inconsequential. She could speak and lip-read fluently by the time she was two, and we went through public schools together seated side by side. There was no special education back then, but my mother would not hear of sending her away to what were politely referred to as "institutions." During classes I could fill Kathy in on anything she missed, and she and my mother would stay up late into the night, working on speech drills, math, and vocabulary lessons. For years she was the most popular girl in the school, quick and feisty, bright-eyed and athletic. But then we reached our teens and suddenly we were different. Our friends mocked her brutally and barred her from our old circles, leaving her shocked, isolated, and in tears. Watching helplessly, I was reminded of a flock of birds pecking the outsider to death. I watched in disgust, and I did not forget.

Soon enough came college in the full blaze and glory of the sixties. There was Woodstock and Kent State, Vietnam and the Black Panthers. The wild nonconformity suited me perfectly, and I thrived, attending antiwar rallies, tutoring, and reading everything from Marx and Mao to Thoreau and Jefferson. Then one day I knew it was time to leave my books behind for a while and I left school, much to my father's dismay and my mother's approval. I worked two minimum-wage jobs at once, waitressing at night at roadside cafés and typing sleepily through the days, until I had enough money for an overseas plane ticket and a few months' expenses. Then I tossed some clothes into a pack and began a new phase of my life that would last for many years. I visited Greece, with its murderous military junta; I washed dishes in Istanbul and talked late into the night with the despairing Kurds and Palestinians; I traveled through remote Iranian villages where people lived in terror of the U.S.-backed Shah and his hated secret police, the SAVAK. For a few months I stayed in the Khyber Pass, living with the women in the back of a house and covering my hair whenever a man entered the room. In North Africa I was stunned by the colossal scars left by the colonial era. The world was not what my schoolbooks had taught me. I did a lot of thinking, Everardo, a lot of thinking indeed.

By the time I reached Harvard Law School there was really no question about what would come next. I knew who I was, what I wanted, and why I had gone back to school. I wanted to do civil rights work and nothing else. Unlike my fellow students, I suffered no identity crisis and never interviewed on Wall Street. By the time I graduated, my bags were packed and I headed straight for the Texas–Mexico border to a job at a small legal-aid bureau located next to a pool hall. I loved my work, and I spent my days with the farmworkers, learning some Spanish, hurrying to strike lines, and fighting for health rights, bilingual education, and minimum wages. Then came the early eighties, Everardo, with thousands of Mayans swimming the Rio Grande and running in terror from the death squads and massacres in Guatemala. Their stories stopped me dead in my tracks. I didn't want to believe what I was hearing, for the cruelty and suffering they were describing left me in despair. And yet listening to them, watching their terrified children hiding beneath the tables and chairs, I knew they were telling the truth. Everyone else knew, too.

And yet our immigration courts sent them home, to my initial shock and later outrage. Reagan wished to send money to the right-wing Guatemalan and Salvadoran military regimes. Such funding was illegal if the armies were committing human rights atrocities, which they most certainly were. So the victims were found not to be credible, not to have enough proof, not to have recent-enough proof, not to have proof that things had not changed for the better, and they were routinely sent home to the death squads. A man covered with acid-burn scars, fresh from a torture chamber where his brother had died, was declared to have no reasonable fear of persecution should he be deported. That lit my fuse, Everardo. It really did. Soon I was leaving for what I thought would be a few short months in Guatemala. Now here I am, eleven years later, writing about you and wondering what on earth to do with the battered pieces of my life that are left to me.

And you, Everardo? Your early life is almost the mathematical inverse of my own, the other side of the looking glass. It was hard, so hard to get you to talk about yourself, for you considered it somehow vain and irrelevant, all this talk about your individual self and your past, as if you were somehow of great importance. In your eyes, it was only the team that mattered. I had to coax the stories in bits and pieces from you and later fit them together at my desk back in Texas. I know you were born in 1957, just three years after the CIA invaded Guatemala and kicked out the reformist President Arbenz at the request of the United Fruit Company. The military was then placed firmly in power by the U.S. government, and it stayed there for the next forty years, despite the ensuing bloodbath carried out against civil rights leaders and unionists.

I know you were born on someone else's plantation, the first child of two hungry Mayan peasants. They were working the land for the owner, picking his coffee and cotton, trying to stay alive on the pitiful wages, just like the others in the remote community of serfs there. You remembered your mother, though she died after the birth of her third child when you were still very young. There was no money for the antibiotics to save her life, and her death startled no one. Such sad matters were everyday events. After that, there was no one left in the flimsy shack to care for you, to feed you and your little sisters. Your father worked all day in the fields just to keep you alive. He tried to arrange for another woman to give you meals while he was away, but she beat you and mistreated you, and even then you preferred to starve rather than accept abuse and injustice. Your father watched you grow thinner and thinner, and he began to take you to the table with him to eat in the evenings, to shelter you as best he could. Soon enough you had to go to the fields and work with him, small as you were. It was work or starve.

You remembered the hunger forever, Everardo. But even more you remembered the school in the village just down the road, the one you could never attend. Your first language was Mam and you were learning Spanish, but you wanted to learn ever so much more. You wanted to learn to read and write, you wanted books and an education, you were starving to death for ideas and concepts and information about the outside world. Years later, even after you had devoured libraries of books from cover to cover, you still remembered this early ignorance with a keen rage. For you it was a humiliating stain smeared upon you against your will, for after all you were but an *indio*, less than nothing, a dark-skinned donkey to be worked till it dropped, then tossed aside. You understood all too well that in the eyes of the light-skinned landowners, you were not worth teaching to read. This didn't stop you though. You went to the others and learned a few letters from them. Your younger sister remembers you working over those letters late into the night, slowly puzzling them out until you had some rudimentary reading skills. Still, you were hungry for more.

By your teens you were in full-blown rebellion, running off from the plantation every so often to roam through your green volcanoes, to think things through, to figure things out. Guatemala was your country, some 80 percent Mayan, yet you and the others lived like prisoners or worse. You had no lands, no money, no representation, and no rights. The conquistadors had taken everything with their steel swords and gunpowder, and their descendants now lived happily on the great plantations, mocking you for your color and culture, killing those who sought to rise up to seek their lands or ask for a wage that would feed their children. Like all the others, you knew your history from the elders, how the Mayans of Guatemala had created one of the greatest civilizations of the world, how they had never been fully conquered, how they had fought, every single generation, barefoot and armed only with stones and machetes, since the coming of Alvarado. Every generation had been cruelly crushed, but their hopes were still fiercely alive, even now. Even now the Mayans clung to their own languages, some twenty-six ancient mother tongues, they wrapped themselves in their own handwoven fabrics, and they worshiped defiantly in their secret temples hidden far up in the volcanoes. Assimilation was not for them, for the Mayans have always known their true identity. Battered and starving and ridiculed, they have never surrendered.

During one of your long climbs into the mountains you came across Gaspar Ilom, a young man from the City who was hiding out with a handful of others. His real name was Rodrigo Asturias and he was the son of Guatemala's Nobel laureate in literature, Miguel Angel Asturias, whose raging novels read like incendiary versions of *Les Miserables*. Rodrigo was not one to sit at home and write. He had once worked openly for reforms and had seen the results firsthand. His civilian friends were hunted down and killed and he himself came under frightening reprisals again and again, until he learned that the only chance for genuine change was through an armed revolution. He took a good look at his own country and he saw exactly what you saw, Everardo, even though he came from the other end of the social ladder. He saw a society not unlike South Africa's. He saw a nation where the great majority were Mayan peasants, the original inhabitants, yet where the Mayans had no political rights, no lands, and no power. Eighty percent were illiterate and eighty percent suffered from malnutrition so severe that the average village woman was under five feet tall, with bones too frail to heal after breaking. The infant mortality rate was one of the highest in the hemisphere. Minimum wage did not cover basic dietary needs, let alone housing or health care. Any civil rights efforts were crushed with a frightening cruelty. All this went on as the tiny blond and blue-eyed upper class enjoyed the greatest of wealth and luxury, and looked down upon the villagers as subhumans, useful only for brute labor. Rodrigo decided that major changes were needed to drag his nation into the twentieth century, and that any genuine revolution would have to have equal rights for the Mayan people at the top of its priorities. That, in turn, meant Mayan leadership.

And so you met up there in the volcanoes, drawn together like the opposite poles of a magnet. Rodrigo was already a hunted man and had taken the nom de guerre Gaspar Ilom, after the Mayan resistance hero in his father's most famous novel. You were full of ideas and opinions, eager to throw off the yoke that bound you and the others and smash it to pieces once and for all. You spent the whole day with Gaspar and his friends, talking over issues and hopes and dreams. They asked about your life and the needs of the people, and you answered characteristically, after a long, thoughtful silence, your concise answers wise and serious beyond your years. When you left, you felt that you had feasted all day long. When you left, Gaspar told the others that he wanted you as a future leader more than anyone else he had ever met.

You returned to this small encampment again and again, drawn by the ideas and the chance to think. Gaspar and the others taught you to really read, and they gave you books and an education. You learned world history and politics, science and mathematics. You became especially close to Luis Ixmata, who gave you poetry books and encouraged you to write poems yourself. Even then you had the knack for finding the perfect word to express your thoughts, a musical gem to be offered to the others. In turn, the others listened to you, learned from you. For the first time in your life someone understood who you were, instead of seeing you as a chattel to be exploited and forgotten. And so you became the tenth member of this fledgling group, the Revolutionary Organization of the People in Arms, ORPA. On your eighteenth birthday, you left home forever, telling the others you were searching for work in the City, but leaving for the mountains instead.

For years you and the others organized in secret, building up a base of support, talking with the villagers, arranging for supply lines and evacuation routes. The Mayans all knew you were there and why, but in the seven years you worked in secret, no one ever turned you in to the authorities. Indeed, it was the Mayans who formed the vast majority of the new organization. When I arrived in the volcano years later, I found that over 90 percent of the combatants were Mayan villagers, and a good chunk of them women. You, a villager, were the commander of the entire region, while Marcos, also Mayan, was second in command, and Celia, a *ladina* * villager, was third. Your generation of Mayans, just like all the others before you, had risen up to fight.

You yourself rose up to fight knowing exactly what to expect from the authorities. For a slave uprising like yours, there would be no mercy or fair trials or Geneva convention. The upper class would unleash its army in a hellish rampage that you, Everardo, never hoped to survive. In your mind, the fates had dealt you the card of war and death and there was nothing to do but accept it with dignity. And so you braced yourself as ORPA became public in the late seventies and openly went to war against the military. You and the others linked forces with the other rebel groups, the indigenous Guerilla Army of the Poor, or EGP, from the northwest and the Armed Revolutionary Front, or FAR, from the remote Petén jungles in the northeast to form the Guatemalan National Revolutionary Union, or URNG. Conditions were harsh, for there was little funding. Indeed, you and the others never received or asked for a nickel in salary in all those years. Supplies were scarce and you were often cold and hungry and without boots or blankets or medical care. Weapons and ammunition were scarcer still, but you fought with what you had, rusty hunting rifles and rationed bullets.

Yet morale was high because the villagers supported you always, recognizing their own sons and daughters within your ranks, recognizing all of you, with your tilting dark eyes and sculpted features, as their own. They knew you were fighting for them, and they hurried to bring you food and warn you when the army drew near. Throughout the country you were friendly with the members of the burgeoning pacifist movement of civil rights groups and church programs. You

---

* A *ladino* or *ladina* is a person of mixed European and Mayan descent.

understood one another well enough, for your goals and demands were precisely the same, although your methods differed. Yet you yourself, Everardo, understood far more than this. You understood that all of you were doomed, and that it would be the next generation that would live to see the new Guatemala, a Guatemala that would rise phoenixlike from your own collective ashes.

When the crackdown began in the early 1980s, you were grimly unsurprised. The army began to hunt you and anyone else guilty of seeking reform—civilian or combatant, no matter. Change and sedition were one and the same, for they both spelled the end of the old ways. All around you, your friends began to die. They died at your side in combat, they were blown to bits in bombings, they vanished on missions, and they succumbed to infections caused by their wounds. Those taken alive were found hacked and mutilated, their pitiful corpses tossed into roadside ditches. In thirty years of war, not a single prisoner survived in army hands. In the City the urban underground went down in flames, the soldiers taking safe house after safe house with tanks and bazookas. Children died with their parents. Those who survived the mortars and the fires were dragged away and tortured until they told of yet another house and yet another leader. And so it went, till the underground there was exterminated once and for all.

The army went after the villagers, knowing full well that this uprising was rooted deep in the Mayan people themselves. They said they were draining the sea in order to catch the fish and they set about a scorched earth and massacre campaign the likes of which had scarce been seen since the days of the conquistadors. Within a few nightmarish years, some 440 Mayan villages had been wiped from the map altogether, the charred bones of the dead left scattered through the cornfields. In San Francisco Nentón three hundred peasants died in a single afternoon. In the City the progressive movement was destroyed, the unions crushed, the students shot and beaten to death on campus, the doctors and teachers working with the rural poor vanishing in the middle of the night. The liberal church circles were next, the nuns and priests left dead alongside the bodies of their catechists. Soon the death toll was one of the highest in the hemisphere. None of this surprised you, Everardo. You just bent your head into the firestorm and threw yourself forward, knowing only too well what was yet to come.

Somehow you lived through those early, impossible years. You taught the newcomers how to survive in the mountains too, how to hide, how to listen, how to walk, how to find food. You became legendary in combat, for you fought without anger and utterly without fear, protected by a serenity that none of the others could fathom. It was because you had long since accepted your own death, Everardo. Whatever the price, you were doing what you knew was right, and to your way of thinking there was simply nothing else that could even be considered. You rose swiftly through the ranks, for you were a natural leader and a gifted strategist. Even then, in the early, terrifying era of extermination, your tranquillity was complete, steadying the others and keeping your mind quick and clear.

The hardships seemed not to touch you. The army moved swiftly to cut off supply lines from friendly villages, leaving you and the others without food for days at a time. There were never enough bullets or blankets or medicines or boots, and the army hunted you and the others without mercy, bombing the volcanoes, sending in their paratroopers, setting up ambushes at every turn. And yet you and the others fought on without a backward glance. You all preferred death to a return to the past.

It was the others who kept you alive, wasn't it, Everardo? It was the villagers who hurried to help with the wounded, brought you food and information, and sent their kinfolk to fight at your side. It was the little old ladies who carried your messages into the City, defiant and fearless, who treated you like a son. It was the field laborers who hid you in their homes, despite the risks, silently recognizing you as one of their own. You were all in this war together, you Mayans, and the blood ties that wordlessly bound you together were also what kept your heart and mind alive even in the cruelest of times. You were but one people. You were never alone. This you understood in your very bones, and you loved the others with a depth and ferocity that few outsiders could understand.

Then again, it was the others who formed your Achilles' heel, wasn't

it, Everardo? When Luis Ixmata fell dead in an army ambush, you felt
that you had died with him, that your very heart had been ripped
from your body. His death left you with crushing new responsibilities
as well, for you were now in charge of the entire region, and the survival of so many others depended on you alone. The army was everywhere, burning and killing and torturing, bent on annihilating your
forces forever. You were only in your early twenties, but after Luis died
you thought long and hard throughout the night and pulled yourself
together. For Luis you wrote a poem of farewell that you kept with
you always but never showed to another. Then you squared your
shoulders and took command, leading the others to safety again and
again, gliding in and out of the villages to magically rearrange supply
lines and listen to your people. You fought from the cornfields, from
the mountains, from an ancient Mayan fortress where your ancestors
long before you had fought against the conquistadors. Soon you were
legendary.

The cold winds and the hellish battles never stopped you, Everardo. But then you fell in love with a quiet young woman named
Gabriella, a university student who arrived to fight in your combat
unit, the new *frente*[*] named after Luis Ixmata. Characteristically, you
loved her without compromise or limits, yet you had only six months
together. She died in a remote village during an army ambush. You
had been wounded, and you urged her to run to safety since the soldiers were far too close, but she would not leave you there alone. She
was shot through the heart as you reached for her hand. You never re-
covered. For a year you thought you would go mad, but you knew well
enough you had no right to fail the others. A decade later, I would
still hear you cry out in your sleep as Gabriella died yet again in your
dreams.

It was the same with so many others. You would grow close to new
friends, only to steel yourself as you sent them off to battle and later
learned of their deaths. You disciplined yourself to accept the crushing burdens of command, to send out yet more *compas*, forbidding

---

[*]A *frente* is a mobile combat unit composed of several hundred people. The ORPA *frentes* were commonly named after fallen resistance leaders.

yourself to hope for their safe return but rejoicing when you saw them
again, as if you had been granted some rare and special favor. You
stayed up late into the night, planning new strategies and working
them through with the newcomers, hoping to keep them alive, finding ways to keep them alive. Then you lost your second *compañera*, Rosalvina, a young villager like yourself. You sent her on a mission and
the army took her alive, a fate everyone knew was far worse than a
quick and merciful bullet. After that you did not risk your heart
again. Instead you wrapped yourself, priestlike, in layer upon layer of
asceticism and responsibility and you carried on alone. Despite your
rank you returned to combat again and again, but like a mythical
creature of one thousand lives, you went unscathed. As the years
passed, all the other young Mayan commanders Gaspar had trained
and educated with you so long ago went down in a hail of bullets or
vanished in army hands. You were the last survivor. The army wanted
you dead and hunted you like they hunted no other, but it cost them
seventeen long years. You almost reached the end of the war, Everardo, almost.

And so we met, two people from utterly different worlds. Yet we
understood each other on some deeper level from the very beginning.
We both loved new ideas, were fascinated by foreign cultures, cared
deeply about civil rights, and were passionate about the Mayans. We
didn't give a hoot about money or creature comforts. Security of any
kind was not an issue for us. We were quite willing to yield to the
wishes of others about most things in life, but when it came to matters of principle, we were both stubborn enough to drive an outsider
to laughter or suicide, depending on his or her sense of humor. We
hated bullies and notions of rank and caste. We were never equals, for
you were always far ahead of me in wisdom and in vision, yet this
didn't trouble either one of us. You always treated me as an equal in
every way and you were always proud of my independence. In turn,
you were quite whole without me, for your responsibilities were your
life. I respected this and did not try to change you. You did not need
me at all, but you gave me your love so unstintingly that I was completely content. You took the time to really listen to me, to under-

stand me down to my very bones. I miss you, Everardo. Even now after all these years, I still miss you.

The Goose Step
Guatemala, 1985

I THINK IT WAS THE GOOSE STEP, EVERARDO, THAT STARTED ALL OF this. It was Army Day, 1985, and I remember that I was standing on my small hotel balcony, watching the parade below. A military band was playing somber music and troop after troop of soldiers passed us by, armed to the teeth. There was none of the gaiety or communion with the crowd that I have seen at similar events in other countries. Instead, these parading men were intentionally terrifying. Their faces were streaked with black and green paint, the eyes glinting through the masks like watchful beasts of prey. They looked neither to the left nor the right and smiled at no one, gripping their glittering automatic weapons close as they marched straight ahead. Their belts bristled with hand grenades, knives, and enormous metal cartridges. At intervals, great cannonlike weapons and heavy machine guns were dragged to the intersections and fired, the sound so deafening it shook the earth. Armored tanks roared by and Doberman pinschers trotted forward in clusters, growling at the crowd and straining at their leashes. No doubt about it, we were all being warned. And then the soldiers passed beneath my balcony again. They were marching the goose step.

Watching them, something snapped in my head, even way back then. I had not been in Guatemala long, only a few months, but what I had seen and heard was enough to leave me ill and desperate. I had arrived just after Holy Week with the idea of taking some live testimonies about the human rights situation here. The refugees back in the United States needed help, confirmation of their claims that they would be killed if deported to their homeland. No human rights groups were allowed yet into Guatemala, not even the Red Cross, so specific information was not so easy to come by. The Amnesty International and Americas Watch reports were horrific enough, but they were routinely ignored by the immigration courts as too general, too old, too whatever. I wanted the refugees safe in the United States until the firestorm in Guatemala was over. The United States government wanted them out.

When I arrived here I knew quite a bit about your country, Everardo. I knew that the rampaging army had left 150,000 civilians dead or "disappeared"—a death toll higher than that of Chile, Argentina, and El Salvador all put together. Hundreds of thousands of others were in exile. I knew that 440 Mayan villages had been wiped out. In a refugee camp in Mexico I spoke with one of the survivors, an old man who had watched his sons and daughters shot, and then his grandchildren disemboweled one by one. Not unusual, back then, in the eighties.

So I knew pretty much what I was getting into, Everardo. Yet it is never the same, hearing about it and knowing it, compared to seeing it for yourself, meeting and loving and then losing the people I once knew only from the printed pages. It is never the same.

And then I arrived in your homeland, Everardo, and it all began. I hurried to meet with the band of women who had recently formed a group for the disappeared. The GAM, it was called, the Grupo de Apoyo Mutuo. The women had met the year before, after the army swept the student council leaders and union members from the streets of the City. They had never been seen again, and their despairing wives and mothers had searched the prisons and morgues again and again, appalled by what they were seeing, and determined to save their loved ones. They had banded together and organized quite brilliantly, demanding that the army return their family members. They became all too successful in attracting international attention, and the military finally attacked with all its mad cruelty during Easter week.

The first to die was Hector Gamez, one of the few male founders in the group. He was forced into a car by armed men in broad daylight, in front of terrified witnesses. The next day his body was dumped into the dusty streets not far from his home. He had been savagely beaten, his skull crushed, his liver ruptured, his tongue slashed out of his head. Death had come slowly, not from the beatings, but from wounds dealt by a blowtorch. Word reached the streets quickly enough, and the forensic physician who so bluntly reported on the injuries was shot dead a few weeks later. The women were horrified but they did not surrender, for their loved ones were still missing, still suffering only God knows what. They flocked to Hector's funeral by the score, the Mayan members arriving barefoot, with their children strapped to their backs. Beautiful Rosario, another founding member, gave the funeral address, holding her small child in her arms. By the end of the week she lay dead in her coffin, together with her younger brother and her two-year-old son. According to the army, the three died in a tragic car crash. The sobbing witnesses told a different story, that Rosario had bite marks and cigarette burns across her breasts and that the baby was missing his fingernails.

When I arrived, the women were still under constant threats, the army raging at them across their telephone lines, armed men lurking menacingly near their homes. Still they did not give up, and a tiny woman named Nineth continued to lead them every Friday afternoon to the National Palace, where they wept and chanted through their borrowed megaphones and marched around and around the square, ignoring the menacing cars with the black glass windows parked nearby. They needed international observers, people to stand close by, for the army even then shrank from the view of the outsiders. They did not want their funding cut from places such as Washington, D.C., and they vehemently denied any responsibility for human rights violations, despite the obvious. They preferred even then to kill in the privacy of some dark corner.

And so I got to work, Everardo. I was pretty green and my Spanish was awful, based as it was on the Tex-Mex dialect I had learned from the farmworkers back home. But there was so much need for protection for these women, and for others, that the church people began to bring them to me one by one to hide and rush out of the country as quickly as possible. Within a few months, my hands were full and my mind was raging.

Soon I found myself on my small balcony, watching the troops march by below in their menacing black boots, arms and legs stiff in a goose step. I fantasized about heaving boulders or pouring boiling oil down on their heads as they passed. Inside my room, cowering in a corner, was a terrified teenager named Miguel, a Mayan peasant who needed to leave in a hurry whether he wanted to or not. He had been badly tortured and was lucky to be alive. Even in my room he cringed from the sight of the uniforms below. His golden face was ashen and pale as he fought off a dead faint.

Miguel was from a small Mayan town near Lake Atitlán, a place of idyllic beauty and army terror. He was from a poor family himself, but he did so remarkably well in school that his proud father sacrificed heavily to keep his studies going, with the aid of a generous church scholarship. At the age of sixteen he was in the eleventh grade, unheard of for a villager. He was out one day in the hills, tending the sheep as he worked on his trigonometry problems. A patrol of soldiers came by, the officer pulling out a list of names on a crumpled paper. You, he growled, show us your papers. Maybe you are on this list. Miguel hurried to produce his identification card and was relieved when his name appeared nowhere on the ominous-looking paper. But then the officer penciled his name in at the bottom and ordered him tied up anyway.

They bound Miguel's hands tightly behind his back and pulled a hood over his head, dragging him for hours to a remote place in the forest. He knew he was going to die. The officer told him that his math papers were secret codes for the guerrillas and that he must now decode them, confess, and explain where the weapons were hidden. Miguel protested that they were only his school papers—logarithms—and that they should go and ask the priest in the village. The officer responded that all priests were subversives. He told Miguel to prepare for death, and Miguel requested five minutes for prayer. The officer kicked him in the face. There's your five minutes, he said. Then they placed a thick plastic bag over his head, tightening it until he began to suffocate and his lungs seemed to burst and he finally lost consciousness. When he awoke, they were tossing him into a deep pit filled with trash and stinking of urine. His hands had gone completely numb, but his arms ached terribly. At midnight they hauled him out with a rope and said they were taking him to be shot. Instead, as they reached the square a quiet soldier told him to go, to run home, and to never speak to anyone of what had happened. Never, to anyone. When the priest brought Miguel to my room the teeth in his lower jaw were badly broken and he had black rings of dead flesh around his wrists. When I saw him off at the airport on his way to Canada, he was a pitiful and thin adolescent, walking uncertainly down the runway all alone, far from the family and village he had never intended to leave.

The Canadian embassy continued to take people like Miguel, hurrying them out of the country and rushing to offer them English lessons and job training. The U.S. embassy turned them all away and I learned never to go there, for stories abounded of information being shared with the army. Worse yet, I began to hear consistent stories of North Americans wandering in and out of the torture chambers. The army finally took offense with the Canadians, and a diplomat's car was hit with machine-gun fire, the diplomat and the driver miraculously escaping. Then a young woman named Beatriz was granted a visa, but she never made it to the airport. She was left dead the next day in a gutter, naked and filthy, hacked and battered, her head cracked open from a blow to the side of her face, perhaps with an ax. It was her hands, though, that haunted my sleep, for they were neatly sawed off at the wrists and lay mute and disconnected on the gravel nearby. On her chest was a bloody note: "We'll be back for the rest."

I was shocked senseless, for I had somehow believed that once connected to the embassy, everyone was safe. But the truth was that they were merely safer. As I thought it over, I remembered other embassy stories that left me numb. I remembered the story of the Spanish embassy, and how four years ago more than forty Mayan civil rights leaders had marched from the Quiché region to protest army atrocities. They had peacefully occupied the building to highlight their demands and were chatting quietly with the Spanish ambassador when the security forces attacked and burned the building over their heads. Their ambassador escaped with his life, but most of his staff did not. The villagers all perished in the inferno except for one, who was terribly burned and placed in a hospital. That night he was dragged from his bed and left dead and mutilated, all alone, in a field.

Then there was the Belgian embassy, only a year ago. A young unionist had been picked up and taken to a secret army house, tied to a bloody mattress, and beaten within an inch of his life. Later he was hung from a meat hook and beaten some more. Others were there too, including vanished friends from the labor movement, all hideously tortured. The young man finally promised to turn in certain "allies" if they would take him to a specific intersection at a certain time the next day. None too bright, his captors agreed and drove him there in a car with black glass windows. While they waited two women passed, and inexplicably the two men ran after them. The unionist's hands and feet were tied, but he managed to leap from the car anyway and hobble up the front lawn of the Belgian embassy, where he had asked them to park. The two men ran after him and opened fire, shooting him on the embassy lawn and leaving pockmarks on the walls as well. Desperate to live, he made it to the doorway and survived to tell it all.

I walked down the main avenue that night, thinking it over, and looked up to see a Jeep Cherokee careening ominously through an intersection, the windows totally black. The Guatemalans, quick on their feet, had vanished into the shops and cafés that line the street, for they knew all too well who would be driving a car like that. I took a step backward, heading for a doorway as the car sped past me, and in that split second I heard the screams of agony coming from the back in that blacked out, secret space.

After that I took to the countryside, Everardo, for I needed a change. But if anything, things were worse. As I hiked through the jungle I found the charred remains of dead communities, the survivors rounded up and fenced into strategic army hamlets ironically known as "model villages." They were starving, terrified, forced into so-called civil patrols that required reporting on their neighbors, upon pain of death. Those who refused either found themselves dead or placed for days on end into pits of cold water that reached their necks. Far off in the jungles were other survivors who had fled, not into Mexico, but into the Sierra Madre instead. The army was hunting them, calling them Communist subversives, bombing their hiding places to rubble. I spoke with a small child in an orphanage, and he said, Her mouth was full of blood. His eyes were dull, vacant. I asked *who* had blood in her mouth, thinking he was telling me of a playground friend. He answered, My mother. She could not get up. She didn't hear me.

Around me everywhere was the rubble of old church programs and social services deemed too subversive to survive. There were vacant buildings with charred walls that had once housed the cooperatives. In one town, an old church on the hilltop had been converted into an army barracks. The villagers explained that it was once the church of Father William Woods, an American priest shot down in his small plane by the army. On board with him were three other U.S. citizens—a young volunteer, a doctor, and a mother of four small children. Father Woods, the villagers told me, was a very good man. They had been hungry, and he had brought them there and helped them find land that they could buy for low monthly rates, then taught them to pool their resources to buy medicines, a generator, and agricultural equipment. The village became very successful—too successful. That's why, one man commented matter-of-factly, they had to kill Father Woods. Gone were all the old programs, the health promoters, the teachers, the literacy clinics, and the rural medical services. The army had wiped them all out, civilians and church folk alike, just as they had crushed the unions and the student movement in the City. In every village the people ran to beg me for medicine when I arrived, for the army had taken all their supplies, leaving them with nothing. I took to carrying extra antibiotics, vitamins, aspirin, anything I could, because in every village I found a child dying. In one remote town a baby died in my arms, choking on his own blood and tugging mutely at my hair, hoping for rescue. I tried to get him to a hospital but no one was allowed to leave the village after dark. For years I dreamed of those tiny hands pulling hopefully at my hair, Everardo. No wonder you stood up and fought.

Slowly but surely, I began to meet the *compañeros*. Sometimes they were on a remote trail, dressed in olive green, good-naturedly motioning me onward or chatting briefly. Most of the ones I knew, though, were the secret ones, the ones who were everywhere and yet so completely invisible. They had learned to be invisible in order to stay alive, in order to keep their families alive. It was only after a very long time that I began to recognize them. Some were old friends who rushed to take refuge in my hotel room in the City on their way out of the country forever. These were doctors and lawyers and unionists and church people whose efforts at civilian reform lay in ruins about them. Others were sharp-eyed peasants who had met with me a dozen times during my visits through their towns. First they would tell me they were merely humble peasants caught in the cross fire. Then they would mention that the guerrillas were decent enough and wanted only what was right for the people. Then they would tell me more, wanting me to understand, to really understand. They were civilians, all of them, and yet all of them, hating the army, were playing a role in the resistance. Some had family in the mountains, sons and daughters who were carrying guns. Others ran secret clinics, tending the wounded. Some arranged for the vast network of food supplies, or hid the hunted in their basements, or operated medical evacuation routes. Some found weapons wherever they could and risked their necks bringing them to the hills. Others were watchdogs, hurrying to warn the *compañeros* whenever the army was drawing near.

At first I was taken aback by the numbers, for I had always understood the URNG to be but a handful of surviving combatants. But now I began to get things into focus. This had been but one more Mayan peasant uprising, joined by those city folk who had attempted social reform and had managed somehow to survive. The army had miscalculated badly in its use of mass murder and shocking violence, for unwittingly they had brought together many disparate sectors of society and joined them in a resistance force that was truly to be reckoned with.

I watched them die one by one, civilians, collaborators, and *compañeros* alike—it seemed to make no difference. I attended a funeral in the City and wandered through the enormous cemetery, looking for the family and passing wall upon wall of catacomblike cubicles, the graves of the poor. The walls seemed unending, holding perhaps a hundred cubicles apiece, and I began to look at the hand-painted inscriptions on the plaster seals, reading dates and looking for names. Suddenly I noticed that almost all read XX, or unidentified, the generic symbol used for the bodies of death-squad victims found at the sides of the roads, tossed into ravines, or grimly sprawled in the city parks. I walked farther and farther and past more and more walls. XX, XX, XX, XX. They seemed to go on forever. Men and women, dead and mutilated, dragged here on flimsy stretchers, held for a day, and then sealed into a tiny cubicle forever. And their families?

After a while back in the City, I knew that my days were numbered in Guatemala. I had caught the army's fatal attention and already the men with dark glasses were on the street corners and crowding my hotel lobby. They wanted me to see them, to get the message. Leave while you can. Or else.

And so I started to pack, for no longer could I offer any protection to the Guatemalans, or move about unnoticed through the villages. I could no longer help; my time was up. As I packed, a union friend was picked up and badly beaten. I spoke to him one last time, offering to take him to the Canadian embassy. He refused, vowing to continue his work no matter what. If we don't try, then what's the use, he said, shaking his head. A few days later he walked toward a bus stop with his three-year-old son and the death squads opened fire. Miraculously they missed him and he found himself standing in horror over the body of his little son. The bullets had struck the child in the neck, shattering his spine and paralyzing him for life. The hospital was on strike, for the army had taken all the medicines, but the doctors took the child as a special case. Appalled, I ran to buy extra antibiotics and bandages on the black market. Later, I found father and son crying together in the hospital room. The father was weeping for his son. The little boy was weeping because he wanted to ride his tricycle and could not understand why he was unable to move. The sight gagged me and I rushed to buy a bus ticket and finish my packing, for I felt that I was about to lose my mind. The next day another unionist was cut to pieces in front of his office. Common crimes, the police reported. No human rights violations here. The people roared in protest and flocked to the funeral. My bus trailed just behind the procession as I left the country for good.

Back in Texas I came unraveled, for I could never again work on something far from Guatemala. I could not forget my friends. They were still dying back there, those people I had come to love so, and the U.S. authorities were still lying. No need to cut off aid, things are ever so much better, just give it all a fair chance. The real problem here is common crime; perhaps they need more police. Guatemala is a violent culture, that's just their way, perhaps it's right to let the army help keep law and order. Isn't that up to the Guatemalans?

Finally, I lost it altogether and decided to write a book. The press had never been allowed to cover Guatemala during my two years there. I had known any number of excellent U.S. journalists who had tried, who had sent home boxes of information and well-written stories, only to be told that the American people did not care about Guatemala, that it was not an issue of public interest. Those who pressed too hard were transferred to another country or had a hard time finding work. Yet how could anyone know what the U.S. public was interested in if no one ever told the public about what was really going on? Why were Salvador and Nicaragua on the front pages every day and yet nothing about Guatemala, even though the death toll there soared above all other countries? I decided to write my own book about the war and the people I had known. I left my job and started writing and arranging for interviews. More than anything, I wanted to speak at length with the combatants themselves, for there was virtually nothing known or written about them, other than official communiqués. After the City underground was wiped out, they had adopted clandestine security measures that made it impossible to find or reach them. But this I would have to arrange. It would take time, but it could be done. It was worth it.

And you, Everardo, you stood up and fought. You starved through your childhood and then you left for the mountains and you fought for seventeen years. You started the war and you knew you would end with it, that you were feeding your very life and soul into the resistance. There was nothing that could change your mind or break your incredible will. Good for you, Everardo. I am proud, so proud, to have known you.

The Volcano
Summer 1990

IT IS HARDLY A MATTER OF LOVE AT FIRST SIGHT, IS IT, EVERARDO? You think I am a CIA agent, and I, half-blinded in the sun, think you are an adolescent standing over there, almost frail-looking, in the shadows of the forest. We will laugh about this later on when we become inseparable, amused by the perils of first impressions. We will marvel at how our true selves, let alone our intertwined futures, could have been so invisible to each other. It is as if we passed each other by, oblivious, then turned around for a second instinctive glance, a glance that would fuse us together against all logic for the rest of our joint lives.

It all begins a few weeks earlier, when permission finally comes from the Guatemalan underground for me to climb the Tajumulco volcano and interview women combatants for my book. I am thrilled, for I have waited two years now to enter a combat zone, contenting myself instead with interviews in various safe houses and clandestine clinics scattered discreetly throughout the region. The stories and the people I encounter in these furtive meetings are quite extraordinary, but I must see the *frente* for myself. I must understand how it operates, who is up there, and why. I must see it with my own eyes or the book, for me, can never be valid. The *comandancia*[*] has always deemed the trip too dangerous until now, for they will risk no foreign lives to chance

---

[*]The *comandancia* is the team of top-level commanders of a given resistance organization, such as ORPA.

skirmishes or ambush, but at last I receive the terse message, the small green light. I may spend thirty days in the Luis Ixmata *frente* of ORPA. I should prepare to leave at once.

I outfit myself carefully and in accordance with their instructions. All clothing must be dark green or black, including underwear, gloves, and scarves. Even the smallest item drying on a makeshift clothesline could be visible from the air and cause a bombing raid or aerial attack. I should take a lightweight pair of boots, the hollow rubber kind that I remember so well from my previous years in Guatemala, the kind that glide across the sucking mud holes like snowshoes across the mounding snow. The pack itself must be small and easy to run with. I should take a small plate and cup and a tin spoon, a sturdy flashlight with batteries large enough to last, but not the shiny metallic type. No more than two changes of clothes, but plenty of socks, the cheap nylon kind that dry quickly in the sun. A few toiletries, a dark sweater, and perhaps a few tins of food and a bit of chocolate for the *compañeros*. I add several thick notepads and extra pens, and after consulting with some friends in an underground clinic, I pack some hard candies, spices, and cartons of cigarettes. For my arrival in customs, I add some bright-flowered hippie-style skirts as camouflage. These I will leave at a friend's house once I'm safely across the border.

I stay quietly ensconced in a small room for a few days, receiving last-minute instructions on codes and maps. Then word comes that it is time to go, and a curly-haired youth with crooked teeth and a good smile appears with an aging car. We drive through the deepening shadows on a remote, ever-curving road for several hours, chatting pleasantly as if on the way to an afternoon tea instead of a dangerous rendezvous. I hold the map in my hands and we check off the kilometer points together and swap stories until we reach the fork in the road that signals we are ten minutes from contact. It is time to be serious now, very serious, and I follow his instructions to watch our rearview mirror without turning around. He slows slightly, for we are rather early, and precision in arrival could mean life or death. We both know well enough what happens to any person, foreign or otherwise, caught by the army while approaching the "*subversivos.*" At the five-minute point, my friend tells me to put on my boots, and I take off the black cotton Chinese slippers I am wearing and quickly pull on the boots. At two minutes I put on the dark jacket. Then we roll down my window and watch for a villager carrying the correct bundles in the correct hand and wearing the shirt with certain designs on the sleeves. We find him almost immediately, strolling down the roadside with a relaxed gait. We slow, but he does not look up until I speak, reciting the lines I have been given. He turns his head cautiously toward us then, wary of my accent, and in the half-light I make out the open face of a villager with dark, intense Mayan eyes. They lock with mine for a moment, exchanging silent confirmation; then he recites his own coded lines and swiftly pulls open my door.

In a few seconds I am out of the car with my pack and he has me by the arm, pulling me into the heavy foliage and down a small rocky trail. We come to a large tree surrounded by enormous vines and shrubs that conceal us completely, and he quickly strips off his shirt and pants, revealing olive green fatigues beneath. Then he bends to retrieve a heavy rifle from the brush. We say nothing, but he communicates with his eyes that all is well and pulls a small walkie-talkie from a tangle of green vines, whispering several code words into it. There is a crackled response and a sudden clattering of boots; then four other *compañeros* appear in the shadows. They look quickly at me, evaluating my readiness, then give me welcoming hugs, calling me their sister and telling me that they are glad I have arrived safely. The older one scoops up my pack and moves on ahead of us to scout, and we stride off at a fast pace behind him. There is no time to waste, for we are deep within army territory. I worry some about the small huts in the distance, wondering if we are visible, but the others smile and tell me not to worry. These are the homes of friends.

For many hours we move at a half run through the darkened forest, skirting around open fields and jolting down steep, rocky paths. The young *compañero* just in front of me holds his flashlight pointed straight down so that the light skims the terrain about my feet. His fingers are positioned just over the bulb, keeping the pinpoint of light soft and dim. He and the others call to me in low voices to warn me of pitfalls and slippery spots, taking gentle hold of my wrists to help me over particularly bad terrain. Together we cross river after river, stepping across moss-covered stones in the cold rushing water. Inevitably I fall in, soaking my socks and the bottoms of my dark jeans, and end up wading across, smiling as they try desperately not to laugh. They cross so effortlessly, like gazelles, that my wild thrashing is preposterous to them, but they do not wish to hurt my feelings. Instead they help me wring out my socks and smooth my hair, murmuring words of encouragement. By late that night we know one another well enough that when I slip and splash we laugh out loud in unison. During our brief breaks, I learn that sweet-faced one is named Daniel and that he has been in the mountains now for nearly fifteen years. The older, sturdy one is Abram. The three younger ones are Eloy, Carlos, and Antonio. Perhaps in their late teens, they are rosy-cheeked and playful in the cold shadows, but also wary. Their dark, ever-alert eyes, like those of so many villagers, suggest they are old beyond their years.

As the hours pass, I grow used to the rapid pace and catch my second wind. It is beautiful here, the sharp black outlines of the volcano etched against the night sky with its scattering of brilliant stars. A rich silence envelops us, for we are far from any sounds of roads or towns now. There is only the murmur of nearby streams and the rush of the wind through the thick branches above our heads. Carlos and Antonio take turns mimicking the coos and trills of wild birds to amuse me, and I notice that we have begun a difficult climb. When Daniel calls us to a halt, I look at my watch and find to my surprise that it is nearly two o'clock in the morning. We are out of the military's grim reach now, and it is time to rest. We are safe here.

Abram and Daniel throw some heavy canvas wraps on the ground and smooth them out and we curl up together under yet another layer of canvas and lightweight blankets. Eloy takes the first sentry shift and the others quietly agree among themselves as to who will take the next turns, so that everyone will get some rest before dawn. Then we lie down to sleep, fully dressed, boots on, a neat pile of rifles within easy reach. They have learned the hard way always to be ready for surprise events. For a while I am wide awake, far too amazed by my new surroundings to fall asleep. But as I grow warmer beneath the covers, the exertion of the last few hours overtakes me. When I open my eyes again, it is dawn.

Daniel and Abram are already up and about and cooking some wild roots over a small fire. Later, they explain, it will not be safe, for the flames will be visible from the air. We must eat quickly now in the pale light and then move onward. Antonio hands me a small portion of the boiled roots and I chew them slowly, surprised by their sweet taste. More than anything I am thirsty, as if all the fluids had been sucked from my limbs the night before. The others seem to intuit this, for a tin of cold water mixed with powdered milk and sugar appears and I drink it down gratefully.

Soon we are off again, the tarpaulins rolled neatly into Daniel's pack, the fire out and the ashes scattered so as to leave no trace that we were ever here. Eloy takes a fallen pine branch and gently sweeps away the vague imprints that our bodies left on the ground as we slept. The others look quickly about for mislaid scraps of paper or other telltale signs. No clues can be left for random army scouts, no signs that this is a trail used by the *compañeros*. Such errors lead to ambush and certain death.

Today the hike is more difficult, for my legs have stiffened during the night and we are no longer running across the low, uneven ground of the coffee farms. Now we are climbing so sharply that I keep grasping for vines and rocks above my head to pull myself upward. Even the flatter stretches are difficult, for the earth is soaked through with the daily rains and gives way under my stumbling feet. The trail is very narrow, and we skirt around and around the hairpin turns of the green mountainside. Carlos and Antonio hover close, ready to take my arm or hand if I totter too near the edge of the cliffs, and they banter back and forth with each other to distract me from the climb. Their voices are soft and somewhat singsong, with the birdlike accents of Mayan highlanders, and as I listen to them I realize that I am indeed back at last in Guatemala.

The thought makes me giddy. I have been miserably homesick for this land that I was not born in. With the faint light, the lush scenery is fully visible to me now, the enormous lily-like leaves covering the slopes below, together with the twists and turns of thick vines, wild shrubs and grasses, and short angular pines. The entire valley is incredibly green. As I gaze downward, I see the pale morning mist drifting slowly up the mountainside toward us from the dimly lit villages below. For me this is home. I cannot stay away.

Gradually the sun emerges, and although the winds continue to chill, I begin to grow wildly thirsty again. The *compas* stop frequently to give me sips of water, warning me not to drink too much. As we hike upward, the muscles above my knees begin to throb and I curse myself for not thinking of running hills instead of distance in preparation for this trip. I am nearly forty now and irately note the changes in my once-sturdy body. Daniel and the others encourage me gently, promising that the upward climb will not last long, that soon a downward stretch will come. They are right, but the shift downhill does little to alleviate the pain growing throughout my legs, for the slopes are so sharp and jolting that my muscles are worked even harder by the descent. They know this, and soon a soft voice begins to reassure me that the downward part will not last long, that in just a bit we will be climbing again. And so they encourage and cajole me as we climb farther and farther up the cliffs of the volcano, stopping in shady clearings here and there for short rests and drinks of water. The younger ones have lost their initial shyness now and pull at my braids and tease and throw their arms about me, villager-style, as if I were some long-lost cousin just arrived for a visit.

At last we reach the upper volcano ridge and cross a ravine. The trail becomes dangerously narrow now and a thick rope is bolted to one side of the cliff, with heavy knots for handgrips. We cross step by step, hanging on to the knotted rope, then climb through a last cluster of pine trees. Out of nowhere a sentry calls softly to us and Daniel waves his rifle and calls back the password, adding a joke in Mayan that provokes a smothered giggle from behind the screen of giant leaves and vines.

We walk a few more yards into the sunlight, and suddenly we are in a small clearing with a campfire and low wooden stools made of tree trunks. To one side is a small shelter with a well-camouflaged roof of interlaced pine branches and flimsy green and black sheets of plastic. Inside are cooking supplies, a clothesline hung with sundry socks and shirts, and small benches. A cold, clear stream encircles us just a few feet below and I see two young men on their knees down there, scrubbing their laundry on the rocks and splashing each other.

As my eyes adjust, a large, sturdy man hoots out a welcome and sweeps me off my feet, whirling me around. It is Marco, my friend from one of the underground houses so far from here. I interviewed him long ago when he was recovering from a bullet wound, and he made me roar with laughter and weep over the stories he told of his many years in the war. It is strange to see him now in uniform, his rifle slung easily over one shoulder, and I remember that he is second in command here, a man of responsibilities, despite his relaxed manner. I cling to him, happy and surprised to see him, and he sits me down on one of the tree stumps and hurries to bring me a pan of cold water. Daniel and the others tarry for a moment, then, quite untired by the climb, they move off to their different tasks of chopping wood, gathering water, and teaching reading and writing to the new combatants. Marco gives them their assignments in a quiet voice. Then he explains that many of the women I have come to interview are still away on a mission but will be back in a few days. Meanwhile, I can interview as many other *compañeros* here as I wish; he will make all of the arrangements. I must be very tired from the climb. Have I any blisters that need attention? Any torn muscles? Jorge, the doctor, will be returning this evening if I need anything. At night I will be staying with Emma, the sassy-faced woman bending over the cooking pot. She looks up and sends me a humorous smirk of welcome as he tells me this, and I immediately like her. Short and robust, she is in her thirties perhaps, with a shock of unruly black hair, bold eyes, and curved lips set at an impish angle. She is so roguish and at ease, I can't help smiling back.

Marco puts an arm around my shoulders and points out the different faint footpaths. That one leads to my tent, up there behind the boulders. Emma will show me which one later on and help me to set out my things. I mustn't unpack completely though, for up here one never knows what could happen; we must be ready to move quickly, even in the middle of the night. The trail over there leads to a small swimming hole for bathing. Up there is the communications post. I can always find one of the officers there if I need anything—Celia or

Emma or Comandante Everardo. That's him, in fact, to the right at the edge of the trees. Marco points up the slope and I see a young man in olive green standing motionless in the shadows of the pines. He is neatly proportioned, with short, sturdy arms and legs, and he stands very straight with his rifle in hand. He waves politely as we look up at him but his face, though intriguing, seems impossibly young. It is very wide at the cheekbones, with fierce black eyes and full vulnerable lips. His smooth gold-colored skin shows not a line or wrinkle. Surely I am looking at the wrong person. I glance about, searching for someone else back there in the shadows, someone older, more grayed and stooped under the weight of such responsibility. The young man watches us for a few moments, his head up and his eyes sharply alert, and I have the sense of being scanned and evaluated, read like a book. Then he turns and walks off into the forest with a silent, catlike gait, without so much as a backward glance.

And so it is, the first moment we meet, Everardo. You are wary and I am confused, looking for someone utterly different. But I remember this first glimpse of you, with your fierce eyes and lithe mountain walk, as clearly as if it were yesterday. I will remember it always. There is no detail about you, no fragmentary image, that I could ever forget. These memories, at least, the years cannot take from me.

The Camp
Summer 1990

FOR THE FIRST FEW DAYS MY LEGS REMAIN STIFF AND SORE. I HOB-ble about the camp, getting to know the *compañeros* and learning my way across the faint trails of the volcano. I go with the others to gather firewood on the nearby slopes and help clean and scrape the wild roots and greens for dinner. Emma takes me to bathe in the ice-cold waters of the swimming hole and in the afternoons Leonardo, a seasoned combatant with perfect Mayan features, sits down to teach me a few words of the Quiché language. Hobbled from a tumble over a cliff, he is waiting for his knee to heal. The *compas* are all shy at first, but after a brief watchful phase, they tell me their stories bit by bit, careful to leave out names and places that could lead someone to harm. Still, my small tape recorder frightens them and so I learn to listen carefully as we chat over daily tasks, then fill my notebooks late at night in the dim glow of my flashlight. Soon, without noticing, we fall into a comfortable routine. There are well over a hundred *compas* here, with several hundred more away on missions. Gradually, I come to understand that this is merely a communications and transit center, with the combatants flowing in and out for training, instructions, medical care, and R and R. Soon the location will be changed, lest the army finally figure out their exact position. For the same reason, the radio codes must be rewritten every week.

I grow to know the *compas* one by one, starting of course with sassy Emma, my tent mate. Almost immediately, we become fast friends. She teaches me the ropes, explaining how the camp is organized, which *compañeros* are in charge of what and, naturally, provides me with a rundown on the personal lives of one and all, including her own. Like Daniel, she has been in the mountains for nearly fifteen years and was one of the first women combatants in the *frente*. This fact she takes as nothing special, though she is a pretty *ladina* with some schooling and could easily have lived a middle-class life in the City. She came up here, she explains with an easy shrug, because they were hunting down her unionist father in the City and she didn't want to go into exile with her mother and brothers. Who, after all, would want to leave Guatemala?

Slowly, I learn to walk properly in this new terrain. Eloy and Antonio, close friends since our long climb, show me how to tread lightly on the shifting earth as we descend a slope, letting my feet slide downward a bit, then lifting them up as if I were swimming across the muddy surfaces. Emma teaches me to throw my weight forward slightly as I move, telling me not to fear the brief skidding of my feet, explaining that I must not fear a fall. In the end I will fall less often, she says, and of course she is right. Crossing the streams takes more practice, but they show me again and again where to place my feet, how to balance. I continue to stumble and splash, but they no longer fear my anger and my clumsiness becomes a great joke between us, something to gently tease me about. They also tease me about my size, which they consider quite remarkable, for most of them are villagers, malnourished from birth. At five three I am by far the largest woman in the camp and taller, in fact, than most of the men. Weeks later I will try to give my boots away but this will be impossible, for they measure a woman's size seven, far too large for anyone up here to wear.

The days become seamless. At dawn everyone rises and heads for the small, dim clearing for morning exercises and stretches. Together we do sit-ups and push-ups and back bends and then jog around the small periphery and up and down its steep edges. The drills are far from militant and are usually carried out with a flurry of giggles and teasing comments, ending up with a playful game. The favorite is a startling form of leapfrog, with the target person standing straight up while the others take turns flipping over his head. They are all built like aerial acrobats, light-boned and tight-muscled and quick as cats. I never tire of watching them. Later Marco makes the announcements and assigns the day's tasks of cooking, wood gathering, and sentry shifts. Then we disperse and wander down to the kitchen fire for a breakfast of tamales made of toasted roots and hot coffee with sugar and sometimes milk. Inevitably as we eat, a small cluster of *compañeros* appears with their packs strapped to their backs and their rifles and ammunition pouches slung across their shoulders, heading out to a mission below. They give the ritual exchange of hugs to each and every person at the fire, for though casualties are rare these days, anything is possible. One must never take a life for granted.

I pass the daylight hours with the different combatants, helping with chores and listening to their stories. I quickly come to love them, with their straightforward, affectionate ways and wild humor. Yet their stories tell of so much more, of a discipline I find hard to fathom, of a clear-eyed commitment, of a fierce vision for the future that I am only beginning to comprehend. Many are second-generation combatants, for their mothers and fathers fought before them, as did their grandparents and even those before them, against the relentless heritage of the conquest. Most are Mayan, thin and small, with sparkling diagonal eyes, sculpted cheekbones, and the chirping accents of the highlands in their voices. Others, like Emma, are from the City. Some are university students and teachers, others unionists or co-op workers, many even leaders from the church. All left home on the run, leaving everything they had ever known behind.

Their stories overwhelm me, leaving me sleepless at night. Day after day they tell me of their lost villages, the people massacred and the homes burned to the ground; of close calls and comical escapes; of loved ones dragged away and left battered and dead in the streets; of terrifying battles. Some stories make me laugh, like the tale of the pet squirrel who stole everyone's food, then fled to the highest branches to mock them from above. Others leave me in despair, for they tell of lost friends and lovers, of army tortures and cruelties that I cannot bear to imagine. I weep over these late into the night. With time, I begin to have nightmares again about my own two years in the City so long ago, remembering the terror and the endless piteous dead in the morgues.

From time to time, I am reminded of the army's rage nearby. The small dark planes circle endlessly overhead, motors droning, and as we move beneath the protective trees it seems so impossible that they cannot see us. Yet the bombs fall at quite a distance, randomly flung across the upper face of the volcano, blasting ugly scars into the cliff sides and making the ground beneath our feet shake and tremble even from so far away. The sound is terrible, of wrenching earth and shattering stone, and it echoes deep into my inner ear.

When it's over Everardo appears out of nowhere, gliding across the encampment, making sure that all is well, touching my elbow and asking discreetly if I am in need of anything. I have come to love his quiet manner, his way of being everywhere at once during times of trouble, then vanishing like some woodland spirit once everything is quiet. In my many days here, I have never heard him raise his voice or bark an order. He simply appears from behind the trees, speaking in his soft, low voice with the others. Somehow all is arranged without more ado. No curt salutes or militaristic clicking of boot heels are needed up here. Late at night while the others play and tumble about the campfire, he sits quietly reading, a small book in one hand and a flashlight in the other, his lips moving slightly as he thinks about the words on the page before him. One by one the younger *compas* approach for a few quiet moments of talk, to ask him for advice or to confide a problem, whether of love or health or fear or simply war. Just as he is the first to rise, checking in with the sentry as the others stumble sleepily about, he is also the last to leave the campfire. I notice him night after night, sitting erect at the edge of the fire, listening attentively to a young *compañero*, nodding his head and reaching forward with his small hands to give a reassuring pat or embrace.

I watch him carefully, hoping for a chance at a long conversation but not wanting to distract him from his work. We have spoken often enough now about small day-to-day things, and he has taken great care to attend to all my needs with grave courtesy, even taking Leonardo's place one afternoon to teach me some new phrases of Quiché. We have spoken about the history of the organization, and he has told me much about the early era, when they worked in secret for nearly seven years in the southwest. He thinks all my questions over slowly, silent for a bit as he forms an answer that is inevitably flawless. It is clear even from these conversations that this is a man of unusual intelligence. I want to hear more of his own life but am afraid to ask, for I know he does not fully trust me even now. At night I still feel him watching me from across the campfire, his black eyes as alert and unblinking as a wild deer's in the forest, thinking over my presence. I must yet wait.

The Talk
Summer 1990

EVEN FROM SO FAR AWAY, THE BOMBING RIPS US ALL FROM OUR DEEP slumber. The sounds of shearing rock and battered earth echo toward us across the mountainside like some dread long-distance thunder, making us roll from our blankets before we are even fully awake. As we fumble for the tiny flashlight, Everardo runs on swift, silent feet past our tent and taps on the makeshift walls, calling softly for Emma to meet him at the communications post. She pulls on her boots and vanishes into the darkness after him, leaving me wide awake and very worried. Soon I hear the crackle of the radio from the ledge above and her firm clear voice calling series after series of coded numbers and passwords into her small receiver. There is no response.

I find the others at the campfire, talking quietly with Marco. They are wide awake and calm enough, neatly dressed, their faces scrubbed and alert. Dawn is breaking, but it is still very cold in the weak light. They wrap their arms around one another, sharing a steaming tin of hot coffee and waiting patiently for word from the radio post. Two of the older ones have brought their packs, ready to move whenever the orders arrive. All carry rifles.

After a bit, Everardo appears and they gather around his small figure. There has been an ambush; a cache of explosives went off. No one is dead, but some *compañeros* have been injured and need to be evacuated. Two must be carried, and an escort must be sent to bring Jorge, the doctor, back from the western slope. An extra patrol is needed to reinforce the combat unit in the valley as well. He quietly calls out names and one by one the *compas* disperse and reappear almost immediately, combat-ready, with neatly laced packs and cartridge belts in place, machetes strapped to their backs, and rifles looped easily across their sturdy shoulders. They seem relaxed enough as they exchange embraces, but they move and speak now with a quick, surgical intensity. Within minutes they are gone, moving lightly across the shadowy trails and calling back soft good-byes. I wince as I see Daniel and Eloy leaving with them.

There are no boisterous exercises this morning, and Marco smoothly divides the day's chores among the remaining *compañeros*. Antonio takes a double sentry shift, Emma will not leave the radio post, so Carlos will take her turn at gathering wood. Beto will cook; Julio will bring extra medical supplies from their far-off hiding place. The ranking old-timers, Celia, Abram, Juan Carlos, and Marco himself leave for the command post to work with Everardo on strategies. I wander back to the tent and straighten the blankets on the rickety bed of tightly lashed branches. Emma has left her flashlight behind, for she can find her way to her radio post with her eyes closed, but she has not left her gun. I tidy up and write for a bit; then as the morning passes, I wander up for a visit and to find out if there is any news.

I find Emma at her radio table, cheerful enough, and busy decoding the most recently arrived messages. Sheafs of scrawled-over paper and plastic-wrapped charts filled with tiny letters and numbers clutter the space in front of her. She laughs at my mournful face and tells me to straighten up, that no one has been lost, and that Jorge can cure anyone, no matter how serious the injury. She winks and reminds me of the old saying that bad grass never dies, telling me to think of all the trouble the *compas* have caused throughout the years. If they aren't bad grass, then who is? Eh?

I stay with her and read quietly for a while, enjoying her roguish company even though she hasn't time to speak much with me. From where I sit, I can see Everardo's low green tent through the thin screen of pine trees. This morning he has been everywhere at once, gliding from post to post, receiving information, checking on sentries, and arranging the medical supplies into neat piles. Now he sits on a small stump, ankles crossed and a large notebook spread across his lap, surrounded by *compañeros* moving swiftly about with maps and messages. He pores intently over these, lifting his head from time to time to give quiet instructions, signaling with his small, deft hands. Then as I watch, he stands and straightens and moves rapidly down the trail toward us, documents tucked firmly beneath his arms. He greets us with small pats on the shoulder, his face smooth and serene. Are we well? Have we need of anything? He takes a seat on the flimsy bench and picks up Emma's papers, reading them silently, marking a few passages, then writing down the responses for her to send. They go through these together, word by word, to assure no misunderstandings, for these could lead to deaths. Despite his calm, I can see the edges of fatigue gathering around his eyes and lips. For many days now he has been working ceaselessly. I know because I have been watching.

When he finishes with Emma he rises again and vanishes down the

slope, heading for the small clearing with the campfire. I catch sight
of him as he reaches the upper bank just across from us, and I am fascinated as always by his soundless walk. He stops abruptly at the
heavy metal corn grinder, and I realize with a start that no one has
been grinding corn or roots for the evening meal. It is a task that takes
many hours and normally begins early in the day, but in the confusion
somehow the grinder has remained idle, a large bucket of cleaned
roots and loose corn kernels waiting at its side. This is no small error,
with incoming *compas* weary and hungry after a difficult battle and a
rough climb across the volcanoes with their injured friends. They will
be arriving soon and there must be food to nourish them.

I watch, waiting for Everardo to shout for Yemo or Raul to come
and start up the grinding, for they are not far away from where he
stands. He makes no sound though; instead, he stoops lightly to un-
strap his rifle and lay it against the nearby tree. Then he lifts the heavy
bucket and pours a portion of the roots into the cup of the grinder,
filling it to the brim. Gripping the mill handle, he begins turning it
round and round, his small arms tracing neat circles in the air as he
leans his weight into the task. I myself have tried my hand at this job
under Emma's supervision, and I know exactly how heavy it can be,
but he works gracefully, almost effortlessly. Watching, I remember
that he was born a villager and lived a life of hunger and hard labor
before he left the plantation forever and came to the mountains to
fight. The familiarity with which he bends to his task gives silent confirmation. This man is no stranger to hard work. Nor does he consider it beneath him.

After a few minutes Capitán Celia comes down the trail, her maps
in hand, her stride bold and confident. She stares at Everardo as he
bends over the grinder, then calls out quickly for the others to come
and help. Yemo arrives at once, and also curly-haired Ariel, who is
nursing a bad leg, and Marco. The chores are quickly rearranged and
Yemo good-naturedly takes over at the wheel. Marco shakes his head
and throws an arm about Everardo's shoulders as they move off together up the trail. Musing, I watch them for some time. Not a voice
has been raised nor a harsh word given, for there is no need up here.
Matters have simply been resolved, in the style of the *compañeros*.

Soon a small patrol arrives with the wounded, and Jorge Medico rushes into the camp just a few minutes behind them, out of breath from his long run back up the mountainside. His kindly face is pale and worried-looking, and he hurries straight to the campfire, rolling up his sleeves. Together they lay the injured out on the ground near the fire, pulling up trouser legs to inspect shrapnel wounds, and examining a bad shoulder. One man has a bloody head gash but is quite clear-minded and conscious. After a short while Jorge looks up, smiling at us, and announces that none of the injuries are serious and that there is no need to worry. The *compas* must rest and keep their wounds clean and well bandaged, but they will be fine in no time. The others sigh with relief, remembering aloud about the time Jorge did full abdominal surgery on a dying *compañero* in a cornfield. That man lived, and so will these friends. Jorge will see to it.

They rush about now, eager to fetch water and medical supplies and wide strips of sterile gauze. Packets of long-hoarded special food appear, cookies and bits of chocolate, and a tin of dried meat. These are passed eagerly to the men lying on the ground, who huff that perhaps they should get hurt more often. Everardo arrives and sits down with the *compas* for a while, welcoming them back and conferring with Jorge about their care and needs. He banters back and forth with them, adds a few coveted cigarettes to the communal stash, then glides off to Emma's station to check for messages from the rest of the unit, for though the wounded are back, the others are still far away and still in potential danger. For him it is not yet time to rest.

At last the day draws to an end and the clearing fills with shadows. Ariel is stoking the fire and tending the large cauldrons of beans and tamales, lifting the lids carefully to avoid the billowing steam. His leg still drags as he moves, for it has been slow to heal from the bullet wounds that once shattered the bone. He spent a year in a hospital, but he has steadily refused to take a post in one of the towns, insisting that he belongs with the others up here in the volcano. In his early twenties, he is still young and sassy and flirts impudently with Emma and Celia as they pass by. This makes them laugh, for he is fragilely built and at least ten years their junior. They yank at his curls and drape their arms affectionately around his slight shoulders, hissing back feisty answers that make the others chuckle aloud.

As they jibe back and forth, the long-awaited patrol finally arrives at the camp, calling out passwords and hoots of greetings. The other *compas* rush to embrace them and pull them to the fire, helping them stash their heavy packs in a neat pile and offering back rubs and pans of cold water. Now that everyone is safely home, the mood turns raucous. The *compas* sit together in an intertwined heap on the ground, arms flung about one another, cuddling close and chattering in Mayan and Spanish at the same time. Tin dishes of hot food are passed around, and as they eat the wild jokes and preposterous, teasing stories begin. Ariel wraps a thin arm around my shoulders and tells me I am his kind of woman, making everyone roar as I am at least twice his size, but he only gives an unabashed smirk, then turns to tickle Yemo with a large rubbery leaf. Soon Everardo appears and sits down to work with Bartolo, but the *compas* quickly pull him into a makeshift game of soccer. Together they scramble after a small plastic ball in the tiny periphery, tumbling about and bouncing it off each other's heads, careful not to trample their injured friends. After a fierce tussle, they end up in a giggling heap on the ground as the ball vanishes over the ledge and into the river below.

We settle into our coffee then and Emma brings out a tiny Chinese checkerboard, challenging me to a match. The others surround us, helping to illuminate the board with their small flashlights and calling out advice to both of us at once. Emma wins the first game and I the second; then I play against Ariel and Yemo. The mood grows quieter, comfortable, and some of the *compas* begin to stumble off tiredly toward their tents while Ariel and Marco scrub the cauldrons and haul water for the night. As I finish up with Yemo, Everardo sits next to me, picking up a small plastic piece and wordlessly offering a game. The others are delighted and clap and cheer him on, making him laugh at their uproar. It is quite dark now and growing cold, so we move closer to the fire and begin to play. He beats me soundly the first round, and the others groan and hug me, urging a rematch and pointing to different places for me to move my checkers. As they chatter out support strategies Everardo looks up, worried that perhaps he could hurt my feelings, and he lets me win two games in a row. I accuse him of this but he denies it gravely, telling me I am simply the better player.

I pour a second cup of coffee and bring one for him and we settle close to the flames. His face is open to me now, the dark eyes ever cautious, but the slight lines about his mouth are friendly and relaxed. I have grown accustomed to this face now and it no longer appears young or even frail to me, despite the smooth skin and tranquil look. The jaw is strong and square and well sculpted, balancing the broad cheekbones, and the mouth, though soft, is firmly set beneath dark brows and a small Mayan nose. It is the eyes, though, that are ancient, flashing a depth of painful experience and wary intellect that make them fathomless. They are the eyes of a man who has aged beyond death.

Looking at him, at those fierce eyes, I tell him that someday I would like to hear his story, at least the parts that he can tell me. He stares, evaluating this dangerous request, and I struggle not to avert my gaze, realizing that he needs to read me. Our eyes lock and for a long while I sense my mind being turned inside out and gently ransacked without a word being spoken. Then he asks politely if I am cold, if I need another sweater or wrap. I tell him no, and we fall into a long Mayan silence, strange for me yet quite comfortable, and he thinks the matter over for some time. At last he settles back against a stump and asks me if I will go first, tell my own story to him. Fair enough, I think to myself, amused at this deft turn of the tables. I will go first.

For a few minutes I feel silly, not knowing where to begin or what would be of interest to a man who has battled from the volcanoes for some fifteen years. But as I speak, telling him about my mother and father, brothers and sister, and my childhood in Connecticut, I begin to realize that there is nothing that this man is not interested in. His mind is like an enormous vortex, spinning everything inward toward his hungry center. He asks about public schools and private schools and field trips and museums and child nutrition programs and special education and my opinion on bilingual classes. We move on to my experiences in the sixties, of race rights and the Vietnam War, of details about Freedom Summer and descriptions of Jimi Hendrix and Janis Joplin and my evaluation of the impact of Watergate. I begin to grow tired, but his dark eyes are enormous now, unblinking and eager, and I am suddenly anxious to feed this remarkable and voracious mind. I tell him about Afghanistan and we discuss the role of women in Islamic societies, and the perils of cultural interventionism, but he shakes his head and says that no culture exists that is worth enslavement. I talk of Peru then, and he devours my description of the wild animals in the Amazon basin, asking over and over about the turtles and the alligators and piranhas and eels in the water, and the clouds of electric blue butterflies. We move on then to China and dissect the good and bad, the repression in Tibet, the advances in public welfare, such as literacy and nutrition, and the schools and public medical programs. What works and what doesn't, and how would I compare it to the United States, and why?

By the time I reach my years at legal aid, working with the migrants, and my time in Guatemala, most of the *compañeros* have left for bed. There are only Ariel and Marco now, preparing tomorrow's beans to simmer throughout the night, and Bartolo, writing out his reports on the week's mission. The sentry sits far above, watching over us, but Everardo is not tired, despite his long day. He continues to interrogate me about my experiences in Guatemala, where I traveled, what I saw, and what I thought. What did I like about the people? Why? What else? When he finishes, I feel as if he has seized me by the ankles and shaken me upside down, my thoughts and memories bouncing like small gold coins onto the ground at his feet. I am exhausted and a bit taken aback by this mental shakedown, but as I look into his face in the firelight, I see that he is utterly content, savoring the discussion like a sip of fine rare wine. When I tell him I must sleep, he thanks me for the gift of this good discussion, this good stimulus, and walks me to the edge of the clearing with an arm around my shoulders. As I start down the darkened trail he holds a lantern up high, lighting my way. By the time I reach the tent, I know I am falling in love with this extraordinary man and I curse myself for being a fool.

The *Compañeras*
Guatemala, 1990

I DON'T HAVE LONG TO WAIT FOR THE REST OF THE WOMEN COM-batants. A few days later, they arrive with their different patrols within a few hours of one another, and they descend on the camp like a wild band of gypsy queens, sassy, flirty and full of life. I am quite enchanted, and I spend the entire morning with them, watching them pitch their tents anew, unpack their gear, and nonchalantly comb their long black hair free from their tight braids. They are quite young, most of them, and have ultrafeminine pseudonyms* like Larissa, Brenda, and Clarita and they wear bright woven bracelets and tiny ear-rings of beads and rhinestones. They take me in as a matter of course, as if I were a package addressed to them, simply awaiting their return.

When they finish with their tents, they invite me to the river to a special bathing hole and I clamber down the steep, rocky slopes, try-ing to keep up and making such a racket that they burst into high-pitched giggles. Larissa, the smallest one, hovers close by, smiling but watching carefully to be sure I don't fall. The trails are narrow and slip-pery from the constant rains, making it easy enough to take a danger-ous tumble into the ravines, especially for a stranger like myself. This they would never allow, for after all I am a guest, and a rare one at that.

After a rough downward hike, we end up at a small lagoon with a tiny waterfall that serves as a perfect shower. The women strip down

*All *compañeros* use pseudonyms in order to protect themselves and their families.

to their underwear, pulling small washcloths and scraps of hard colored soap from their pockets and piling their uniforms on enormous
green leaves to protect them from the mud. Laura, the older one,
stands guard with her rifle, and after a quick look around she motions
to us that all is well. One by one the others plunge in, laughing and
teasing and calling to me to join them, splashing water at my feet. I
pull off my clothes and wade in, shocked by the cold clarity of the
mountain water, which they seem not even to notice. They happily
lather their hair and scrub their small, sturdy bodies from head to
foot with their bits of soap, then duck under the surface to rinse,
popping back up for a lusty gasp of air. They scrub me too, marveling
at my big feet and playing with my hair, pushing me under the surface as if I were a large and interesting doll.

I crawl out after a bit, chilled to the bone, and sit in a small patch
of dim sunlight to watch while the others scrub out their dirty clothes
on the rough rocks. They are smooth and husky with gold-brown
skin, reminding me of so many playful seals as they splash and chatter in the water. Only their neat pile of rifles tugs at my attention, reminding me that there are no children here and that these women have
just returned from combat.

They show me how to spread the thin uniforms out smoothly on
the larger rocks so that they will dry as if pressed by an iron in the
chill winds. Then they climb back into their clothes and twist their
hair into loose knots at the backs of their heads, helping one another
with pins and barrettes. I gasp as Clarita puts her uniform back on
wet, for she has washed both sets of clothes. But the others only laugh
and tell me that the thin fabric is quick to dry and that the dampness
will help keep her cool on the rough climb back. We tarry for a while,
chatting and swapping bits of information about each other—where
we are from, our ages, what brought us up here in the first place.
Larissa arrived after years in a distant refugee camp, drawn by her
memories of a flight through darkened cornfields with her mother.
Elena's husband was beaten to death and she barely had the time to
get her children to safety before the masked men returned to her
home, looking for her. Laura's brother was burned alive in the Spanish embassy during a peaceful sit-in for Mayan rights. We are quiet

for a bit, thinking over these hard stories; then we gather up our things and begin the return climb.

As we arrive at the main campfire, an unspoken recess is declared and the other *compas* arrive from remote parts of the base, lavishing the women with fond embraces and small gifts they have collected in their absence: bits of embroidery and weavings proudly worked by the men, tiny penciled cards, and as always, the hoarded cigarettes. The men listen to the stories and news eagerly, asking me with great pride if I do not find their *compañeras* quite remarkable, and I respond that I do indeed. The women, too, have brought things from below, and I have to smile as they display chocolates, tiny plastic earrings, packets of coffee and spices, and miniature tubes of lotions. The *compas* carry no money of their own, for they receive no wages, and it is clear that they have caught the admiring eyes of more than one villager outside the volcano. It is easy enough to understand, for their feisty laughter is infectious and their bright, bold eyes, ever watchful, make them striking indeed. They unload cookies and molasses candies, passing them around, and suddenly Marco appears with a box of strawberry cake mix packages sent from below with the routine supplies. He shakes his head ruefully as we laugh out loud. Cake mix? Well, why not?

Marco sits down with us and quietly rearranges the day's chores, lapsing in and out of both Spanish and Quiché as he speaks. The younger women will catch up on their studies for the afternoon, and Estella will work with Celia on the reports. Antonio, Johnny, and Pablo will take the solar-energy panels to the next slope where the sun is brighter, and mix up the cakes and bake them in the clay oven at the old base camp there. I think Marco is joking about this, but soon they are off with me in tow, their backs piled high with the wood-framed panels and a large pack of shallow pans tied to one side. Up here nothing is wasted—especially not food, and certainly not cake. As we trudge off I see Clarita and Eloy sitting together under a large tree, their heads bent together over a brightly colored book. He is teaching her the alphabet, calling out the names of letters while she points with her pretty hands to the page before him. She is relaxed and happy, but it is Eloy's face that catches my attention. He is watching her fixedly as he softly calls the letters, and on his face there is a look of deep affection and fierce pride.

The old base camp is not far away, but we must pass the ravine with the knotted rope, then descend and climb back up the other side. I am surprised at how much easier it all seems now, at how much stronger my legs have grown during my short time in the volcano. As we take up a rhythmic pace, I admire the vast green valley below, hung with floating mists. So beautiful a country yet so grim a war. I begin to daydream, remembering friends long dead in the City, wondering who is still alive, who has fled into exile, and who the newcomers might be. There are always newcomers, I have learned, young and strong and waiting to take the places of the dead. They have fought, now, for five hundred years. How many more generations will it take to undo the mass destruction of the conquest?

Despite myself, I start thinking of Everardo. We have become fast friends, though he is still rather guarded with me, uncertain as to exactly what makes me tick. Until he fully knows me, he will not quite allow himself to trust me, and this I understand well enough. Mislaid trust could lead to deaths. In any event this friendship, though dangerous, is worth a bit of patience. At the campfire at night I read my battered novel while he finishes with the others, then comes to sit close by, signaling silently that we can now resume our conversation from the night before. Together we talk over the news and share stories, sipping slowly at our cups of rationed coffee and helping with the fire. I piece together his early life bit by bit: his childhood in a remote village, his mother's death for lack of antibiotics, their deep and endless hunger as they worked the plantation fields of the very rich. He, like the other Mayans in the village, existed as but another dispensable life, quite without value, like a paper plate to be tossed away once soiled at a picnic. It was only when he rebelled and ran off to the mountains to fight that he learned to read and write, a gift that he values even now above all else.

From the others I learn that he was a founding member, legendary for his brilliance and fearless combat style. They tell me with pride of his startlingly rapid ascent to the *commandancia* at an early age, and of his first *compañera*, Gabriella, who died at his side during an army ambush. I also learn that his second *compañera* was a villager named Rosalvina. They were together only a few months before the army caught and killed her. In all the years since there have been no others, for he chose instead to live priestlike, focusing on his work and shunning the distractions of a broken heart. I ponder often on his story, thinking it quite remarkable, but when I tell him this he becomes reticent and remote. One simply lives the life one is given.

We reach the base camp and Johnny and Antonio spread out the solar panels on the steep embankment while Pablo unpacks a metal pot and hauls fresh water from a nearby stream. Then he shows me the large clay oven with its deep interior, telling me how they once experimented with baking tortillas and tamales within. They had been tasty enough, but it only worked out when there was plenty of extra time, a rare occurrence. Still, it was nice to come back here, to prepare something special. He sets to gathering wood, chopping it into short, even chunks and stoking the fire until it roars and glows. Then he mixes the cake batter with the water, stirring it to get out all the lumps, and showing Antonio and Johnny how to do the same. They stir away for what seems like a very long time, but Pablo rejects a number of proffered batters, insisting that they are not smooth enough and that the others should do a better job. Finally he is satisfied, and the batter is poured bit by bit into the dozen or so small tin pans and then set to bake in the oven. When they are done, they remove the steaming cakes and place them on large rubbery leaves, then refill the tins. Soon the air is redolent with the smell of baking and strawberry flavoring, making me laugh. They, too, are amused by our surreal activities, but they shrug and remind me that when there is, there is, and when there ain't, there ain't. We must enjoy this as much as we can, for who knows what tomorrow could bring.

By the end of the afternoon we are done, and we wrap the cakes tightly together in the giant leaves, then place them gently into the packs. We move off down the trail and back toward home, eager to return before it becomes too dark. As we walk, the afternoon rains start up, and we pull our thin black sheets of plastic close around our bodies. Soon my legs and hair are soaked through all the same, for the wind drives the rain in sheets into my hood and splashes it up from the ground. For a while I am cold, but then the heat of the climb makes me forget, and I appreciate the dampness against my face as I trudge along the disintegrating trail. Soon we are crossing the ravine again, clutching the knotted rope hand over hand, the *compas* moving easily down the narrow ledge, even with their huge packs and bundles of tin pans. When we reach the campfire I expect the cakes to be smashed to bits, and I am amazed when Pablo unrolls them, intact, from their green wrappers. A few are a bit misshapen now, and others cracked, their steaming texture turned cold and firm during the hike. But they will do quite well indeed.

As evening falls the clearing becomes crowded with the *compas* from the newly returned patrols. Greetings and embraces are rapidly exchanged, and everyone ends up in the affectionate heap of intertwined arms and legs that I always find amusing. Bartolo sits arm in arm with his old friend Isaac, catching up with the news while Beto uses his shoulders as a backrest. Clarita leans with her elbows on Estella's knees and both of them chatter at once with Laura, who is flirting outrageously with Pablo. Antonio and Carlos form an interlaced square with serious Abram and giggly Larissa, each resting against the knees of another. When the food is ready they get up reluctantly to receive their rations, then hurry back to the huddle, anxious not to miss out on any of the stories. Later we each receive a small strawberry cake to warm at the fire, then eat it slowly with our portion of sweetened coffee. I am surprised at how flavorful it seems, for after weeks of beans and boiled rice and toasted roots, my palate has become keenly sensitive. The others congratulate Pablo and eat their cakes with relish, even though most do not like sweets and find artificial flavorings quite odd. More than one have confided to me that they find foreign food in instant packages to be . . . well, terrible. They tell me this gently, inquisitively, baffled as to why one would make such bad foods when one has the money to choose something truly delicious.

After we finish, Laura and the others haul out a battered tape recorder and announce that tonight there will be a dance to celebrate everyone's safe return. This idea confounds me, for where indeed would one dance up here? The clearing is slippery with mud and surrounded by heavy trees and thorny foliage on one side and by a sharp drop to the river on the other. As I watch, though, the *compas* move away the tree-stump seats and stack their rifles carefully against the walls of the lean-to kitchen. A few scratchy chords sound out, and after a moment I realize I am listening to the sound of the Beatles. Estella and Clara have already moved to the corner of the clearing and are dancing rhythmically with Beto and Antonio while Eloy claps out the beat. Larissa pulls quiet Abram to his feet and he dances too, moving his hips back and forth and holding her small hands for the pirouettes. Brenda pulls in Daniel, and Emma invites Pablo. Soon the tiny space is full, and I watch amazed as they dance with their machetes strapped to their backs, heavy boots laced to their feet, skirting carefully around the drop to the riverbed and the muddy downward trail.

After a few songs, a salsa tape goes on and the women choose new partners, taking care that everyone be invited. I muse at the role reversal up here, for most of these *compañeras* were village girls in long skirts and tidy braids just a short while ago, demure and apparently submissive. So much for appearances, I think to myself. *Sic semper.* Suddenly I realize that Everardo is sitting next to me, and I start openly. As always, he has approached without a sound, and he sits so motionless that he is nearly invisible in the shadows. He laughs as I jolt to attention, and he reminds me once again that it is best to remain alert up here in the mountains.

We sit together in the comfortable silence that I have learned to love, watching the dancers and enjoying the music. Then the tape is switched again and Bruce Springsteen begins to sing. Everardo asks me about the English words, and confides that the music is interesting but that he likes the softer sounds of a marimba, or folksingers like Jara or Rodriguez. I am about to agree when Emma and Estella call over to us, telling us to join in. Emma shouts that I am the guest of honor tonight, and that since I am a woman, I can pick my own partner. Who will that be? She is impish now and smirks openly, for she knows very well that I am fighting my feelings toward Everardo. She insists that he feels the same way about me, although he certainly reveals nothing of the sort. Now I am in a quandary, as she well intends. I can't very well ask someone else while he is sitting right there at my side, yet I am timid, afraid to show him any familiarity or disrespect while our friendship is still so new and fragile. I glance up at

him and find his dark eyes fixed on his boots, his quiet face shy and
worried. Estella and Larissa join in calling me to the clearing now and
the others hoot encouragement. No way out being evident, I place my
hand on Everardo's sleeve and ask if he will dance with me. He looks
up nodding with his usual grave courtesy, and as we rise to our feet
together, everyone breaks into loud cheers and wild applause. Chants
of his nickname, "Comanche," fill the air, together with the raucous
music and the claps and shrill whistles of the *compas.*

I pull him into the midst of the dancers and safely out of the center of attention, for even in the shadows I can see that he is blushing.
At first he keeps his eyes on the ground, but after a bit he raises them
to mine and we smile at each other, admitting wordlessly that this joke
indeed has been on us. I know he does not care much for dancing, as
it is so foreign to his villager sense of decorum and reserve, but he
sways gently to the rhythm and takes my hand firmly enough to turn
me through the twirls. His back is still very straight, machete strapped
tightly in place, yet he dances gracefully, and his eyes now lock with
mine. Again, I sense that mental ransack as he searches my thoughts
without uttering a word. As we dance, Yemo begins to clap his hand
back and forth over the bulb of his flashlight, providing us with a
strobe effect. For me, the night is now complete.

After two dances, Everardo leans toward me and murmurs that I
should invite another, that no one should be left out. I turn to invite
Daniel, a favorite friend since that first day, and when I look back,
Everardo has vanished from the clearing. Daniel and I dance a waltz,
and he holds me affectionately as we glide across the mud and rocks.
Then Carlos and Antonio pull me into a polka, and we bounce with
the others in a spirited hopping step, bumping into other couples
until we all break apart, out of breath and laughing. I sit out a few
after that and chat with the others around the fire, watching the
whirling couples. After a while the party begins to wind down, for it
is late and the *compañeras* are tired from their long weeks away.

I pick up my small flashlight and head down the trail toward
Emma's tent, careful not to skid on the muddy rocks and remembering to move to the right of the large tree to avoid a malevolent pot-
hole. This much, at least, I have learned in my time here. Now that

the rains have lifted, the sky is very bright, with a luminous moon, and the chill clean air is bracing. When I pass the large boulder, I realize that Everardo is walking beside me.

Not one for words, he glides silently at my side, looping my arm through his in a manner both easy and confident. I am moved by this wordless admission of affection, but I am afraid to speak and break the spell. After a few more steps I turn to look at him, and without further ado he pulls me gently into his small, firm arms and kisses me full on the lips, shattering forever my intended self-restraint. It is a sweet kiss, slow and soft and almost innocent, and when it is over I cling to him and trace the edges of his full Mayan lips with the tip of my finger. It is such a fragile mouth, vulnerable, belying the fierce strength in his old-man's eyes. As I cling to him, he swings me easily into the shadows and kisses me again, and then again. When he finishes he takes my wrists in his hands and holds me away from him. I love you, he tells me, but in this life it is all so impossible. He stares at me for a while, his eyes unmasked for once, allowing me to see his mixed emotions of happiness, love, and wistful discipline. Then he touches my hair and repeats that it can never be, vanishing down the trail before I can speak a word.

I retreat to Emma's tent and lie wide awake and shaken for the rest of the night, knowing that some wild spirits have been let loose by this momentary crossing of forbidden boundaries. Good or evil? It makes no difference, for I would not relinquish the memory of this soft kiss for anything on the face of the earth.

The Departure
The Volcano, Summer 1990

THE DAYS MOVE BY SWIFTLY, BUT I AM TOO ENGROSSED IN MY WORK to notice their passage. I stride about the green volcano with the others, watching them work and listening to their stories, then lie awake at night, haunted by what I have heard. I wonder how on earth I will write this book, with all its tragedy and wild beauty, and how on earth I can make these people real to those outside the mountains. I think about my lawyer friends and the far-off libraries at Harvard with their carved wood panels and quiet students, and my old circle of artist and dancer friends from the California coast. They would understand and even like the *compañeros* if they could only know them. But how can I make that happen? I have never written a book before.

I grow more and more angry about the stories tossed about by the powers that be, both in Guatemala and in the United States, to somehow justify army conduct here. The *compas* are mere middle-class intellectuals, young university hotheads eager to be the next Che Guevara. The *compas* are Mayan sheep blindly following the lead of some outside Communist forces, too stupid to think for themselves, and needing to be rescued. The *compas* are Cuban and Soviet invaders. This last makes me smile to myself at the campfire. The Cold War is over and everyone here has diagonal black eyes and they chatter in Mayan to one another. Outsiders? They were here long before the conquest was even planned. The *compañeros* are terrorists. Yet the 150,000 grisly murders of civilians have all been committed by the army.

Watching the *compañeros*, my resolve begins to grow. I will tell who these people are and why they are here, and somehow, God alone knows how, I will find a publisher. Until these people are known and understood, they will continue to die, the bullets that cut them down paid for with my own tax dollars. I remember 1986, the men in dark glasses in my hotel lobby, their vests bulging with ill-concealed weapons. They forced me to leave back then and silenced me by driving me out. It won't happen again.

Even as I focus on my work, Everardo comes unbidden to mind, and I chastise myself for behaving like an adolescent. Since the dance we continue to see one another at the nightly campfire, picking up the threads of our conversations where we left off the night before, roaming through topics and issues as if exploring a remote and beautiful wilderness. Although he remains careful, he has in many ways become quite at ease with me, finally confident that I will not use our friendship to extract forbidden information. He opens slowly now, blooming yet untouchable, and I can only watch with love but with no hope of possession.

Since our kiss on the trail he stops often to visit during the day, to speak quietly for a few moments or, if no one is looking, to steal a swift and shy caress. He gives me his affection honestly enough, but he steadily refuses to make me his. The relationship is impossible, he says, for I cannot stay in the mountains and he will never leave. This is the life he has been given; these are the people he loves. If the relationship with me cannot be real, then he does not value or accept it, no matter what we feel for each other. Nor will he dally, for women are not toys. Even though I respect this verdict, it also breaks my heart.

As the weeks pass, I watch the life of the camp unfold before me. A recently arrived volunteer, a nineteen-year-old student named Joel, is shot through the heart in his first battle, and Jorge cannot save him. They bury him in the soft earth of a cornfield far below, then redistribute his few possessions, shaking their heads in quiet grief. His friend William leaves the mountains in horror, deciding that this life is not for him. Capitán Celia, young and slender, and yet the veteran of so many long years up here, leads a patrol off on a combat mission, vanishing down the trails with her light, swift stride. Ariel's leg stays bad, the bones too frail from childhood malnutrition to ever heal properly, but he stubbornly refuses to leave the mountains. Like the others, he sees transfer to the City and separation from the others as a terrible fate. Marco and Estella, after a bitter quarrel and long separation, finally reunite and are teased mercilessly by the others. The shy villager Guillermo learns to read. Before I know it, Emma's radio crackles the message that my allotted thirty days have come to an end. I am to leave the next morning; the car will be waiting for me just after sundown. As she decodes this from her scrawl of numbers, her eyes fill with tears, as do mine, for we have come to be very close indeed.

I pack, disconsolate, tossing my still-wet clothing, all black in color, into my small bag and giving away my spare shampoo, plastic sacks, soap dish, toothpaste, extra socks, and cheap nylon sweater. The *compas* receive these as if they were invaluable gifts and give me hand-painted cards, woven bracelets, and special bits of food in return. I visit them one by one in their tents for quiet good-bye talks, and they tell me of their hopes for the future and the reunion we will all have someday when the war is over. I go to Everardo's tent last of all because I do not want to say good-bye to him. We will never see each other again and we both know it, but I do not want to face this fact quite yet. Someday later on, back in Texas, when it does not hurt as much I will think about it all, but not today.

As the afternoon draws to an end I find myself reluctantly standing at the opening of his low, flimsy tent and wishing I was someplace else. He is sitting inside on a tree-stump stool, engrossed in a small book, but he looks up as I arrive and signals for me to come on in, pulling up an extra stool for me to sit on. The inside of his tent is neatly ordered, his pack laced and ready to go, documents in tidy piles on the small bed of roped-together pine branches. His rifle and flashlight are stacked near the entryway, in case of emergency, but he has not unstrapped his cartridge belt or machete or even loosened his boots. We sit in silence for a bit and then he puts his arms around me, holding me close and gently stroking my hair. I tell him that I love him and will miss him, biting off the other words that rush to my lips, knowing that I must not push against the boundaries he has set for us. He tells me that he loves me also, that my friendship has been a great gift for him, that he will remember me always but that he will never write. We sit again in silence as the light grows shadowy outside, and then he reaches deftly into his pack and pulls out a small recorder and a cassette carefully wrapped in plastic. He will give me this cassette he tells me, for it is his favorite, the music of his home, the mountains, and the *compañeros*. When he hears it he sees his life pass before him, and when I listen to it when I am far away, I will think of all of them. Then he pulls me close again and we listen to it together, the lyrical music of Vangelis called the "Hymn of the Wilderness."

The next morning I leave at dawn with a small patrol, Antonio and Carlos again, and Larissa, Abram, and David. Everardo and the others come to the campfire to give us the ritual embraces and farewells, and I sadly tell them all good-bye for the last time. As I reach Everardo, I can see from his quiet face that he has already given me up to the past, for he is standing very straight, his dark, old man's eyes betraying only acceptance of the world we live in, of the way things must be. As I lean to kiss his cheek, he tells me once again that he will never write. Then we swing off down the trails and I cannot help but look back. I see him standing motionless in the shadows of the trees far above, watching as we take leave of the volcano.

The route downward is grueling, though short. The old trail is badly damaged by recent bombings and is now prone to dangerous rock slides and collapsing earth. As it is no longer safe to use, we take an older trail, which seems to plunge straight downward, some parts so steep that we are half-sliding, half-falling instead of walking. The vines and brambles have almost reclaimed the narrow pathway and Abram and Carlos move ahead, slashing an opening for us with their machetes and calling back to warn us of sharp drops and pitfalls. We help each other downward one by one, sliding down the sharper faces of the cliff side, then reaching back to brace those behind us. A slip could lead to a dangerous tumbling fall down the muddy banks of the ravine and result in a badly fractured leg, or worse. Soon we are all sweating and grumbling about the trail, and the *compas* begin their crazy banter to distract one another. The trail deserves a name like all the other places, but whom should they name it after? Who deserves this honor? Perhaps General Ríos Montt, the former president?[*] He was certainly into torture as a pastime.

Finally the pathway levels out a bit, then merges into a larger, well-kept one and we are able to move more freely. It is already late afternoon, so we do not stop to rest, continuing instead across the green slopes until we come to an open area with a large pool of clear water. Here, at last, Abram calls for us to sit for a bit and drink some water mixed with powdered milk and sugar. It is sweet but cold, yet we dare not build a fire. The villages are not far away, and once again we are in army territory. We must begin to speak in lowered voices and take care to leave no telltale bits of paper or refuse behind. As we rest, Carlos and Larissa stand sentry duty, watching for unexpected enemy patrols.

I am badly scratched and sweaty from the climb, with mud caked under my nails and smeared across my face and arms. Within a few

---

[*]General Ríos Montt was the president of Guatemala during the worst of the massacre campaigns of the early 1980s. His name is roughly the equivalent of Genghis Khan to the Mayan people.

short hours I must be able to pass as a tourist once again, so this will never do. I borrow a scrap of soap from Abram and wash in the cold water, taking off my shirt and scrubbing my arms and neck. Soon I am clean enough, but the damp leaves me shivering in the cold, and I am grateful when Abram announces we must move on.

We walk carefully now, Carlos and David moving silently ahead as scouts, and as night falls I see the glowing lamps of nearby villages in the darkness. After a final stretch we move off the main trail and into a cornfield, where we sit in silence on the soft, fragrant earth. To my surprise I hear the unfamiliar sound of a passing truck, and I realize that we have already reached the road. Abram comes up to me and whispers that the car will arrive in twenty minutes and that I should prepare for the meeting point. With that I open my pack and reach for the small black plastic bag I have stowed for thirty days now, taking out a flowered skirt, sheer white blouse, and black cotton Chinese shoes. My boots, cracked and caked with mud, will stay behind, for they are too telltale now to bring through army checkpoints. I take them off and hold the shoes in my hands, then pull on the thin skirt and blouse. Larissa spreads out a small plastic sheet for me to kneel on as we wait. Scrubbed and stripped of my heavy shirt and work pants, I feel terribly exposed and shiver in the cold night wind. The *compas* worry, too, that the full moon will reflect off the exaggerated whiteness of my blouse, and they drape one of their olive green shirts about my shoulders, knotting it under my chin.

As we wait, the *compas* come to me one by one for a hug and whisper good-bye. We hold one another very close and I know that I will miss them terribly but there is so little that we can say now. They ask me to write and send chocolates and I promise I will. They tell me not to forget them, as if I ever could. Larissa cuddles close, keeping me warm, telling me to tuck my fingers under the long sleeves of her jacket. Antonio combs my hair.

Then we hear a car slow and stop, the engine still running and the lights turned off. Abram takes my arm to guide me out of the cornfield. We run swiftly out of the cover of the tall maize, then across a rocky surface that cuts deeply into my bare feet, for I cannot put on the slippers till I enter the car. There must be no telltale mud. When we reach the door, I am gasping for breath and the olive green shirt is still knotted about my shoulders. I try to untie it but cannot, for the fabric has dampened in the moist air. Abram pulls it swiftly over my head, hugging me once more, then pushing me gently into the car. As I close the door, he vanishes once again into the shadows.

Suddenly we are on the road and I am sitting in a comfortable car, my serene curly-haired friend once again taking me for a pleasant drive. He chats quietly with me, as if I had never left his vehicle some thirty days back, as if it were all a dream. I am grateful for his gentle talk, since it is difficult for me to keep my composure, to refrain from turning around and searching for one last glimpse of the *compas*. This I must not do, for there is a car just behind us, and they might well be watching us. After a while we turn onto a main road and my friend reaches out and gives me a giant bear hug, welcoming me back. Then, looking askance at me, he hands me a comb and reaches into a bag for a large bottle of cheap perfume, for I reek of telltale wood smoke. As I rearrange myself with the comb and a bit of lipstick, he douses me with the perfume and satisfied at last, hands me a small box of chocolates.

Soon we are in a town, with bright lights and people lined up at a movie theater. There are cars and babies and brightly lit store windows and telephone booths and park benches and buildings strung with electrical cables. The noise and the lights seem strange and disorienting. I am on my way home.

The Letters
Spring 1991

THE LETTERS BEGIN TO ARRIVE LIKE GOOD-LUCK CHARMS FOR A bracelet, tiny and filling my life with short-term sparkle. They find their way to my cramped office in Texas one by one—small scraps of paper folded neatly and backpacked out of the volcano, then set loose in the whirlpool of international mail. I am surprised at first, for Everardo had sworn he would not write, and he is hardly a man who takes words lightly. Yet these tacit admissions that he still cares fill me with joy, as I have been quite unable to put him out of my own mind. Months have passed since I left Guatemala and I have crammed the time with books and music, long-distance running, and endless hours of writing in remote farmhouses. Slowly, the wound of losing him, or rather of never winning him exactly, has healed, and I am convinced that though I think of him often, he is firmly in my past. The arrival of the first letter with its familiar neat writing shows me that I am wrong and that I have made no progress at all. After the initial burst of happiness the pain returns, leaving me wishing for what I cannot have.

He says little in his notes, telling me only that he is well and that the others are in good health, that the clandestine broadcasts of their shortwave radio program, the Voz Popular*, continue from the volcano despite army jamming, that he hopes I am happy, and that he sends me an embrace. I respond by sending him a small container of spices, neatly separated in plastic bottles, and a painted card telling him I wish only the best for him. This takes months to reach him, but finally an answering letter arrives, heavily creased and a bit smudged from the rains. They have passed Christmas in the volcano with their traditional special dinner and reunion with one another. All is well. He encloses a tiny pin looped through with a scrap of colored ribbon, hand-lettered with the words *Feliz Navidad, URNG.* I study it for a while, then tuck it safely away with his other notes and the woven bracelet he made for me as a farewell gift.

After a few more long-distance exchanges, another small card arrives, telling me he is in Mexico with the *comandancia,* and making my heart jolt. They have summoned him to work on the peace talks, for the next issue of the agenda is equal rights for the Mayan people. He

---

*The Voz Popular, or Voice of the People, radio station began its first broadcasts from the volcano in 1987. The programs were aired in Spanish and Mayan and covered human rights issues, current events, and Mayan history and culture. In response, the army bombed the volcano on a daily basis and sent in wave after wave of soldiers, but it was never able to silence the broadcasts.

has been assigned to work on their position papers and to prepare the negotiation points with the others. The city is difficult for him and disorienting, and he misses the volcano, but the work is going well. He would like to see me again.

I put the letter down, half-wishing I had never received it, for it stirs up far too many dangerous desires. No good could possibly come of this, for it will either end badly in the unromantic and smoggy surroundings of Mexico City or it will make me yearn despairingly for something that cannot be. He will return to the volcano soon enough, leaving me behind once again with his impossible self-discipline. Then what?

Against all common sense I find myself booking tickets to Mexico, as in the end it seems to matter little how things turn out between us. I need to see him again whatever the consequences, to speak with him once more, to find out if he really is as I remember him. Dressed in street clothes and in ordinary surroundings, will he, too, seem ordinary? Will we quarrel, given the time and chance outside the magic of the green volcano? Or will we simply reach a dead end in our relationship, blocked by the vast differences that lie between us? We ended well once and we should count our blessings and leave matters as they were. To return is to risk losing my favorite memories, to risk defacement of the beloved images in my mind. Then again, perhaps in the long run this will be for the best.

When I arrive in Mexico I fall easily enough into the old routine for meetings with the underground. I have been coming here for five years now to work on the book, waiting for interviews to be arranged and instructions given for connecting with the *compañeros*. I take a taxi to a small, crowded plaza, then walk for a bit until I am certain no one is following me. Then I check into an anonymous hotel, registering under a false name and paying for everything in cash. Things have been difficult under Reagan and Bush. My sanctuary friends have served time in jails and other solidarity members have been trailed and harassed for years. I must take care not to lead anyone to the *compas* themselves, for the death squads have never been squeamish about crossing the border into Mexico. Nor have the U.S. authorities hesitated to pass information along to the death squads. The connections are a tricky business and they must be taken seriously.

I change my clothes, pulling on the jeans, sandals, and woven shirt of the tourist population, adding hoop earrings as a finishing touch. The result is apparently good enough, for as I move back to the street I am immediately surrounded by hawkers offering me guided tours in English. I wave them off and find a quiet restaurant near a park where I can sit and sip a mug of thick Mexican chocolate while I watch the streets from the window. After a bit, when all is still quiet, I slip away and use the phone at the back, leaving my hotel name and number with one of the many intermediaries.

Back in my room I can only wait, for now it is the *compañeros'* turn. They will approach the hotel slowly, leaving the car with its license plates several blocks away, walking through the crowded streets and window-shopping a bit, then sending a friend to take a look around in the hotel lobby. If all is well they will enter and go swiftly up the elevator, checking for cameras—which I have already checked for myself—and for anyone loitering about near my room. Later they will send for Everardo, but not until they are quite satisfied that I am indeed alone.

Finally the telephone rings and a friendly voice tells me my dental appointment has been set for an hour from now, and I answer that this will be fine. I am anxious, but my efforts to rein in my feelings are crumbling and I am glad I have come. I comb my hair and kick off my shoes, then sit down to watch the news on Mexican television, laughing at the wacky commercials that come on between the grim broadcasts.

Before I know it, there is a soft knock from the hallway and I snap the TV off and hurry to answer. As I swing the door open Everardo glides in, moving so swiftly that I am taken aback. He looks a bit older, more tired perhaps, and he is dressed in plain black pants and a borrowed shirt with sleeves so long he has rolled them to the elbows to free his hands. As I lean to give him a kiss on the cheek he pats my shoulder gently then moves to sit in one of the straight-backed chairs at the small table. I quickly join him, asking if he has eaten and if he would like something to drink. He gravely accepts a coffee and I order from room service, meeting the waiter at the door and placing the blue-and-white cups and saucers out myself. Formalities done, we sit and look at each other, uncertain as to what changes may have come between us during the long year apart.

He is the same but for the clothes, and he looks at me with those fierce familiar eyes, unabashed at having called me here, at having admitted his affection. His wariness is back though, that guarded look rooted in a lifetime of caution and crisis. There is a glimpse of something else as well that I cannot quite define, perhaps a deeper sadness, a weariness. We talk easily enough as we drink our coffee, and he asks about the book and the cases I have worked on, curious about my life in Texas. In turn he tells me about the *compas*. Most are well, though Celia's partner was killed and she has left the mountains to grieve. Ariel, with his weakened leg, was shot to death at the edge of a small town. Santiago was captured alive with Karina—very bad. He shakes his head and again I sense the sadness and share it. Ariel dead? Grimly, I remember the flirtatious young man with the curls and the bad leg and the fierce determination to stay in the mountains forever. The others are doing well and there are several newcomers, good ones. The radio station is still being heard across Guatemala. Marco and Emma send their special love.

He tells me what he can about his new work, admitting that it is difficult for him to be here in Mexico City, but accepting the necessity of it all. We talk about the peace process now and shake our heads in unison, thinking it a fine idea but fraught with danger. Who will make the army comply with what they sign? Who will make the death squads really stop their killing, even after a cease-fire? Yet try we must, he tells me, for the war has dragged on for more than thirty years now. Try we must. He grows quiet now, thinking about the difficult future and the cruel past, and after a while he takes my hand, troubled and in search of comfort. My heart goes out to him. As I study his face in the dimming light, I know he will not send me away a second time. I will not let him.

He glances at his watch, realizing how late it has grown, and tells me that he must go soon, that there is yet another meeting. I stand up and he thinks I am calling an end to our visit, so he stands also, reaching for his jacket. Mixed emotions flutter across his face as we look at each other—wistfulness, fatigue, caution, resignation. I walk around the table and take his jacket from his hands, neatly folding it across the back of the chair while he watches me in silence. His expression turns to uncertainty and then to hope as I turn and place myself firmly in his arms.

I would not let you resist me twice, Everardo. Even now, after all that has happened, I can tell you that I have no regrets. You were worth it all.

The Carnival
Mexico, Spring 1991

OUR RELATIONSHIP BEGINS A BIT UNCERTAINLY, FOR WE ARE HAPPY with each other yet quite baffled as to how to make things last beyond a weekend fling, which appeals to neither of us. His schedule is exhausting but he sees me when he can, even if only for quiet walks through the nearby park, where he takes solace in the vines and trees. The greenery steadies him in this sooty, frenzied city so far from the volcano. At dusk I often find him there sitting cross-legged on the ground, reading from a small book and jotting notes in the margins.

I cherish our time together no matter how brief, loving his musing silences and seeing things as if for the first time through his eyes. We explore the flower and fruit market together, test windup toys from the street vendor, and browse through the crowded tiled bookstores in search of his favorite poems. I know he is tired and worried, yet there is so much he can never tell or share with me—where he went, what he worked on, what problems are leaving him sleepless at night. I worry about the darkening circles beneath his eyes. He would like to speak, to confide, but he has no right and he is not one to flirt lightly with his commitments. I understand and accept this, yet it keeps a distance between us, as if we were speaking through a sheer wall of bulletproof glass. We can hear and see each other, but we can't quite touch.

One day he tells me he can leave the city for a weekend of rest, and he shyly asks me to go with him. Together we travel to a small colonial town not far away and check into a hotel that I remember for its luxuriant gardens, filled with flowering shrubs and vines. This pleases him greatly, but he worries a bit about the rustic architecture, pointing out that the door is flimsy and could easily be knocked down in the middle of the night. His comment makes me stare for a moment, realizing what his life must have been like all these years, always running, always hiding, always waiting for annihilation.

We settle in and unpack, and for a while he is intrigued with the remote control of the television set, playing with it intently until he has it figured out to the last detail. Next comes the telephone book with its bright yellow pages, which he leafs through until he is familiar with its underlying logic and organization. Then he takes my small radio apart, finding it a bit dull, since it's no different from the ones the *compas* have in the mountains. He was expecting something new, more sophisticated, something to give him ideas for the Voz Popular back home. I offer him the colored tourist pamphlets explaining the history of the town, and he devours these while I call for lunch, asking the waiters to serve it to us in the garden outside. By the time they ring, he has memorized the map.

It is bright and sunny outside and we take our time over the food. Like most Guatemalans, Everardo craves meat after a lifetime of hunger and eats his steak slowly, savoring every bite. I ask if he would like a second portion but he shakes his head, explaining that he is content with his ration, that it is enough. It has made him happy, he says with shy gratitude, as if I have given him a special gift. He eats the roasted onions and avocados with the same reverence, eyes half-closed, as if trying to etch the meal into his memory for future use. There is food enough in the mountains now, he tells me, but this was not always so. He remembers the early days when they had nothing—no food, no medicines, no boots, no guns, no real chance for survival.

He settles back against the tree and tells me about a long-ago illness that came upon him when he was all alone, struggling up the volcano from a difficult mission. As his fever raged, he realized he could walk no farther and so he crawled to the banks of a stream. There he scrabbled out a small pit with his hands and laid out some food, then buried himself in the cool mud. He knew the army was on his heels and that he was far from the safety of his friends, but he resigned himself to his fate. He had no choice. Two days later he awoke, very weak but still alive.

Afterward we stroll through the narrow streets, admiring the hand-painted pottery and ornate silver jewelry in the shop windows, then stopping for a chilled Mexican beer at a small café. He sips thoughtfully for a bit, staring out the window, then confides that it is hard for him to be here alone with me, without the others. He has never been apart from the group before, the team. It is so strange. He takes my hand as he speaks, not wanting to hurt my feelings, and I muse over his self-identity, so Mayan communal that one-on-one feels like an amputation to him. Watching his face, I see that he is slightly off balance yet determined to try this new experience, this new way of being. He wants to give it all a fair chance. He wants, most importantly, to give me a fair chance.

That evening there is a carnival nearby and we venture out to see it. He has been vaguely sad for several hours, though affectionate, and I hope that this will distract him from his worries. We stroll past the clowns and jugglers and mime artists, then stop to try out the bumper cars. He has never been on such a ride before, though he has watched them from a distance. So we climb aboard a pale blue car and spin madly about as he tests the steering wheel and finds that it has very little connection to our movements. We crash whether he turns left or right, which makes him laugh and lean out of the car to study the zigzagging tracks that guide us. Afterward he leads me to a small patch of grass nearby and we squat down together in the shadows. From there the underpinnings of the cars are clearly visible, with their interlocking turntables and huge metallic gears. He is fascinated and cranes his neck to watch, to understand how it all works.

Next, we observe the cotton candy machine with its puffs of

brightly colored sugar foam, the accordion player with a small costumed monkey, and a clumsy magician who fails to impress us. We
stop then for drinks of fresh-squeezed juice from a jumble of brilliant tropical fruits in a street stall, then wander past a strip of ped-
dlers, their wares spread out on the clean grass of the park. They are
selling music and sweaters, chocolates and toys, lipsticks, combs, and
handmade arts and crafts. He stops suddenly before a young girl in
her teens, her bright handwoven materials stacked neatly on a blanket
before her. She has long black braids and full lips and the tilted black
eyes of the southland Mayans. They stare intently at each other, and
for a fleeting moment I sense the immediate identity and secret language that flows between them, brother and sister that they are. No
words are exchanged. Then she turns to attend to a customer and he
moves on, holding my hand, thoughtful.

We pass by a small shooting gallery now with raucous music and
flashing orange lights. We stop to watch as people take turns trying
to shoot the small target over a brightly lit set. It is crammed with
scantily costumed dolls gyrating to the music of the lambada. When
someone hits the target, the music grows louder, the dolls' skirts flip
up over their heads, and the winner is handed a stuffed animal as a
prize. This result is quite startling to Everardo, who cocks an eyebrow
and silently begs for an explanation. For once I am stuck. How on
earth does one explain a dance like the lambada? The look on my face
is evidently enough, for he laughs and gets into line, asking if I like
stuffed animals.

When his turn comes, the clerk hands him a crude wooden rifle.
As I watch, Everardo lifts it to his shoulder and leans forward in one
smooth movement, focusing on the shifting target with total absorption. He hits it effortlessly with the first shot and the crowd applauds
as I am handed a small blue toy kitten. As he leans forward again, I
recognize his lithe movements from the mountains, the way the rifle
seems to flow from his arm, the way his dark eyes watch intently
through the sights, the way he moves the barrel ever so slightly in time
with the target before he pulls the trigger. As he wins me a pink pan-
ther with his second shot, I am suddenly frightened for him, afraid
the others will see what I am seeing, a combatant who has slept inches

from a rifle for some seventeen years, a hunted man from the underground. With his third shot, he wins me a fluffy white rabbit. The crowd roars its approval and the dolls dance lewdly, embarrassing him, so we move quickly away. No one has envisioned him as I have, in olive green in the volcanoes, firing from the cover of the trees and rocks. They have seen only the dolls and the prizes.

Late that night while he holds me in his arms, I think about the fact that he has killed other human beings, that he has taken life. Years ago this fact would have disturbed me greatly, making it impossible to love this man. But after more than a decade in Guatemala, the notion of armed resistance is something I have long since come to accept as a cruel necessity. The civilian reformists and pacifist resisters are long dead, including so many of my own friends. Unbidden, the memory of Rosario comes to mind, of her baby with his broken neck and missing fingernails laid out in his tiny coffin. The other memories crowd in then, too, the ones I cannot bear. I begin to cry, and Everardo shifts quickly to pull me close, waiting for me to tell him what is wrong.

I ask him about his life then, knowing that he will never flinch from my questions. I ask him about combat, about pulling the trigger against another living being. He understands me and strokes my hair while he thinks the matter over in the darkness. Killing, he answers at last, is the most terrible task of the war. It must never be done out of rage or even excitement or fear. It must never be done thoughtlessly. One must never become hardened. Each life taken must be remembered, accepted as a responsibility. Lives must be taken in combat but not elsewhere. Prisoners should never be killed, for they are but brothers, taken from their families by forced recruitment. They have no blame for what has happened. It is enough to take their guns and send them home. There are no more orphans needed in Guatemala.

I ask if it became easier for him as the years passed in the mountains. After another long silence he answers no, that if anything, it has become harder. I ask what has been the hardest part of the war for him and he tells me it has been the burden of command, of sending the others to fight and perhaps to die. This is how he has lost his closest friends. This is how he lost his second *compañera*. Regrets? Yes, he has many. What would he do differently if he could turn back the clock? He pulls me up to face him and kisses me, then falls into silence yet again. Nothing. He would do nothing differently, no matter how terrible the pain and loss. He has been dealt a life of war. He would have preferred something different, but this has never been a choice he has been granted. He stares thoughtfully into the darkness, then into my eyes, searching for something he does not name. What do I think of him now? I tell him I love him without reservation. He pulls me close again, cradling me against his shoulder, watching the dim shadows on the windowpane until I fall asleep, exhausted, in his arms.

The next day we have a slow breakfast in the garden and go for a final walk through the narrow streets, then catch the bus back to the city. We sit in the rear by ourselves so that we can talk in private. As we lurch off from the station, he takes my hand and tells me he cares for me but that he is also confused, that there are so many things we both must think about. How are we to continue? Soon he will return to the mountains. And me? If we stay together much longer, this will become very difficult. But can we stay together? He knows I care for him, but could we ever be happy together on a permanent basis? Could I ever be happy? I tell him yes, and he smiles but answers that I should think about it more. As for him, it is painful to grow closer in the heart yet maintain his guard always about what he says and does, about what I learn from him. He cares for me, but how can he know I am not an infiltrator? He grips my hand to ease the pain of his words. His heart trusts me, but his mind knows that the heart is the fastest route to betrayal. It has happened before, many times. He can never let his guard down, no matter how much he wants to, for it is unfair to the others. Could I live with that? I am silent. We have grown so close, he tells me. Almost too close, too fast. Soon it will be impossible to separate. He wants to think about things very carefully as well.

When we reach the city, he pulls me into the shadows of an underpass and holds me for a long time. He tells me he cares for me but that he must think it all through. These decisions cannot be made so lightly. He will call me when he finishes thinking. With that he lifts his duffel bag lightly to one shoulder and moves down the street, vanishing into the smoke and traffic. As I watch I am certain that I will never see him again.

Clara
Mexico City, Summer 1991

It is a tiny sitting room lost in the choking air of Mexico City, but Clara, my wild Chilean artist friend, has brought it to life with a vengeance. The walls are crammed with preposterous nudes and fantasy animal masks and hung all around with ivy so long and thick it seems as if we are sitting in the middle of a rain forest. She pours strong coffee into heavy clay mugs painted yellow and blows me a kiss from across the room. Clara is fifty now, and she dresses in long gauze skirts and Mayan weavings, with layers and layers of scarves and jewelry. I watch her from my low leather bench while she applies her black eyeliner and scarlet nail polish. I would like to dress like her but would never dare. Instead, I watch her in admiration and enjoy the coffee and let her tease me about sulking over Everardo. It has been almost two weeks now, and he hasn't called, so I suppose he never will. He is right of course. There are too many gaps between us: language gaps, culture gaps, lifestyle gaps, everywhere I look a gap, and yet I desperately want to see him again. For me it is far too late to turn back, and far too late to stop. I love him too much. It makes no sense, but I cannot help myself.

Clara is laughing at me from behind her coffee mug. She is fanning one tiny hand in the air to dry her nail lacquer and reminding me of all my years of fiery independence, my aversion to cumbersome relationships. Now she has watched me fall over the cliff of an intense and improbable love affair at the age of forty and she is gently amused. We stayed up late last night together, listening to her collection of South American resistance music and watching Charlie Chaplin, her favorite actor, but I was not appeased. She fed me wine and a sharply aged cheese, then figs and even chocolate, her face dimpling when I asked her what on earth was happening to me, the hardheaded gringa realist. When she saw the tears in my eyes, she looked away and held my hand, offering only her silent friendship.

Today I am in rebellion, though. After all, enough is enough, and I am not about to play tourist in Mexico forever while I mope over an impossible relationship. I must return to Texas and put my life back together. So I toss my clothes back into the small nylon overnight bag, not even stopping to fold them, and tell Clara that it's time for me to leave, time to get a grip. She is still laughing at me from behind her yellow mug, but as I glower through the calls for plane reservations, she softens. When I hang up she convinces me to relax, to let her paint my nails as a farewell present so that I will remember her and come back again to visit. This is hardly necessary, as we have been friends for years while I have worked on the book. I sit down at the small table and let her pamper me all the same.

We bicker a bit over the proper shade, she urging a sheer violet hue, me clinging to the safer beiges. Like everything else having to do with colors and textures, her collection of lacquers is extensive—dozens of tiny bottles lined up on a small shelf in her refrigerator. After rummaging about for a while, she selects a coral shade that is less than orange yet not quite rose, and I agree, liking it quite a bit despite myself. I proffer my hands, and while she slides the tiny brush along my short fingernails, I relax, admiring the effect and loving Clara. She is trying to convince me to accept a glittery blue sequin in the center of each thumbnail when the phone rings. It is for me. Everardo would like to have coffee.

I tell him yes calmly enough, then fall into a full-fledged panic. What has he decided? Clara drags me to her back room and opens up her closet to me, draping me in half a dozen fantastic outfits of silks and weavings before I give up and decide on jeans, a T-shirt, and a pair of her exotic earrings with dark green stones, which she swears match my eyes to perfection. The nail polish stays, but without the sequins, which disappoints her, and so she adds a touch of perfume. Finally I am out the door, rushing so I won't be late, running down the spiral staircase. I can hear her soft laughter above me as I walk out into the noisy street.

I take the subway and get out near the Zócalo stop, at the white marble opera house with its fantastic carvings and wall-to-wall frescoes and floors thrown crooked by centuries of earthquakes. Around the corner is the old colonial building encased in deep blue tiles where we are to meet. I look about in the inner hallway for him, but he is nowhere to be seen, so I move back outside to wait. The city has grown both bankrupt and huge, most services like public telephones and buses long since fallen into disorder. It is almost impossible to be on time here, and so I have grown accustomed to tardiness, and amuse myself by browsing among the street vendors' tables.

Suddenly I see him. He is standing motionless there at the edge of the park, where some small trees are struggling to survive the smog. From the look on his face, he has been watching me for quite a while, amused that I have not noticed him. Once again I have the uncanny feeling that he can make himself invisible at will. He looks rested and at ease, as if he had only just seen me yesterday, and I am so happy to find him that I hurry to give him a hug and a quickly stolen kiss. He permits this despite his discomfort with public affection, then looks carefully at my face, taking a reading. I am not sure what he is looking for, but I am too content to ask, and this seems to satisfy him. He takes my hand and leads me inside to a small corner table, then sits next to me and tells me in his old unspoken language that he has missed me.

He asks what I have been doing and I tell him of the bookstores and galleries and my progress on the manuscript. He can tell me little of his own work, and I know I must not ask, so soon we are back to our old game of exploring strange subjects, from eccentric poets to medical advances to technology to foreign cultures. It is not time yet to discuss our own relationship, and for the moment I'm so happy he has called me back to him, I don't need any explanations.

Today there is nothing he does not want to hear about. I describe my childhood trips to the Yale museum with my mother to see the dinosaur exhibits, which always frightened me, and he questions me minutely about the displays and the size of the bones and the anthropologists' techniques and theories. I have to rack my brains to remember, but he is focusing intently on every detail. I know that if I give him a book, he will devour it at once and then entertain me with arcane dinosaur facts for a very long time to come.

But will he still wish to see me for a very long time to come? I am suddenly afraid to look at him but I know that I must, that his face will be, as ever, honest. I twirl my blue china cup in my hands, then glance anxiously up at him. His eyes, dark, intense, and ancient, meet mine unflinchingly. He makes no attempt to hide his thoughts from me. I see kindness, bemusement, and affection in his eyes, but do I see love? I think so, but I am not certain.

I twirl my cup again and it tumbles out of my hands, flooding the wooden tabletop between us. He moves backward swiftly, but the hot liquid splashes against the knees of his jeans. As I watch, appalled, he pulls out a white cloth and halts the flow with his deft hands before I can even move. Then he sits back down as if nothing had happened and pours me another cup of coffee from the fat china pot. When I cannot react, he presses it into my hands and continues to ask softly about dinosaurs. His face is gentle and understanding now, and he wants to laugh but would never do so, for he knows it would be cruel.

I want to throw my arms around his neck but do not dare. I compose myself instead and tell him about the gigantic prehistoric turtle with the scary fins and then the big fish and the savage birds of paradise I saw long ago in the Peruvian jungles. He listens with total absorption, but I am still rattled, and I fidget with Clara's heavy green earrings as I speak. I am too much in love with this man, I admit to myself. It is dangerous.

As I think these words the earring slips and bounces across the tabletop and onto his lap. He is too taken aback this time to hide his thoughts and he stares at me, momentarily mystified, waiting for an explanation to appear on my face. I struggle for composure, then am forced at last to laugh out loud. He smiles back in relief and laughs with me, the soft, free, honest laugh of a child, a rare laugh that always moves me deeply.

He takes my hand in his then and asks if I love him. I tell him yes, though I know it might frighten him. Has he decided to take me back, or has he come to tell me good-bye? He thinks about my answer for a while; then we pay the bill and step outside. I am worrying about what he will decide to do, whether or not I will ever see him again. Before I can speak he wraps a firm, smooth arm around my waist, and without a word takes me home with him for once and for all.

Home
Mexico, Summer 1991

WE MOVE INTO A TINY BORROWED APARTMENT TOGETHER. IT HAS grimy linoleum floors and cheap, flimsy furniture, and the windows are black with soot, but we are completely happy there. It is home, at least for now. We shop in the tiny *mercado* around the corner, buying bread and tortillas, huge ripe tomatoes, avocados, mangoes, cheeses, and rice. Sometimes we buy meat, which I like less, but which Everardo craves after a lifetime of beans and corn and hunger. Then I take to finding a rare tropical fruit each week as a surprise for him. I love the guayabana, sweet and mellow, and he is fascinated by the pomegranate with its juicy crimson seeds. These he lines up on his plate to admire and contemplate. We try tangerines and plump figs, melons, plums, and berries. I cook from time to time, though badly, and he makes fine nourishing soups for me, slicing the carrots and onions and greens neatly on a small round board. Once he buys me a sugar bowl of clear plastic, fat and flowered with a yellow lid, a house-warming present from him to me.

We have few belongings between us. He hangs up his three changes of civilian clothes, on loan from the *compañeros*. I unpack my small traveler's bag, folding my shirts and jeans into the dresser drawers, and set up my heavy ancient word processor on the low living room table. To type during the days, I put the sofa cushions on the floor and sit cross-legged in front of the softly lit screen. He spreads his papers and books out in the dining room when he is home. Mostly he is away, leaving early in the morning and returning late at night, tired and worried, but always with time enough for me. We listen to music, talk, and make dinner. Then we curl up together on the sofa under an old blanket, he making notes for the next day's meetings while I try to read. Sometimes I grow restless and wickedly pull his socks off with my toes or place my head on his notepad and demand the "taxes" of a kiss, which he always gives. On other nights I fall asleep in his arms and awake hours later, only to find the lights turned off and him still reading, tiny flashlight in hand, as he did so long ago in the mountains. He treats me like a precious gift he must not squander. I live in terror of the day he must return to Guatemala.

We hoard his free hours. Once I bring him a packet of tiny colored pellets, the magic rocks I loved as a child, and we place them into a glass bowl and watch them grow into frail crystalline vines and flowers. We pore over a catalog of hydroelectric-energy gadgets together, and he demands translations of the captions, pointing at each sketched propeller blade, nut, and bolt. When we finish he is delighted, and murmurs to me late into the night of his dreams to light up the mountain villages of his homeland with affordable power. We talk about China and Nicaragua, the Berlin Wall and the inner cities, medical care, education—what works and what doesn't and why. He wants to learn to drive, and we draw an automobile dashboard on sheets of paper and discuss gearshifts, gas pedals, brakes, and oil changes. He listens, his eyes fiercely absorbing, and I know when we finish that he will drive well the first time he sits behind a wheel. He tells me of Gabriella, his first love, cut down by army bullets as she tried to pull him to safety. They were in their early twenties then. Later he weeps as he dreams and I know he is watching her die once again, helpless to save her. It breaks my heart to listen, so I shake him gently awake and we lie wrapped together, saying nothing more until dawn.

Slowly but surely we work through our differences, which are numerous yet seem superfluous. We become committed partners of a strange three-legged race, struggling to match each other's gait and speed. He watches me, probes and questions, looking always for ways to accommodate, as if I were a fragile piece of equipment he must learn to work with properly. For a while we have a tug-of-war over cooking, with me wanting to go out, experiment with Japanese and Indian foods, to avoid the kitchen with its looming pots and pans whenever possible. He wants to stay at home; to him our apartment is a luxurious and wonderful cocoon and cooking a relaxing and fun affair. Sharing tasks does not resolve the matter. We are baffled by each other, and he sits me down to talk, watching my face and asking questions, curious. I tell him of how kitchens seem like prisons to me, so hot and sticky, how the woman's place traditionally is in the kitchen and how this woman doesn't want to be there. He nods his head quickly, this making perfect sense to him. I ask why he likes to stay at home and he reminds me he has never had a house before, only the shack of his childhood, complete with hunger and misery, and then his years in combat tents, in the cold and under fire. As he speaks, my mouth drops open with shame, for I have not seen the obvious. He laughs and kisses me, and from then on we take turns cooking at home as usual, and on weekends, unbidden, he takes me somewhere special, to a secret garden he has learned about, or a new painting exhibit or a street festival. Remembering that I like to dance, he brings home new cassettes of music and we salsa or slow-dance, cheek-to-cheek, in the hallways.

We decide to settle in and houseclean and buy gallons of lemon- and pine-scented soaps and bottles of powder cleansers. We spend two days scrubbing, and slowly but surely the windows emerge fresh and clear and the linoleum of the kitchen floor regains its original color. I sweep the living room and buy fresh sheets, bright yellow because I know he likes this shade, that it reminds him of the sun. He beats the dust from the furniture and scours the faucets in the bathroom. When I return with the laundry, he has washed the glass light fixtures and is on his knees in the bedroom, cleaning the floor with a scrub brush. His pants legs are rolled up neatly and he has removed his shirt to keep it clean. He looks up happily as I walk in, his old man's eyes affectionate in his open villager's face. I pause for a moment, for it hurts me to see him there, on his knees. In my mind's eye, I suddenly see him back at the plantation where he grew up, ridiculed and abused for his Mayan ancestry, hungry, illiterate, fit only to be used and broken and tossed aside. On his knees was where they wanted him. I love him because he fought on his feet instead. I kneel down and put my arms around him and take the brush away, trying not to cry. He watches me in surprise, searching my face for clues, yielding the scrub brush but wondering silently what difference it makes, since between us all is equal in the end.

Nights
Mexico, Summer 1991

HIS LIPS ARE PREPOSTEROUS, SO CURVED AND FULL AND FRAGILE, like some wild orchid easily crushed underfoot. They pull into a crooked shape over his uneven teeth when he speaks, giving him a battered look during the daylight hours, but at night they are perfect, and terribly vulnerable. I love to lie in his arms and trace the outer edges of his lips with my fingertip while he stares at me with his fierce black eyes. If I kiss him, he continues to stare, searching my face and probing my thoughts until I feel that he will soon bore a hole through my mind for direct consumption. When I tease him about this he returns my kiss, his eyes wide open, fierce and searching as ever. It pleases him that I make no attempt to shield my thoughts from him, that I do not run for cover.

He is a sweet and affectionate lover, and when he pulls me firmly toward him I know that he is reaching for me and for no one else, and that he will accept nothing less from me in return. I feel as if he is melding us together, bone to bone and mind to mind. He rejects anything other than total commitment as worthless, his intensity frightening at times, yet I have no wish to resist for I love him profoundly. When he sleeps, curled up next to me under our bright yellow coverlet, I remember Guatemala and tremble at the thought of ever losing him.

I tell him I want his child. I know this is complex for him, for he will be away for long periods of time until the war ends. It would be hard for him to have a child and not to raise it, for he does nothing halfway. We are lying folded together, his cheek against mine, and I can feel his long lashes fluttering like a butterfly's wing against my skin. He thinks about my words for a while, then moves his small hand down to my belly. I know he is thinking of his own family, whom he has not seen since he left for the mountains seventeen years ago. He has learned that, inexorably, attachments bring pain.

After a long silence, he tells me he would like a child too, that this would make him very happy. His lips press into my hair, caressing. I worry that it may be too late, that I may not be able to become pregnant, that I am already awfully old. The thought makes me anxious and sad, but he pulls me closer, telling me that we can only try. Life gives what it gives. We can ask for nothing else.

He tells me he loves me in English, which he is learning with startling speed. I tell him I hope the baby looks like him. He tells me he would like a girl, one that looks like me. He pulls me into a half-sitting position now and looks into my face to see if I am as happy as he is with this new idea of a child.

We are silent for a bit; then I tell him the child will somehow have to look like both of us. We laugh at the thought and we stare at each other's utterly incompatible features. His eyes are so dark and diagonally tilted; mine are green and saucer-shaped. His nose is low and aquiline over full lips; mine is high-bridged over a small mouth. He pulls thoughtfully at a strand of my gold-brown curls, so different from his own straight, glossy black hair. Then he looks at me, his face suddenly serious, almost blank, betraying nothing. Maybe we'll have a giraffe, he offers. This catches me off guard and I choke on a laugh, then swat at him with the pillow, which he easily deflects. He keeps a valiant poker face, but he has to turn away to hide the half smile at his lips.

I cuddle back down into the crook of his arm, getting drowsy, tracing the edges of the round white scar over his heart. A bit of shrapnel struck him in the breastbone long ago, miraculously bouncing off instead of killing him. The scar is shockingly pale and rough against his smooth brown skin, a bad reminder of his long, long years in combat. There is an old gash on his upper lip too, from a tumble over a cliff, as well as a thick scar on his left arm from throwing himself through a barbed-wire fence under machine-gun fire. On his upper back are scattered marks from a shotgun blast, and his legs are covered with shrapnel scars from hip to ankle. This has been no easy life, yet when I ask about it, he is neither bitter nor proud. It is the life he has been given—to be accepted with dignity and without complaint.

Without the network of scars and his old-man's eyes, his body would seem so very young. He is small and sturdy, very strong, but with none of the roped muscles or hard, hairy edges of a North American. Instead, he is smooth and supple and clean-lined as a dolphin.

I tell him I love his eyes. He tells me he loves me, but not my eyes so much. They are too pale and strange, like the eyes of a hawk. Always honest, my Everardo. He loves my hair though, he admits, because it is rebellious and out of control, like I am. At this I start laughing into the pillow. I tell him I love his hair too, and play with a fine black strand. He sits up and watches me carefully, ever suspicious of light compliments. I pull closer to him, and his skin is warm and sleek to the touch.

Drowsily I go for broke and tell him I love his skin. This is too much. He quirks an eyebrow at me, amused by my onslaught but slightly irate at my excess. I tell him that skin like his should be illegal. He pulls another poker face, then tells me drolly that in my country, skin like his *is* illegal. I reach for the pillow again, but he pulls me into his arms instead and soon we are fast asleep. As always, I drift into dreams cradled against his chest, listening to the beat of his heart.

Even then, Everardo, I watched you sleeping with a sense of awe that you were still alive, that you had managed to survive against all odds. Even then, I never took a day of your life for granted.

Texas
September 1991

MEXICO CITY BEGINS TO BEAR DOWN ON EVERARDO. IT IS DIFFI-cult for all of us, with its choking air and birds falling dead from the skies, victims of the intense pollution. Nor is there peace. Rather, it is a bit like New York, the streets teeming with scurrying people, honking buses, cars, and trucks, and screaming drunks and vendors. There is no silence and there is no space. He finds the uproar relentless but grapples with it gamely enough, determined to learn to adapt, to extract what is good and interesting about this strange existence. Who knows when life will grant him another chance.

We explore the museums and bookstores when he is free, and listen to the street musicians from Peru and Bolivia, with their cane flutes and strange ancient lutes. Yet I sense him growing more and more unhappy, stifled. He takes to collecting subway and bus maps for the entire city, memorizing them until he can tell me easily how to reach even the most remote barrio. We seek out parks and gardens, even those that are far away, for his need for greenery and silence is growing by the day. The uproar leaves him off balance, and the maze of neon signs and shop windows is disorienting. To him they all look alike, giant edifices of stone and paint and flashing billboards, just as the trees and rocks in the mountains were indistinguishable to me. He has to stop and think carefully to recognize the intersection leading to our home, then check the names of the streets to be sure he is not lost. I point to the Sanborn's and the Xerox center nearby, telling him to use those as markers. He explains that this will never work for him, since there are so many Sanborn's and so many Xerox places here. Instead he has learned his way home from the trees growing down the divider strip in the road. He points them out to me, the one with the bent branches next to the tiny withered one, then a space, then a tiny pine. These things he can count on, for no two trees are alike.

The work begins to weigh heavily on him as well, lines of worry etching themselves on his smooth face. He reads late into the night and arises at dawn to return to his neat piles of documents and notes on the living room table. Equal rights for the Mayan people. The issue is so close to his heart, how to boil it down into a few terse pages of demands? What is there to compromise or give up when his people are starting with nothing? He begins to tell me more about his childhood, the virtual serfdom, his mother's needless death, the hunger, the humiliation. He tells me how he yearned to go to school, to learn something more than how to pick the coffee and cotton of another. He despised his own ignorance. His young cousin was able to go to the next village once, to the one-room schoolhouse there. She went for one year and learned some letters. More than anything he had wanted to go with her, but he never could. With his father, he was bound to fieldwork in order to stay alive. It was the same for all the others, his own people. How to articulate and summarize now, in a few neat phrases, the pain and slavery of some five centuries? His mind is too full for the use of mere words.

We talk for a while about perhaps leaving the city, packing up his books and papers and working in some quieter place, more green and restful. He is pleased with the idea, and we think over different places in Mexico. I tell him I wish I could take him to Texas, to my remote house in the trees where I have been writing. If we stayed for a bit he could meet my family. My mother and father, brothers and sisters, they will be together over Thanksgiving. He has already questioned me minutely about my relatives. Now he demands a detailed explanation of Thanksgiving and a description of the house, together with a

short history of the state of Texas. Next he asks for a map. Two days
later he tells me he can go to Texas with me. It has been arranged.

I don't know what to say, for he has no real papers and the north-
bound route is smack in the middle of the drug war, with fierce black-
booted Mexican *federales* and DEA agents everywhere, checking
everything. I politely suggest that perhaps now is not the time, but he
tells me not to worry, that it has all been arranged. For the first time
in a while, he looks happy, lighter of spirit. He asks me again about
the house and the trees and I warn him that Texas is never green, just
brown-gold and desertlike, although certainly quiet in the countryside. He is very interested and we pore over maps for a bit together.
Then he tells me that I must go on ahead without him, that all will
be well. I don't like this thought at all and try to argue with him about
it, but he tells me that I must trust him, and that I must trust the
other *compañeros*. They would never agree to his travels if it was not
safe. Indeed, they will be transporting him for most of the way. Close
friends will help him cross.

In the end I yield, knowing that if he says it is safe then it is, for
he takes his work far too seriously to risk it all on whim or fancy. Our
tiny apartment begins to fill with somber *compañeros*, who spread out
maps across our tabletop and quietly sip the coffee I bring them. They
work out routes and dates together, jotting down notes and propos-
als and asking me for the names and numbers of trustworthy friends
in case of emergency. I warn them that even the old sanctuary networks have been destroyed, with church people under arrest and
standing trial. Conditions are hardly good. They tell me not to worry,
that it can be arranged through others whom they know and trust.
They would never risk Everardo. I stare at their steady, intent faces,
their meticulous notes, and the small pistols strapped neatly to their
ankles. Suddenly I am not afraid. I remember my own trip into the
volcano, running through a region where I did not exactly blend in. If
these people could get me to the top of Tajumulco—no small feat—
then why am I distrustful now? Perhaps, I admit to myself, there
seems to be more at stake now. Now there is Everardo.

After a few short weeks, all is ready. Two *compañeros* arrive to use our
apartment while we are gone, an older man and a woman with a limp,

both here to see physicians. We leave them our pots and pans and blankets and radio, taking only our clothing and papers. Everardo sees me to my small truck, for I will be leaving first and we will meet in a few days inside the Texas border. It has all been worked out to the last detail, and I have precise instructions, together with backup plans and emergency numbers and contacts. I am no longer frightened, but as Everardo kisses me good-bye, I cling to him, loath to leave him for even a day. He leans into the truck cabin for a moment, gently pulling my seat belt around me in a wordless admonition to drive carefully. Then he shyly hands me a small thermos of hot soup he has made for me as a surprise. He does not wish for me to be hungry, he tells me. Then he strokes my hair and pushes the door shut. When I hesitate, he presses the lock down, the clicking sound my signal to leave him. I switch into reverse and back out of the tiny parking lot into the wild, honking scramble of Mexican traffic, then take one last look back. He is standing on the curb, not waving, but his face reflects his quiet pride in my independence. He is pleased that I can drive across this country, dealing with hostile checkpoints and a foreign language without him.

I drive like hell. I floor the gas pedal and careen through the mountainous curves far faster than I know I should, because I am afraid some chance delay will keep me from the meeting point with Everardo. To be sure, there is a backup date and place, but this does not assuage me. I floor it anyway and drive the entire distance in two days flat, flying across stretches of desert filled with prehistoric-looking palm trees and villages lined with walls of heavy cactus plants. I play endless music to distract myself—Sylvio Rodriguez, Mercedes Sosa, Bolivian flute players, and then Victor Jara, long dead in the Chilean stadium. I listen to Pachelbel's Canon, then an African drum concert, then Handel's *Messiah* and Mozart's Requiem, which always leaves me dizzy. Then I listen to the Beatles and Joan Baez, and finally to Everardo's favorite, *Opera Sauvage* by Vangelis. As I swing back up into the mountains, I understand why he loves it so, for its strange chords and lilting harmonies immediately remind me of the mountains, with their cold streams, lush foliage, and rising mists. It also reminds me of him, of his life, overwhelming, haunting, and yet somehow utterly serene.

Finally I reach the border, somewhat deafened from my ten-hour personal concert, and I bicker nastily with the grouchy customs agent. He feels I haven't answered his questions promptly enough, and he searches the truck in revenge while I huff and puff from the sidelines. Then I am off again, heading straight for the small town where I will hopefully find Everardo. I begin to worry again, although I know I shouldn't, and I check into the hotel that we agreed on in advance, asking anxiously for messages. There are none. I have little to do now since I have arrived nearly twenty-four hours early, so I wander aimlessly to a movie theater for a showing of *Rambo*, then over to the Dairy Queen for dinner. I like this small town, so much like home for me, for I spent years in this region when I first practiced law, working with migrant farmworkers. It is not Mexico, but it is not really the United States either. Rather, it is a unique blend of the two, with English and Spanish mixed together in every sentence. The radio in the Dairy Queen blares ranchero music and the news from a Mexican station. I am the only Anglo in the room.

I sleep restlessly, jabs of adrenaline waking me throughout the night like a punch to the stomach. At dawn I go out for breakfast tacos and lots of black coffee, then return to the room in case of a call. I spend the rest of the day irritably watching soap operas on television and trying to catnap, for there is still a six-hour drive ahead, perhaps even longer. Everardo will hopefully be with me then and I must be very alert and, above all, very careful. I know the remote roads like the back of my hand, but now is not the time for speeding tickets or fender benders. This matter I take seriously enough so by early afternoon I turn off the television and pull the blinds, forcing myself to sleep in earnest.

At five my small alarm goes off and I shower quickly and place my suitcase back in the truck. No one has called, so all must be well. I worry all the same. Will he be there? What if he isn't? I drive back to the Dairy Queen and circle the block slowly, looking for the ubiquitous and dreaded *migra* vans with their ever-alert U.S. Immigration officers. Tonight, mercifully, there are none in sight, so I pull into the small parking lot and hurry on inside. The bright lights make me blink as I enter, and the ranchero music is blaring away just as it did the night before. The booths are filled with families and young couples, all of them with dark hair and tilting eyes, all of them speaking Spanish. At the booth in the back is Everardo, sitting up quite straight and examining a chocolate milk shake.

Marriage
Texas, September 1991

THE TINY HOUSE DELIGHTS EVERARDO, SURROUNDED AS IT IS BY A forest of twisting scrub oak and stunted pines. All is arid and brown-gold here, as I have told him, but he revels in the silence that surrounds us and in the variety of birds and wild animals that we encounter on our daily hikes along the trails. There is no one out here to disturb us, and he feels safe and free at last, back in his element. We buy books in town to identify the hawks and doves and *chachalaca* birds we see, as well as the different species of trees and wildflowers, for he wants to learn the names of one and all. The prettiest blossoms we take back to the house to press flat between clean sheets of paper as keepsakes for the future.

He begins to sleep more soundly now, but he still works voraciously during the days, rising long before I do and setting the coffee to warm on the stove. After my morning shower I find him sitting cross-legged on the small sofa, writing thoughtfully on a thick pad of lined yellow paper and bending to leaf through the reports spread out around him. We breakfast together then go out for long runs along the dusty roadside, both of us grateful for the clear air and open spaces. Later we curl up and work through the day, he with his documents and I with my manuscript, stopping now and then for coffee and for hugs. From time to time we venture out to the small town nearby for food and mail and news of the outside world. A few trusted friends come by to visit and we prepare small and intimate dinners together, sipping wine near the fire he builds and chatting late into the evenings. He likes my friends, though he is cautious as ever, and he loves to hear about their work, their families, their lives, and their opinions, which he mulls over long after they leave. Together we try out vegetarian recipes, which disappoint him, and then Chinese and Indian dishes, which he likes. Soon, so easily that we barely notice, we settle into a routine, lulled by the safety and silence of this remote farmhouse.

One night he suggests a hike into the dark forest so that we can watch the stars, and I readily agree. We lace on our boots and take the large flashlight and a flimsy blanket, then trudge off down the rocky trail toward the pond. It is a beautiful night, chill and clear, the black sky set with stars and a luminous quarter-moon. I stop to stare upward, but he takes my hand and breaks into a half run, urging me rapidly up the steep hillside and across the slippery floor of the forest. It is so easy for him, this run through the darkness, his eyes so long accustomed to night marches and maneuvers. It is so much harder for me, nearly blind on this uneven terrain. He never lets me stumble though, and soon I catch my wind and find the run exhilarating. After a while we stop to strip off our jackets, sweating in the cold night air and laughing at this whim of his. I look around and see that we have reached the pond, its cold dark water sharply etched against the grassy banks beneath our feet.

He spreads out the blanket and we lie down together, cuddled in each other's arms while he points out the different constellations to me. I tell him the Greek myths behind each bright cluster, and he answers with the Mayan version, always so very different. A falling star winks across the sky and vanishes, extinct, and we grow silent, enjoying the panorama above us. As we lie there I wrap my arms about his neck, unable to wish for anything more than what I already have. If I could change anything, I would change nothing.

He pulls me closer and asks if I have been happy with him, if all the complexities of our relationship have been too difficult. He is looking keenly into my eyes, and I know he will not accept a flip or easy answer. I think for a while, stroking his face, then tell him that I love him so much that the hardships seem unimportant, even though they exist. And our differences? There are so many of them, do I not find these burdensome? Again, he is watching me intently, almost fiercely. I answer that so far, our differences seem to be enriching, that we do not have to be the same in all ways for me to love him. At this he wraps his arms around me, burying his face in my shoulder. Do I want to stay with him no matter what happens? Do I understand how difficult things will become? He does not say *may* become. For him there is no question. I think again, for I know what he is asking me—or rather warning me about—and it makes me shiver. I tell him that I cannot leave him, not ever. There is nothing else to consider. He gives me a half smile. But do I want to stay forever, or am I simply unable to leave? I grip his arms then, pinning him to the ground and laughing. Just see if you can get away from me, I say. Just try it, buster.

At this he laughs with me and gently takes my hands in his, telling me that he loves me also, that I am the *compañera* of his soul. Our time will be so short, he says, for things are always so in times of war. I begin to protest this grim thought, but he hushes me gently and continues. He loves me and will share his heart and life with no other. He would like for us to have children and grow old together in some small house in a forest, like this one, after this terrible war is over. Perhaps life will never give so much, but this is what he would dream of as perfect happiness. Do I feel the same way? Do I have the same dream? I answer yes, but he is still not satisfied. He wants more from me than love alone. He wants to marry.

This takes me somewhat aback. For most of my life I have been fiercely single, preferring my freedom to the inevitable compromises of a relationship. I was married once and didn't like it at all. But I know what Everardo is asking. He wants more than my love, which he already possesses. He wants to bind our lives together once and for all, for there to be no more questions, no more testing of the waters to see if we can be happy together, no more wondering if the relationship can work. He will soon return to the mountains, and he wants to create a permanence between us before he leaves. He wants me to decide, to choose him forever, yes or no. I tell him yes. He holds me very close, murmuring that we have so little time left, that we have already been together for longer than he was ever given with the others. We must not waste a day. Again I wish to protest, but he silences me with a kiss, then cradles me in his arms until I fall fast asleep.

And so we marry, in that small farmhouse in the woods. It is simple enough to prepare the small ceremony, for neither of us will tolerate any pomp or formalities. We spend a few days planning our favorite foods, inviting our most trusted friends, and decking the windows and mantelpiece with fragrant pine branches that we gather ourselves. We write our own vows, working them through together late at night, tailoring them to fit our notions of what a true marriage should be. We want no rings, for Everardo has never drawn a salary and the idea is foreign to him and ridiculous to me. Instead we decide on the *compañero* tradition from the mountains: We will exchange spoons.

His grim warnings that night at the pond have rattled me, nonetheless, and I begin to worry. What if something happens to him? My attorney's mind begins to whirl. There are no photographs of us together, for these are prohibited for security reasons. Everardo is as clandestine as anyone can get. I become more and more anxious, wanting something concrete. We cannot marry in a court or church because he has no papers. I check the law books and find that we can marry legally enough at home, as we have planned, as long as we are clear that this is marriage and not palimony or a temporary affair. This reassures me but I am still uneasy, wanting something I can hang on to in case of an emergency. Finally I talk him into the unthinkable step of giving his true name to a few of my closest friends: Efraín Bámaca Velásquez. They must know who he is; they must be my witnesses.

A few nights later, with the gas lamps glowing in the windows and my friends of many years gathered close, we swear to take each other as husband and wife, to stand by each other in sickness and health, in heart and in mind, together and from afar, to cherish our differences and our individuality, to trust and to love each other forever and beyond death. As he holds me afterward, shy before our friends, he speaks the intertwined lines of a poem he has written for me, exquisite words that years later will sustain me through all that comes.

Weeks later we drive northwest to New Mexico for our honeymoon, toward reservation territory. It takes me a while to figure out where we can go safely, so for some time we stay happily enough in our small house. Yet I want him to see more than the forest around our cabin. At the Four Corners I do not fear the traps of the *migra* cars or the roadway checkpoints. Everardo will simply blend in as just another original American, which of course he is. We drive and drive, and the rose-and-cream-colored buttes and plateaus delight him, as does the craggy desert. We are not able to tarry long, though. Soon an urgent message comes from Mexico, telling us to return at once.

As we pack, I am saddened, for here at least I feel that he is safe and sound, far from the death squads and fiery shrapnel of the Guatemalan war. We plan to return soon, for Thanksgiving or maybe Christmas, but I am learning quickly not to look too far ahead. He senses this and places a sweater in my closet and a few books and poems in my desk drawers. Then he takes me gently in his arms and tells me that I am his family now, just as he is mine, and that his true home is wherever I am. Our small room in Mexico will soon vanish, but our home here will stay. It is ours, and the war cannot last forever. But I must remember that peace is a very long way away.

The Wineglass
Mexico, 1991

WE REACH THE CLAMOR AND SOOTY STREETS OF MEXICO SOON enough. Everardo is glad to be back with the *compañeros*, even though he loved the peace of Texas, for without the others he is not completely whole. The news here is not good, though. The peace talks are bogged down, perhaps irrevocably. The war is moving forward.

He is working too hard, and I begin to worry. He stays out later and later at meetings with the *comandancia* and when he comes home he is exhausted and preoccupied, fine lines of tension tugging at the corners of his lips and eyes. A critical phase of the war is coming and the *compañeros* will either make great advances or suffer grim setbacks, but they must move forward. There will be deaths, perhaps too many. I can read the risks as they etch themselves onto Everardo's sad, tired face. Soon it will be 1992, five hundred years since the arrival of Christopher Columbus, and some five hundred years since the Mayan world ended in flames, mass murder, and slavery. We both brood silently about this, finding it ominous, but we do not discuss it. Some things, after all, are best left unsaid.

His friends come by for coffee and private talks in our small salon and I give them plates of food, which they quickly pronounce delicious but scarcely touch. We chat quietly for a bit; then on cue I leave them alone to pore over their maps and coded messages and to spread their papers and books across the low wooden table. They leave their pistols within easy reach; it is my job to watch the streets below for strange vehicles or armed men. When the *compas* leave hours later, they hug me close and murmur that much will depend on Everardo in the coming months. Everardo, of course, says nothing of this, for he would consider it vain and boastful. He refuses to exist apart from the team, and he wears his new responsibilities like a deadweight instead of a crown.

He showers me with affection, treating me as if each day together could be our last. In the mornings he combs my unruly hair and he takes to leaving small gifts about the house, tucking them discreetly away so that I will find them later, once he has left for work. A pair of tiny silver earrings appears on the kitchen windowsill, and once I find a row of chocolate seashells lined up in a neat row on my computer keyboard. My favorite is the love note written on bright yellow paper and folded into the shape of a bird. I notice it dangling gently from the dining room ceiling when I sit down for my morning coffee. As I watch it sway back and forth, I realize with a start that Everardo will be leaving for the mountains soon. He will tell me when he is ready.

Sleep evades him, though he is clearly exhausted. He lies stoically through the nights, holding me close and staring thoughtfully at the lighted city outside our small window. Sometimes he drifts off, but only to dream, and I wake to hear him catching his breath, tormented by some remembered horror. He cries out for Gabriella, for Luis, who taught him to read and write, and for so many others, all long dead. I wake him then, and we talk for a while in the soft darkness, and he tells me who they were and why he loved them and how they died. Once he tells me of Rosalvina. So many years after Gabriella's death, he had risked his heart for a second time, with this young woman who had come to the mountains to fight in the *frente*. Like him she was a Mayan, a Mam speaker, a villager, and though so terribly young, he came to love her deeply. He wished more than anything to keep her safe, to protect her, but as commander he could give her no special privileges, nor would she accept them. He sent her out to find supplies and she was caught by the army and tortured to death. Years later I will come across her photograph, wrapped neatly in protective plastic, her face young and pretty and as fiercely intelligent as his own. I will remember, and her image will break my heart.

He takes to writing poetry in the middle of the night, and I find him sitting cross-legged on the living room chair, like a small, wise owl at rest on a perch, working intently at fitting words to thoughts. He lets me curl up on the sofa next to him, and from time to time he reads me bits of what he writes, intricate lines as wild and beautiful as his own mind. By dawn he rolls them up into neat twists of paper and lights them afire one by one, holding them deftly between his fingertips as they burn. I protest, but he only smiles in response, his dark eyes focused on the glowing scraps. The poems are but fragments of thoughts, unfinished ideas of the moment, unfit for the outside world or for the immortality of paper and ink. He will not allow them to survive.

One night we decide on a movie and dinner at a nearby restaurant. He accepts, reluctant to leave his beloved apartment after a long day away but hopeful that I am right and that it will ease him into sleep. At the theater we settle into velveteen seats and watch Mel Gibson and beautiful Sigourney Weaver cavort their way through a child's-play version of revolution somewhere in Southeast Asia. They fight and flirt and court each other, then drive through a fiery military barricade to prove to one and all that they are wild and free. The flames and barrage of machine-gun fire leave them untouched, and they drive off laughing and alive and in love. Everardo pulls me close to him and I feel tears on his cheek, and I know without asking that he weeps because this can never be our own reality.

As we walk toward the small corner café, he tells me sadly that life will never give so much, that I must know this and be strong. He had six months with Gabriella, less with Rosalvina. Both are long dead. Already we have had more than this and he has never been so happy. But ours is a life of war and it will treat us cruelly. We must know this and prepare. He pulls me to him and kisses me fully on the lips, for once ignoring the people in the streets. I cling to him and beg him to take me with him to the mountains. He understands but shakes his head, his dark eyes filling again with tears, which he makes no attempt to hide from me. "No, please, no," he murmurs into my hair. "You must not make me suffer." To this I have no response.

We stand for a long time in the street then, hanging on to each other and crying. He holds me so tightly that I can feel his heart through his light sweater, beating rapidly against my own. As I stand there wrapped in his arms, I realize that I have lost myself in this man, that our lives are bound together as if the bones of our ribs had merged into one, never to be severed. His death would shatter me like glass.

We stumble into the back garden of the corner café and order two goblets of wine, cuddling together in the shadows of the old trees. I stroke his gold-brown cheek and we talk about our hopes for a child, for a home somewhere, for bits and pieces of time together until this terrible war reaches its end. We order more wine and I become drunk and he tipsy, as we talk and hold each other tightly. I ask what he will want to do after the war ends, and he sighs, for he has known no other life but war and slavery. He sips slowly at his wine, musing, then tells me that someday he would like to speak in public, in one of the towns, something he has never done before for he has always been too shy, too private. He would like to speak to his own people, tell them what the war has been about, why they fought, what it has cost, and yet how it was all worth it. He would like—but only one time—to stand up before the townspeople and speak from his heart, break his lifelong silence.

As he speaks I listen, and in the darkness I can see him standing in some far-off village, speaking in his beautiful low voice for the first and last time in his life, showing the people his very soul with words. The image mesmerizes me and the glass in my hand suddenly slips. I catch it before it falls, but it shatters into small sharp pieces, cutting my palm. The sound of the breaking glass startles both of us, and Everardo quickly bends to take my hand in his and press his white napkin against the bleeding. He looks deeply into my eyes then and says no more of his dream, for we both know that it has come to an end.

Christmas Eve
Mexico, 1991

ALOUD THEY ARE SAYING VERY LITTLE, GASPAR ILOM AND EVERardo. Yet when their eyes meet it is as if, despite the surrounding uproar, there was no one else in the room. They sit side by side on the narrow blue sofa, Everardo small and straight and solemn, his ankles neatly crossed, Gaspar enormously tall, his long arms and legs fitted awkwardly into the small spaces around him. Their drinks are virtually untouched and they silently exchange glances of deep affection, trust, and comprehension. Both see their very life histories, intertwined since so long ago, reflected in the eyes of the other and they are utterly at home together. There is no need to say much. Watching them, I am very moved.

All around them is the clutter and clamor of Christmas Eve. We are in a safe house and the *compas* are everywhere, bustling back and forth with great platters of food, starting up a fire in the fireplace, and playing with the small children who seem to be everywhere at once. Some of the old-timers have been here in Mexico for many years now, in exile but still working, arranging for medical care, handling diplomatic work, and setting up training and education projects. One by one, they have cautiously permitted themselves the luxury of a child in this safe haven, a happiness so impossible in the fiery days of the City underground back home. Now there are half a dozen little ones romping about, playing, and demanding explanations for everything they encounter. I have to laugh as I watch them, for not surprisingly they are high-spirited and precocious beyond their years, and ridiculously stubborn and rebellious. With endless patience, their gray-haired parents help them learn to tie bows on the small Christmas packages, pitch them colored rubber balls to catch, and take them into the redolent kitchen to watch the preparations and sneak small treats.

It is Everardo's first Christmas outside of the mountains. He will return to war right after New Year's, but he has tarried this extra week so that we can be together for just a little longer. Quiet as he is, he does not care much for all the seasonal uproar in the streets, but he has gamely ventured forth with me to see the lights and decorations in the old quarter of the city. Gifts have proven more of a problem, for even though nothing more than a pretty card or a small box of chocolates is required, he cannot imagine giving anyone a gift that is not somehow personal or meaningful. Otherwise, why bother? And so we search for many hours until he finds the perfect decorative cards that play small musical tunes when opened. At first he does not wish to write on them or even sign them, for he finds the music alone to be message enough about his feelings. To him it makes no sense to clutter up such a thing with mere words. In the end though, he takes a pen and sits up late into the night, thoughtfully tailoring a few spare lines of greetings and farewell to each friend.

Now he sits and smiles slowly at Gaspar, at ease and affectionate in a way that I have rarely seen him. There are dark circles under his eyes, for now he sleeps very little, between the heavy work load and the dreams that come to haunt him in the early-morning hours. Yet he sits so straight, his serenity giving him a special dignity. As I hand him a cup of steaming fruit punch, his fingers close gently over my own, telling me he is with me always. For the hundredth time, I find myself fighting off tears.

I cannot ask him to stay. His honor and commitment to the people of Guatemala are far more important to him than any personal relationship, no matter how much we love each other and no matter how painful our separation. I have always understood this about him, and it is one of his qualities that I love the most, his utter lack of self-indulgence, his ability to give his last breath of life to what he believes is right. Extreme perhaps, his character, but it is pure and real and there is nothing I would change about him, no quality I would dilute. I know that he loves me fully, and that is enough. If I could do everything over again, Everardo, I still would not ask you to stay.

Instead we talk over other possibilities, curled up together on our rickety sofa into the late hours of the night. I beg him to take me with him, and at first he is appalled by the idea. I am too old; I do not know the terrain, they are entering a very dangerous phase of the war; I would never survive. I tell him I don't care about the risks. He closes his eyes and holds me closer, whispering that I must not make him suffer. I tell him I am far stronger than I look and hoist him a few inches off the ground to prove it. We are almost the same size; I am a bit taller, though he is a bit heavier. He is impressed by my feat and also amused, congratulating me on my sturdy back and shoulders and thinking over the situation. I could never be a combatant, he explains carefully, for my age and lack of experience could get the others killed. I could never really join the *frente*, either, for I am not Guatemalan. He hastens to add that this changes nothing between us and reminds me of the army's constant and rather ridiculous claims that the *compañeros* are all foreign invaders, from Russia and Cuba and China. This is a grassroots rebellion, and they cannot risk tarnishing their reality by taking in foreigners, especially one as obvious as I am.

I sulk over this for a while, for I know well enough that he is right. Instead I come up with another approach. Perhaps I could go up the volcano for long visits, very long visits. At this he laughs outright, hugging me and telling me he loves me. Then he sits me up straight and reminds me that the *frente* is not for tourists. No one else brings their family there, because it creates a situation of risk for everyone, the combatants as well as the relatives. Anyone caught going in or out would be killed by the army, for mere friendship with the guerrillas has long since been a death-penalty matter, no trial needed. The *compas* could get killed trying to bring people back and forth. In case of an emergency or ambush, they must be able to move swiftly and silently, as they have been trained to do. They cannot take civilians with them. It would be unsafe. There can be no exceptions made for me, especially for me, because he as Comandante can never have any special privileges. None at all, ever.

I keep on trying, though. I ask if I could not perhaps go to the mountains from time to time as a civilian health worker. I remind him of Charles Clements, the U.S. physician who spent time with the FMLN in El Salvador. Perhaps I could get some training and go up for periods of time when he cannot get down to see me. He rejects this idea at first, but as our last days together pass by, we discuss it again and again and he begins to soften slightly. Perhaps if I got some training so that I would have something to give, perhaps if I could get into good enough physical condition, perhaps . . . He mulls it over, but we never come to a firm decision. We just agree that he will go to our house in Texas when he can. For shorter visits, we can meet in Mexico. If too much time passes and he is unable to leave the *frente*, perhaps I could go there to do medical work if conditions permit. He will not promise, but he will consider it. For me, this is enough.

As we all gather around the Christmas table, huge platters of corn tamales are passed back and forth, together with fruit punch, grapes, and walnuts. Marimba music plays on an old cassette, making us all homesick for the highlands. The others are just beginning to propose toasts when the telephone rings and I am called to a back bedroom. A message has been left for me and relayed over here. I must call home at once. The message makes me immediately uneasy and I duck out the back door to use a public telephone from the street, for the safety rules prohibit any long-distance calls to or from a safe house. Such calls, especially international ones, are too easy to trace. I dial and re-dial, but it takes a very long time to get through on the Christmas telephone lines. Finally I reach my answering service. The news is bad, for my best friend of twenty years, Debra, has just been diagnosed with terminal cancer—melanoma. It has spread rapidly and without any symptoms until now, but there is already a serious brain tumor and her liver is disintegrating. She has three months to live. Would I please come home at once?

I return to the house in a state of shock and sit down with the others, listening to their merry jokes and toasts for the new year and trying to hide my thoughts. Everardo immediately senses that something is wrong and quietly reaches under the table to take my hand, his dark eyes wordlessly signaling concern. It is hard for me to eat, but I pick at my food then join in the toasts, closing my eyes and wishing we were both home. We wait together through the festivities as the modest gifts are opened and the children go down to the handmade crèche at the stroke of midnight. My mind spins back and forth between Everardo and Debra and I feel torn in half. He never lets go of my hand. When the others urge us to stay or continue on to yet another house for a roast turkey and some dancing, he quietly turns them down and takes me swiftly back to our apartment.

Late that night I tell him everything and he pulls me close and tells me it is right to go to Debra, that for now, no matter what, I cannot go to the *frente* with him. It is simply too dangerous, for they will be in a new region, with terrain that is difficult even for the villagers. Perhaps in March, if all goes well, he can return, or I could go to him. It will all be clearer by then. I cling to him and promise to go to Guatemala in March if he cannot leave the *frente*. He smiles sadly but doesn't answer me at first. Instead he strokes my hair and reminds me yet again that one can never be sure of what the future may bring.

During those last few days together we were inseparable, weren't we, Everardo? You came home early every night and we held each other as if every minute could be our last. We read poetry and cooked and even danced together in the hallways. I was terrified and you were serene. I tried to talk about our future, but you would tell me only how you loved me and how happy I had made you. The day we parted, you wrapped me in your arms as if to take one last breath of life before your return to the mountains. Then you silently walked me to the street and flagged a taxicab to take me away. I didn't want to leave you there, but you touched my face, then closed my door. We both flinched at the sound. As the cab sped off I turned for one last glimpse of you there on the street. You were standing very straight, your eyes burning black even from the distance, fixed on my vanishing car. You did not wave.

Debra
New Hampshire, March 1992

SHE LIES QUIETLY ENOUGH IN HER TANGLE OF HOSPITAL MONITORS, tubes, and wires. She has, after all, never been one to complain or to judge, my friend Debra. Watching her sleep, I remember our shared campus room so many years ago, my side messy with half-read books and scattered notes, her corner meticulous, with artistic photographs neatly positioned over her well-made bed. On Sundays we practiced calligraphy together, hers in Japanese, mine in Mandarin, our ink pens and rice paper spread across the small kitchen table. Twenty years later she is still beautiful, but she is dying.

As I hold her hand, I wrestle with the fact that I can do nothing for her. She has cancer, a deadly melanoma, which spread fiercely throughout her entire body before any symptoms gave her warning. Now it is too late, but she has decided to battle it through with brutal levels of chemotherapy anyway. I understand her fierce resistance. Tall and slender, she is an athlete and a ballet dancer, never one to smoke or drink. Two months ago she was bicycling across Oregon, taking in the rugged beauty of the mountains and rivers with her ever-appreciative dark eyes. Then a brief bout of flu left her in a hospital bed with the news that she had three months to live. It was an ambush, foul play, unfair, unacceptable. She is right to fight back, and Everardo was right to send me here.

I hold her hand as she sleeps and watch the fluorescent lines and dots on the screen that tell us she is still alive, that her heart is still beating. For the moment we are alone, just the two of us, and I relish the quiet time with her. When she wakes up, I will surprise her with the bagels I found upstairs and a paper cup filled with foamy cappuccino to remind her of her beloved New York City. I know she cannot eat these things yet misses them visually. She will know why I have brought them to her, and she'll smile through her stiffening lips and pretend to take a few bites. Then we will go back to holding hands and saying nothing, for there is nothing left to say.

While she sleeps, I try not to worry about Everardo, whom I miss terribly. He has gone back to combat in the Guatemalan volcanoes, struggling onward in the grim and endless civil war there. As I watch Debra's monitor, I see him, in my mind's eye, under fire, his small Mayan body tucked neatly behind the rocks for cover, his black eyes ever watchful. For the hundredth time I remind myself that he has survived up there for seventeen years, through the rains and the hunger, the bombings and the battles. The hard-won mountains are his now, under his command. I know I should not worry. He will be back in Mexico soon enough, maybe even this week. We will talk on the phone then, he from a noisy public booth in the streets, and I will tell him all my troubles and how much I love him. A borrowed apartment is waiting for us. When Debra is dead, Everardo will heal me.

When I glance back, I see that she is awake and watching me with her beautiful dark eyes. Her soft gold-brown hair is gone now, lost to the radiation treatments that leave her so weak and ill, and yet she seems unchanged. Propped up on her pillows she is still graceful, her long, slender arms and hands at rest on the white hospital sheet. Her face is smooth and serene and sad. Though she still gamely battles her cancer, I know that she has accepted her own death. Success is no longer an issue; she is now struggling as a matter of principle, but quite without hope. She is strong enough to do this. Will I be strong enough to watch?

A nurse enters and fiddles quietly with the IVs, attaching new bottles and taking Debra's pulse. She opens her mouth as if to speak in her brisk nurse's manner, but then she senses the mood and remains silent. Instead she points at the new medicine bottles and nods, and I know she is warning me that soon they will take effect. Last night they made Debra agitated, her mind crackling with disjointed thoughts, her sleep cycles destroyed. This morning they will do the same. It cannot be helped.

As the hands of the hospital clock move slowly toward midday, the predicted restlessness begins again. We turn on the television, but it is hard for Debra to concentrate, the stories seeming to unfurl at an interminable and distorted pace. Noises in the hall seem shocking instead of muffled. No position in the bed seems tolerable, but she is so enclosed with the tubes and wires that it is difficult to move about, to set herself free. She wants to walk and stretch her cramped limbs, but it is impossible. We consult with each other about what to do next, as if it were a rainy afternoon and we were uncertain as to what sort of cookies to bake.

We decide on a bubble bath. She has a collection of tiny colored bottles filled with incredible fragrances, and we take our time mulling them over, deciding on which one to use today. She selects a rose-colored potion in a curved miniature flask. Then we call the nurse and shyly ask for permission to use the large tub down at the end of the hallway. She grants it, of course, with a quick nod of the head, and Debra instructs me on how to loop the tubes and cords about the IV stand without disturbing the flow of chemicals into her body. She stands up weakly then and wraps an arm around my shoulders, leaning heavily on me but happy to be on her feet. I hold her with one arm and pull the IV stand with the other, and together we move very slowly out of the tiny room and down the hallway, waving to the nurses and admiring the snowy trees through the windows.

The bath area has a scrubbed tile floor and a huge metal tub that fills easily with warm water. Debra measures out the rose-colored liquid and a cloud of floral scent touched with spices floats through the room. We nod at each other, pleased, and she pulls at her hospital shift. I help her with the ties in the back and ring for the nurse to help lower her into the tub. She is deathly thin, and I am terrified that she will slip from my hands and break one of those sharpened, fragile bones that seem to be cutting through her skin. Once safely in the water, she leans back and closes her eyes, breathing in the beautiful scent, appreciating the moment. I pour water over her back and ease a washcloth back and forth over her shoulders, trying not to press against any of the swelling tumors scattered through her flesh like buckshot from a gun.

We do not stay for long, but to her it is an eternity, and soon she is toweled dry and gliding back to her room on my arm. Halfway there her feet give way and she worries that I cannot carry her, though she weighs nothing at all. I tighten my arm around her waist to reassure her, fearful of breaking one of her ribs, and a nurse soon materializes to help us the rest of the way. Debra collapses onto the bed and in a few moments slips back into a peaceful sleep, which I know will not last long.

As I sit, watching the television with the sound turned off, a nurse returns to the room. I wait for her to bend over Debra's bed, but instead she motions to me, pointing to the hallway. Her lips form the word *telephone*, and I clamber to my feet, wondering who would call me here. Perhaps my mother, to tell me she will be late, that she has once again prepared some special treat for us and is waiting for it to come out of the oven. I suddenly long for my mother.

I lift up the receiver, expecting to hear her gentle voice, but it is not her at all. Instead I recognize the long-distance static and Miguel's crisp words in Spanish. He offers no introduction, and for a moment I am disoriented. It is Mexico calling, the underground. What on earth can they want, to risk calling me up here? There is a brief pause as Miguel's disembodied voice waits for me to acknowledge recognition and to pay careful attention. I mumble a few words in Spanish in response. Satisfied, he explains that it would be best if I would come to Mexico at once. The tone is kind but firm, signaling subtle command. I start to protest, to explain where I am and why, then stop myself, remembering that they already know this. If they are calling me it is because something terrible has happened, but what could it be? Then I understand. Everardo. My mind goes blank with terror and I beg for an explanation, but Miguel only repeats that I should come at once. I hear the repressed note of sadness and in that moment I know the unthinkable has happened.

I stagger back to Debra's room, trying not to faint, the nurses looking at me quizzically and asking if I am well. I take out a tiny pad of Japanese paper, a long-ago gift from Debra, and begin writing notes, reminding myself to go to the bank with the nighttime cash machine, to call and reserve the 8:00 A.M. flight, to find my passport, to throw some clean clothes into a travel bag. My writing comes out uneven and manic. I try to tell myself it could not be Everardo, that something else must have happened, that they have forgotten about Debra and didn't realize what they were asking. Tears are rolling down my face, and I am jolted by a soft, thin hand squeezing my own. It is Debra, asking me what has happened, searching my face anxiously and reading all of the clues.

It's Everardo, I tell her. The one in the photo I showed you. I try to say more, but I cannot speak, the air in my lungs is like sharp-edged chunks of ice. For a while we sit facing each other, hand in hand. I know she has read my mind, for she straightens herself up on her pillows after a while and struggles to speak clearly, to make sure I understand her.

You must go, she says, reaching up to touch my face. Her fingers are reassuring, filled with release. Words come to my mind like a shuffled deck of cards now. I want to tell her it will all be fine, that I will be back in a few days, that I will see her again, that we will do her fortieth birthday just as we'd planned, with a cake and her friends and films of her favorite ballet dancers. But I can say nothing at all, because I know she will be dead before I can return and that we will never see each other again.

She knows this. We slip back into holding hands and silently watching the white snow falling on the fragile trees just outside her window. It is evening already, with a soft darkness and a glint of moon. I sit in shock, trying to keep my mind from unraveling, and now it is Debra who in a low voice begins to hum a melody for me, comforting, sending me her strength and serenity through her fingertips.

I never see her again. The next day I am on a shrieking jet, hurtling toward the wild labyrinth of Mexico City and Everardo's underground.

Vanished
Mexico, March 1992

I AM OUT OF MY SEAT BEFORE THE PLANE EVEN COMES TO A HALT on the runway. My bag is small and lightweight and I jerk it out of the overhead bin, then scramble through the crowd of weary passengers to the doorway, where the painted stewardess bids me farewell and bon voyage. Then I rush down the interminably long hallways of the Mexico City airport, my heels clattering loudly on the polished marble floors, my heart in my mouth. What has happened, Everardo? Where are you? My God, do I want to know? I shove my way to the head of the immigration line and wait for the heavy ink stamp of entry, then toss my bag onto the customs shelf for a quick official check. Mercifully, the agent glances at me and waves me through, stopping to take a leisurely puff on his cigarette and looking quite bored with his life. I wish I could be bored with my life, I think grimly to myself.

I change a wad of large bills into pesos and taxi to the central plaza, then register in a cheap hotel under a false name. I don't know what has happened, but I know that it is time for the highest security precautions. Something has gone terribly wrong. The *compas* will be counting on me not to forget the rules and I must not let them down. I must not let Everardo down. I pull off my clothes and splash cold water on my face, then change into a nondescript khaki skirt and white blouse, yet another tourist uniform aimed at making me invisi-

ble. Then I take to the streets, the heavy sooty air gagging me as I go
out the door.

The pay phones at the corner are not working, nor do they work
at the next corner or the next, and I grow frantic. Finally, I enter a
small café and sweet-talk the flirtatious owner into allowing me to use
his private line. He smirks and hands me the phone, ignoring the NOT
FOR PUBLIC sign on the wall. I dial with a shaking hand and after a
few tries I hear a connection and a ringing sound on the other end of
the line. I breathe a deep sigh of relief. Now if only someone is home.
I begin to curse as the phone rings on, but finally a familiar voice, lilting with a highlander accent, answers. I give my code name and the
voice immediately becomes intent and crisp. I must go to the "office"
immediately. My friends are waiting. I must observe the strictest of
protocols, the ones they taught me in the long-ago days of my book
interviews in the safe houses. I understand well enough and confirm
with a one-word answer. I must go to the old meeting place at the
park, not to anyone's home. I will be met. I must use the most strin-
gent security norms and be sure that I am not followed. If followed,
I must skip the meeting point and call again. I thank the disembodied voice and there is a long pause; then the slightest bit of sadness
enters the tone. *Abrazos*, says the voice. *Abrazos y adios.* A hug and good-
bye. The streak of fatalism in the tone makes me bang my head
against the stucco wall where I stand. My God, Everardo, what has
happened? The owner stares and makes no attempt to flirt as I hurry
out of his café.

I observe the rules, forcing myself to slow down and pay attention.
Take the metro to the busiest stop, then get out and change to the
green line and get in a car that is not too crowded. Check each face in
the car, then get out at the next stop and check the faces around you
again. Do not leave the station, just reboard the same line and continue in the same direction. Did any of the same faces climb aboard
with you? No? Good. Now get off and walk slowly down the narrow
side streets to the next metro stop. Is anyone behind you? Who? Wait
till they pass you. Do they try to wait for you? No? Good. Keep going,
board the metro, do another test run. Still clear? Head slowly for the
park, buy an ice cream you could not possibly eat, eat it anyway. Look

in the store window, the wide, shiny one that reflects well. Anyone behind you? No? Good. Circle the park a bit now and get to know all the faces. Just women and their small children playing on the swings and slides, so small and happy. I fight down the swell of nausea that has been haunting me for weeks now, since I first arrived at Debra's hospital room. Who is that man in the dark glasses there? Sit on the bench and wait to see what he does. He buys a Coke, then urinates against a tree and leaves. Lunch break. One more circle around the park. No one is there. It's time to head for the side exit. Walk slowly so that the *compañeros* can see you coming and check your back. Walk very slowly. A small sturdy man climbs out of a gray van. Juan Miguel. Don't start crying. He watches as I grow closer, then smiles broadly to show that all is well and hurries forward to give me a bear hug and push me into the vehicle. The connection has been safely made. Now it is up to them.

We say little as Juan Miguel careens through the chaotic streets of the city, checking his rearview mirror and circling about. No one is with us, and at last he tells me to close my eyes so that we can approach the safe house. It is time to compartmentalize, and I must not know the way to this secret place. When the car rolls to a stop, he touches my arm and I open my eyes. We are in the walled-off and luxuriant garden of a private home. For a moment I want to stay here, in the garden with the pretty flowers. I don't want to know what is coming next.

Juan Miguel leads me inside to a small sitting room and motions for me to be seated on the flowered sofa. Then he vanishes and returns with a tall glass of iced fruit juice. At his side is one of Everardo's most trusted friends, Comandante Emilio, his beautiful face looking grim, his small physician's hands folded neatly on his lap, motionless. We last saw each other at the Christmas party, where he was merry and toasting our health. Now his dark eyes are filled with dread and sadness, as if I was the last person on earth he wants to see.

I rise and give him a brief hug and he puts one arm gently around my shoulders, then motions for me to be seated again. He sits across from me in the small wing chair, his straight posture reminding me of Everardo. They are so different yet the same, this man with small patrician features and a university education. Yet the stoic lift of the chin and the pained, defiant dark eyes make them seem like brothers. Like Everardo, he takes a few moments to study me, to evaluate the situation, feeling no pressure to break into words. I wait in silence.

He takes a sip from his glass, then begins to speak. There was a very difficult shoot-out. It was unexpected. The *compas* were out of the volcano now and in the dangerous terrain of the coffee plantations. Everardo knows the region like the back of his hand and was leading. On March twelfth they had divided up, the combatants going in different directions on different missions. The command post was hidden away at a bend in the river. Everardo stayed behind with half a dozen other of the most trusted *compas* to operate communications and coordinate the patrols. Suddenly a young villager appeared to warn them that an army unit was nearby, on a search and scout mission. The *compas* swiftly gathered up the radio, maps, and codebooks and had their packs in their hands when a hail of smoke and bullets broke out. They threw themselves to the ground and took cover in the deep foliage, heads down. Everardo was with Amílcar, but Amílcar was seriously wounded and lost consciousness. When he came to a few minutes later, the army was gone and the others were bending over him, frantically asking for Comandante Everardo. They combed the area and found nothing—no boots, no backpack, no rifle, and no body. He had simply vanished.

Emilio is watching me again, his eyes locking with mine to see what I can bear, what I can comprehend. I stare back, my mouth dry. Then I ask the dread question. Has he been taken alive? Unbidden, the long-ago memory of a young schoolteacher named Beatriz lying dead on a City morgue slab comes to my mind, with her slashed arms and hacked breasts, the piteous amputated hands placed on her belly. I drive the image from my thoughts, gasping for air, and repeat the question.

Emilio does not want to answer but he does, pulling unhappily at his mustache as he speaks. They do not know for sure. The next day the army reported to the press that they had found a body at the combat site, a body in olive green. No one else was missing there, so the body had to be Everardo's. I take a deep breath of relief as he says this. Anything but torture, Everardo, anything but that. I could never live with the thought of your torture. I am not strong enough. Even now my inner ears are ringing dangerously. Emilio repeats sternly that they are not sure, that the reports are strange and contradictory, almost muffled. The army knew Everardo's face; indeed, they had been hunting him for seventeen years. From the contents of his backpack, jammed with top-secret battle plans, codes, military correspondence, maps, and money, it would be very obvious that this was a combatant of the highest rank. The death of a legendary founder and commander would normally be headline news, a major victory for an army desperate to convince the public that it could win this thirty-year war at last. So why the confusion and contradictions? Why the brief mention of the battle, followed by total silence? They have spoken with the villagers. Some heard that a high-ranking combatant was killed, others that he was taken prisoner. Some saw a burlap bag with a body in it—alive or dead, they did not know for sure. There was a helicopter. The body the army reported finding was taken to Retalhuleu and buried as XX the next day. They would try to get a description. They were searching for more information. They were searching very hard.

We sit in silence for a while. XX. Everardo, I remember the catacombs in the public cemetery in the City, wall after wall after wall of the unnamed dead retrieved from the ravines and the City dump and the gutters of the streets, then plastered unclaimed and unnamed in those tiny cubicles. Are you XX now, too? Or are you somewhere else? Where? Emilio rises and touches my shoulder. Everardo was ours to the death; no one ever gave more. We loved him as we know that you loved him. He touches my shoulder again and then leaves the room.

Juan Miguel, his eyes reddened, hugs me tightly and then brings me a glass of brandy. He tries to talk with me for a while but I cannot respond, and he knows that I need to be alone. Without more ado he takes my hand and leads me upstairs to a small room with a cot and a reading lamp. I sit down on the bed as he carries in sheets and a towel and some extra blankets. When he finishes he gently brushes the hair back from my face and bids me good night. Try to cry, he tells me as he reaches the door. You must try to cry. Cry? Everardo, I cannot even breathe.

Grief
Mexico City, March 1992

THE COMPAS DROP ME OFF IN THE CENTRAL PLAZA, LOATH TO LEAVE me alone, and urge me to call in a few hours once I've had my walk, to come back home for dinner. My need for solitude is so foreign to them that they feel cruel and remiss in abandoning me here in the smoky streets of the city. We should all be together so that they can comfort me and press me with special foods and find a hundred ways to show they care and are there for me during this terrible time. We embrace and I wave as they pull away from the street corner, shaking their heads with worry. Yet they understand, and always have, that I am different.

I begin striding down the narrow colonial streets, not caring which direction I take. Nothing matters any longer, Everardo. I cannot eat and I cannot sleep and I cannot breathe, for there is a great knotted noose around my neck pulled so tight that I cannot even scream. I have your picture in my breast pocket, the tiny photo from your fake ID card. I pull it out to look at every now and then and your image leaps off the paper, so real that you seem to be standing next to me. You are far too vivid to be dead. It is impossible.

Somehow I have arrived in the Zócalo, filled with the Aztec and Mayan peoples of Mexico selling their crafts and wares in front of the colonial-style National Palace. Inside are Diego Rivera's famous murals of the conquest, the walls emblazoned with scenes of the glorious Tenochtitlán, the fire and horror of the invasion, and, toward the end of the hallway, the greedy and distorted faces of the capitalist foreigners. Across the square is the massive cathedral, one of the oldest in the hemisphere, its interior hung with solid gold and costly carved mahogany throughout its echoing hallways. I remember the stained-glass windows, portraying scenes of the death and torture of ancient saints, and the enormous cross proclaiming the one and only way to God. I hesitate for a moment, craving the silence of its interior, but I cannot enter, for it sits like a gigantic boot on the ruins of the vanquished Aztec city. Just over there lie remnants of the pathetic temples, partially exposed for the tourists to admire. The rest lie beneath the weight of the colonial buildings here in the square, dead and buried forever. I study the edges of the temple rooftops, remembering the history. It was here that the last survivors of Tenochtitlán fought desperately against the Spaniards, then flung themselves from the rooftops. Their world had vanished before their eyes. In a mural down the street Frieda Kahlo, young forever, hands out rifles for a revolution. Mexico.

I wander about the square and I see you everywhere, Everardo. Isn't that you over there by the ruins? That man with the blue canvas jacket and the Mayan profile, isn't that you? No, I am wrong. It is someone else, someone with a similar build but no fire to the eyes. A lighthouse without its flare, so different. Perhaps over there at the ruins? I hurry to the corner and stare into the stoic face of a villager from the southland; he is unpacking a satchel of hand-carved flutes. It isn't you, but he made my heart jump, Everardo. I must stop this cycle of hope and dashed hope. I must not look for you, for I know full well you are not here. I must not look. So much easier said than done.

I enter the metro station and find myself drawn like a magnet to our old apartment. I should not go there, I know, but I cannot help myself for I am certain that if I bang on the door you will answer, glad to see me, a book or a scrub brush in your hand. As I walk down our street I hear the sound of a rifle shot echoing through my head. They say you shot yourself through the mouth, Everardo. Did you? I know you would have tried, as they closed in on you. Anything but capture. I hear the sound of the bullet again and see the wild greenery of your volcano. Did the incredible light show of your mind end with that crashing sound? Was I with you then? Did my image flash before your eyes one last time? Did you remember how much I loved you?

I reach the apartment building and start up the seven flights of stairs. I am so dizzy now, and the nausea that has haunted me since Debra's hospital room sweeps over me with a vengeance. I should eat, I know, but I cannot. Three floors, four floors—I cannot possibly be this weak. Five floors, six floors, and now at last the tiny landing space at the top and the familiar metal door. I sit down on the last step, ignoring the dirt, afraid to knock but unable to leave. I know you are in there; you must be. If you aren't, then I am dead too. I pull myself up and force myself to knock, for you wouldn't have me run from realities, would you, Everardo? We must accept the life we are given. I knock. There is a silence. I knock once more. Nothing. The metal door remains closed and still, reminding me that no mere mortal can go back in time.

That night I check into a small hotel room and lie on the bed, staring at nothing. I cannot stop vomiting and cramps have begun to pull at my abdomen. At first I am relieved, for my period has been so very late, with all the stress. But as the hours pass the cramping deepens rhythmically, and I am soon face-to-face with the fact that I am having a miscarriage.

I did not take care of our child, Everardo. I didn't even realize he or she existed yet, but I should have. You would forgive me, I know, for that is how you are, but I will never forgive myself. It is all too late.

A Plan
Mexico City, April 1992

DESPERATE, I COME UP WITH A PLAN. THERE IS ONLY ONE SOLUTION here, and that is to open the grave out in Retalhuleu. It is either Everardo buried there or it isn't, and we have to know. We have to. I make Juan Miguel get up early and leave the house to set up an emergency appointment for me with Emilio. My idea is unorthodox, and of all the leaders I have met, he seems like the one most likely to take me seriously. When I tell Juan Miguel about it he rolls his eyes, but he puts on his boots and goes out to make the call. Within a few hours I am walking across a crowded restaurant floor toward Emilio.

He is sitting in a booth over in a corner, a cup of coffee before him and a newspaper in his hand, looking for all the world like any other upper-class Mexican gentleman enjoying a civilized brunch. He glances up as I approach, carefully watching to see that I am not followed, then grants me a sardonic smile of welcome. You rang? The droll lift to his eyebrow as I sit down makes me laugh a bit despite myself and I hurry to tell him that I have a plan, that I have not called him out here just to waste his time. He doesn't answer right away, pouring me a cup of coffee from a large china pot and quietly setting out a pen and paper on the table. All in its time, he seems to be saying. Maybe you are a madwoman and maybe you aren't, and that's exactly what I am going to find out. He gestures for me to enjoy my coffee, then asks what it is, precisely, that I have in mind.

His dark eyes do not leave my face as we speak, and looking back at him I know I have come to the right person. This man will hear me out. I take a deep breath and plunge in, determined to convince him. I remind him that I lived in Guatemala in 1985 and 1986, and that during those two years all I did was human rights work. I helped people get out of the country, took testimonies, went to the morgues, and tramped all over the Ixcán area, writing about the repression in the model villages. Everyone knew I was doing human rights work, including the army, and that's in fact why I had to leave Guatemala way back then. Emilio nods patiently, waiting for me to get to the point. I continue, a bit reckless now. "So why don't we ask for an exhumation of the Retalhuleu grave? I'll get a group of international observers to go with me to attend the proceedings and explain that I met Everardo while I was working on the book and later married him. The army's own files on me will confirm everything and they won't be able to arrest me just for admitting I am his wife. I haven't done anything wrong. I can marry anyone I choose, can't I?" Emilio rolls his eyes just as Juan Miguel did, but he motions for me to continue. "That way I will get a chance to see the body myself. Since Everardo was underground all these years we don't have any dental records or fingerprints. But I remember everything about him. He was just a bit shorter than I am, and almost the same size; we could swap clothes. I remember exactly which tooth is missing, and the gaps in the upper teeth, and the overcrowding that pulled his lip crooked. I can identify him if . . . if . . ." I don't finish my sentence. Even if he is horribly disfigured and decomposed.

Emilio is sitting up very straight now and eyeing me intently. He asks me over and over again how I would be able to identify the body if we can open the grave. I had forgotten that he was once a doctor, as well as the legendary man who led his resistance forces through the times of the massacres. Now we talk frankly enough about medical matters. He does not coddle me at all or mince words. Instead he is testing me, evaluating whether or not I will have the strength to do what I am offering to do. He is building me up by speaking clinically, as if these were the most natural matters in the world. He is teaching me that death and decomposition are, in fact, the most natural of matters and that I must not fear them. As we talk I feel some of my sense of dread fall away.

After a while Emilio switches back to the rest of my plan. As for having the right to marry anyone I choose, I had best remember that thousands of people have been tortured to death for far less in Guatemala—far, far less. I argue that my citizenship will protect me and he reminds me of the North American nuns and priests who died in Guatemala merely because they had defended the poor. Checkmate. He has me cornered there, but I tell him I want to take that risk anyway. It has to be done. He nods thoughtfully but points out that if they know Everardo is married to a U.S. citizen, the stakes become immeasurably higher for the army. It becomes an international incident; they could lose their Washington, D.C., funding. Everything could fall apart if I admit the relationship. He must think about it all, talk with the others. He will be in touch. He puts his paper and pen away in a small case and stands to pay the bill. As he leaves he hugs me firmly, telling me that it is a good idea, a very good idea indeed.

During the next few days the leadership converges on me and we have countless meetings in Juan Miguel's living room. We battle out the details over breakfast, lunch, and dinner and late into the night, weighing the possibilities. This move will frighten the army. If Everardo is still alive, will an exhumation trigger his murder? Won't they kill him anyway? No one has ever come back alive after capture by the army in all these thirty years of war. All captured *compañeros* lie dead and mutilated in unmarked graves. Also, if Everardo is alive, isn't he suffering terribly? In unison, we lower our eyes at the thought. Isn't he better off dead? Maybe yes, maybe no, but shouldn't we try to save him? Yes, but try how? Which strategy? The leaders sit for hours in their armchairs, pistols strapped to their ankles, taking notes, asking questions, mulling it all over. No one likes the subject, for they all loved Everardo, and their faces take on a haggard, pained look as we speak. Chayo, yet another doctor, argues that I am quite mad. The body has been buried in a tropical trench for a month now. It will be horrifying and I am far too close to be clinical about this. Do I understand the face will be a mass of mold and liquified tissue, the softer features like the eyes and lips already eaten away? Do I have any concept of what this advanced state of death is about? The others clench their teeth and fight back tears as he speaks. I tell him I'm going and that nothing can stop me.

At last they decide that it is a good idea, as long as I go as a mere observer and not as Everardo's wife. This would make the proceedings impossible to arrange. Ramiro de León Carpio, the human rights ombudsman in Guatemala, is contacted by telephone. He is nervous, but he agrees to set up the exhumation and to send the forensic results to Mexico City for a final identification by the URNG. Observers are welcome. Yet the weeks begin to pass by inexorably as he files the endless paperwork and, frightened, seeks "courtesy" approval of the Guatemalan army. He dares not move without this, and we begin to lose precious time. I pace up and down crying, as each day makes the identification process more and more difficult, doubtless exactly what the army has in mind. I spend my time calling frantically to every human rights group in the United States, begging for people to accompany me. Most refuse, for it is far too dangerous. We could well be arrested or worse. They are appalled, too, by the political implications of the case, and terrified of losing funding or being labeled as subversives themselves by the U. S. government. Everardo was, after all, a URNG commander, and the McCarthy-like era of the 1980s has left its scars. For a long time now, the FBI has made its rounds of "visits" with anyone perceived to be on the wrong side of the Central American wars. People have been threatened with criminal charges for being too friendly with the left. Solidarity workers have been illegally followed, surveilled, and harassed. One of them, Jack Elder, has been sentenced for harboring and transporting refugees, and another, tiny Stacey Merckt, despite her pregnancy, has served prison time for this. Other church people are still in court and their futures are unclear.

I also consult one by one with old contacts in the U.S.-Guatemala network to seek quiet advice. They agree with the *commandancia*, forcefully arguing that if I go to Guatemala, I must never even insinuate that I am Everardo's wife or else the proceedings will fall apart and be canceled at once. The matter is far too sensitive. In fact, I probably should not go at all, I should just wait for the information to arrive in Mexico. I think it over. There is so little to go on that I don't think a positive identification can be made from mere data or photographs. Also, couldn't the army knock out the correct tooth, falsify the data a bit, find someone who looked rather like Everardo? Couldn't they terrorize the forensic doctor into signing a false report? If I don't go myself, I will always wonder. I talk it over with Emilio, telling him that somehow I am certain that I will know Everardo if it is him, even so late and no matter what. Am I being sentimental? Emilio shakes his head no. I will be able to recognize him if I keep my calm.

And so the plans progress. More and more calls are made to de León Carpio. The leadership has asked him to approach the army intelligence division, or G-2, and ask for forensic photos and dental records of the body found out there at the river. Carpio agrees to this but calls back with bad news. G-2 says there are no such photos or records. Carpio will send what information he has, though. Perhaps this will help. He is working on the exhumation. We shake our heads at this report, for there is no way that the G-2 took no photos or physical evidence, of that body of all bodies. I remember back to Rosario with her baby at her side, both dead on a morgue slab in

Guatemala City. Not even the family could get in to see her until the
G-2 officials finished their own investigation. This was routine even
for civilians they considered "suspicious." They would certainly have
recognized Everardo, for they had been hunting him for seventeen
years. If the face was too disfigured, they would have known from the
contents of his backpack that the dead man was a commander. They
certainly took photos and other records. Why are they lying now?

When the letter from de León Carpio arrives, Emilio calls me to
the small square near Juan Miguel's house. Here's the description of
the body, he tells me. He hands it to me to read, hesitating slightly,
then resolutely placing it in my hands. It is official-looking, the let-
terhead of the *procurador*, or ombudsman, at the top, the text neatly
typed and signed with a flourish. The body found was of a man in his
thirties, dressed in olive green, about 1 meter 60. He was shot in the
back and then committed suicide by shooting himself through the
mouth with his own rifle, destroying his cranium. He had a round
face, broad forehead, heavy eyebrows, wide, thick lips, dark eyes, black
hair, and a turned-down Mayan nose and was clean-shaven, dark-
skinned, and of a sturdy build. The description makes me ill. Everardo, this is you, every feature in your face, your build, your height,
your age. I look up and see my own nausea stamped onto Emilio's
face.

Maybe the army is lying. If they took Everardo prisoner, they
would have this description just by taking a look at him. If he shot
himself through the mouth, wouldn't his face have been more difficult to describe? Maybe it's not Everardo, maybe it's not true. Emilio
looks at me for a long time. We will go ahead with the exhumation,
but I should prepare myself. This is Everardo's description, exactly. I
must prepare to find him in that grave. I start to argue, but he takes
me firmly by the shoulders. This is Everardo's description. Anything
is possible, but I must prepare. I must be ready to find him there.

With that he leaves me, knowing there is nothing more to be said.
I sit for a long time, reading and rereading the letter that describes so
perfectly the image of Everardo lying dead at a muddy riverside, his
brains scattered about him on the damp earth. One by one, hot tears
squeeze from the corners of my eyes, yet I cannot really cry. I long to

but I cannot, for the tears are dammed up in a huge and powerful ocean which, if the dam ever breaks, will drown me for once and for all. How I long to drown, to be swept away, Everardo. But then who would be left to fight for you?

The Visitor
Mexico City, April 1992

THEY BRING ME HIS THINGS. WE SIT ABOUT IN JUAN MIGUEL'S LIV-ing room, trying not to think about the endless delays in the ex-humation arrangements, trying not to think about the exhumation at all, in fact. I cuddle with the children, and Marisa, his *compa*, makes us hearty dinners. We listen to the news and play marimba music from Guatemala. Life goes on, but it goes on a bit wanly, and in fits and starts. The leadership comes by to visit in the evenings, bringing his things, Everardo's things. The items form a pitifully scant pile, for he owned almost nothing. His civilian clothes had all come out of a communal supply and he returned them when he crossed the border. Our kitchen utensils were borrowed from friends and the yellow flow-ered sugar bowl he gave me was somehow lost in the confusion of his disappearance. They bring me his blue sweater, my Christmas gift to him, and his small pocketknife. His Vangelis tape and shaver arrive in a brown envelope, together with a small volume of poetry. The pho-tographs of me he burned before he left, to keep me safe in case the unthinkable happened.

Comandante Annibal, Everardo's longtime friend, sends me his small journal, which was wrapped in plastic and stored for years at a time in a safe house near the border. It is old but well cared for, with a red vinyl cover and still-crisp pages filled with tiny script. I flip through it, but most of the annotations are encoded and make no

sense to me. The dates of the peace talks are marked neatly and perhaps with hope. A small photograph of me, his favorite, is tucked in
the back to await his return to Mexico. As I pull it loose a second
photo, tiny and much older, falls into my lap. I hold it up to the light
and see the face of a very young and pretty Mayan woman, her black
hair neatly combed, her lips soft and full. For a moment I wonder if
she is his sister, so fierce and dark and old are those tilted-up eyes, so
vulnerable the lips. She seems to leap from the inked image, so much
like him, the intelligence so obvious. Yet she cannot be his sister, for
he told me once there were no photos from his childhood. Indeed,
there were no cameras. Then who? I think for a moment and then I
know full well who she is. Rosalvina, his second *compañera*, the villager
taken alive and tortured to death by army forces years ago. So this is
her face, of course, no wonder he loved her, for her fading image is
breaking my heart. And Gabriella? I search, but of her there is nothing, nothing but the memories he shared with me in the middle of the
night after watching her die in his dreams. So, I think dully, we are all
together now, here in this living room.

I thank the others for bringing me these gifts, then wander off to the
side bedroom with its small cot and rough wool blanket. Juan Miguel
follows and leaves my glass of wine at the door, then vanishes without
a word. I unlace my shoes and flip through the agenda book a bit more,
tracing the fading handwriting on the tiny pages with my fingers.

And then you visit me, Everardo. I am not asleep yet; indeed I am
still sitting up on the cot, fully dressed, your agenda book open in my
hands. But I'm not awake or daydreaming either. I am somewhere else,
and you are there too. Or rather, I am someplace else and I can see
you even though I know you are far away. You are in a small dark space
barely big enough to fit in, and you are huddled up, hugging your
knees to your chest. Is that a grave, or a pit, or a darkened cell? I cannot see; it is all so foggy and unfocused. I can see only that it is small
and dark and that you are there. You say nothing at first, but you lock
your eyes with mine, telling me everything with that look. You are sad
and wistful for the life we will never have together, for all that can
never be now. Yet you are stoic, chin as always lifted straight, eyes un-
flinching. I cannot speak to you, but I know you hear the thousand

questions hurtling through my mind like swooping bats. We cannot touch. And then I hear you. I hear your words even though you do not move your lips and I do not know which language you are speaking. But I hear you, just as I will hear you over and over throughout the coming months. You say only three words, yet they reveal everything and drive me to madness.

"I am cold."

Evidence
Mexico, May 1992

SO MUCH FOR THE BRIGHT IDEAS, EVERARDO. BUT NOW WE HAVE TO figure out how to make it all happen. Emilio is working frantically with the others, trying to convince the Guatemalan authorities to open the grave in Retalhuleu. They are in constant touch with de León Carpio, the human rights ombudsman. He has filed the basic paperwork with the courts, but he is understandably terrified and still wants "courtesy" military approval before he sticks his neck out any further. Opposing the army is still a death-penalty matter in Guatemala, even for civilian officials. Easter week comes and goes and Guatemala shuts down for ten days. After that there are still more delays. Meanwhile I burn up the telephone lines calling friends in the United States. Will you please be an international observer? Where? In Guatemala. For what? The exhumation of a guerrilla commander's body. No? Too dangerous? Would you recommend someone else, please. It really is an emergency. Please spell the name. Would you have their phone number? Thank you. Operator, I would like to place a call to the United States.

It all goes so slowly, Everardo, I am in despair. Every day that passes makes things ever so much more difficult. It's been months now that the XX body has been buried out there in the tropical rains of the southwest. How on earth will I be able to identify you? Or even know for certain that it is not you? Are you still alive? For how much longer? And what are they doing to you right now, even as I think of you? Day by day I go slowly mad, trapped in a Wizard of Oz scene, the grains of sand trickling through the hourglass while I frantically tear at the door to free you.

As the weeks pass I become obsessed with the question of how to identify—or, hopefully, to disidentify—the body. How will I know for sure? There is so little physical evidence, so few records. Everardo grew up a peasant; he never saw a dentist, never had braces. Later with the *compañeros*, in the mountains, it was the same. Bad teeth were either pulled by the medic or ignored. On rare visits to other countries, dental work was arranged, but always under false names, with false papers. Everything was done so as to leave no trace. Everardo was the perfect invisible man. So how, now, am I to make him visible enough for the forensic doctors?

He is so visible to me, every detail still etched into my mind. I sit down with a pad of paper and a pen and start making notes. No braces; his teeth were strong and white but very crooked, with a gap in the front that I always found endearing. *Number one*, I write, *gap between upper front teeth.* I close my eyes and conjure up his image. In my memory he smiles for me and I see the familiar tug of his upper lip, pulling unevenly across the crowded teeth on one side. *Number two, upper side teeth, protruding and overlapping.* I close my eyes again and he appears, so real that I break into a sweat. He is laughing now as he holds me close, the bright white arc of teeth in the lower jaw forming a tidy curve. One is missing there, to the side. What did he tell me? Jorge pulled it out with pliers long ago. *Number three, old extraction, lower jaw, right side. Number four, no gold caps or coronas. Number five, all other teeth intact.*

My face feels clammy and I get up to make myself some tea, pushing the damp strands of hair out of my eyes and pacing up and down. This is too hard, I want someone else to do it. But who? Could I remember so much detail about anyone else but him? I know I could not. I dabble the tea bag in a mug of hot water and force myself to think some more. Come on now, think, his life may depend on it.

Think. I know his height and weight, of course—that's easy enough. He is just a bit shorter than I am, a fact that bothered him not one bit. He is barrel-chested but not large. I remember him wearing my unisex shirts and even my men's jeans once. Our proportions are so very different, but we are almost the same size. Age? He is thirty-four, and in just another month or so he will turn thirty-five. I remember our plans to be back in Texas by then and my head begins to ache.

None of this. I shake my head and rub my eyes. No time for this; there is work to be done. Dead or alive, Everardo needs me now. The thought braces me and I sit back down with the yellow pad. What else? I vaguely remember an article about discovering the grave site of some historical figure. The czar of Russia perhaps? The forensic specialists were conducting some kind of tests by comparing the exact proportions of the skull with old photographs of the face. So few exist of Everardo, forbidden as they were for his protection. What if they were to fall into the wrong hands? But now he has fallen into the wrong hands.

Old photographs. I go back to the small package of his things, his tiny calendar, the picture of Rosalvina. I check my jacket pockets. There it is—the false ID card he was using here in Mexico. It has a small photograph of him in the corner. I remember when we stopped at the booth to have it taken, not far from our apartment. It is eerily sharp, this image, the black eyes locked dead straight on the camera lens, the wide cheekbones, the full lips. It is as if you were staring straight into my own eyes, Everardo. The photo makes me cringe. I place it next to my notes and write down *number six, enlarge photograph.*

What else? It may be far too late for fingerprints, but who knows. I lay siege to the city and ferret out some odds and ends that once belonged to us. In one house I find a small box he left behind, unopened and still awaiting his return. It contains some packets of raisins, a pair of socks, a can opener, and his small battery-powered recorder. I find it untouched at the bottom of a storage cabinet and take it home with me to add to the small but growing pile of evidence. Then I remember his things back in the Texas house, his few clothes and books, the pair of worn shoes with the clear imprint of his foot inside. I write these down on the yellow pad as well. Evidence, forensic evidence, a good cold clinical word. It clears my mind and also breaks my heart. Is this what our world has come to, Everardo? A legal file? A small drawer filled with clinical evidence?

Then at last, the call comes. The date for the exhumation has been arranged; all is well. It is time to catch a flight for Guatemala.

XX
Retalhuleu, May 1992

I AWAKEN IN THE DARK HOTEL ROOM, EXHAUSTED AND FOR A FEW moments uncertain as to where I am. Then, in the shadows, I see my friend Sissy in the bed next to mine and remember with a wince that we are in Guatemala. In just a few short hours we will be at the grave site in Retalhuleu to begin the exhumation, but we have a long drive ahead into the tropical lowlands first. I roll out of the bed and stumble into the bathroom to splash cold water onto my face, for I badly need to clear my mind. The last few days have been a hellish whirl of rushed preparations and I have slept very little, but at least we are finally here.

A band of loyal friends from Texas has arrived with me—Jim Harrington, a civil rights lawyer I have known since my days with the farmworkers, and Sissy Farenthol, a liberal politician from Houston. Tony Equale, a former priest, is with us too. Late last night we met briefly with the human rights ombudsman de León Carpio, finding him tense and frightened in his small office behind multiple locked doors. He reminded us that this is a very dangerous case and warned us to avoid wandering about in the streets unescorted. It would be best to remain in the hotel. As for the exhumation, we should be ready to leave at 5:00 A.M. His forensic doctor, Leonel Gomez, will accompany us.

I pull on my clothes and wait as Sissy stumbles about to her suit-cases and the shower. Then we meet the others downstairs and stand quietly in the lobby, saying very little. The grim task ahead has robbed us of small talk.

Leonel comes for us at five precisely, looking crisp and scrubbed and well rested. I climb into the front seat of his car, wanting to talk to him on the long drive out to Retalhuleu to gather up any clues that I can. A round-faced forensic photographer sits in the back next to a pile of legal documents, camera cases, and an ominous black medical bag topped with packets of heavy rubber gloves, a rubber sheet, and surgical masks. Jim, Sissy, and Tony take the rented car and follow us closely through the dimly lit city streets as we head out of town. It is strange being here in Guatemala City after so many years. I recognize the old cafés and shop doors with a jolt of nostalgia and regret. This is not how I had planned to return.

As we head onto the southern highway, Leonel pulls out a thermos of hot coffee and hands it to me, together with a small plastic mug. He is a kindly enough person, brisk and professional in his short-sleeved white shirt and khaki trousers. I ask how long he has been a forensic doctor and he tells me he has practiced for a number of years now and trained, in fact, at a military base in the United States for a while. When de León Carpio became ombudsman, he went to work for the human rights office. He has been happy there, though they are understaffed and need better equipment. I wince as he names the army base and try not to stare at him as I drink my coffee. He is clearly upper-class, blond with languid, heavy-lidded blue eyes and the short, trim build of a collegiate wrestler. Whose side is he on? Obvi-ously he has strong military links, but is he here to cause trouble? Or is he simply being honest about his background? He is open enough—that is certain. He smiles at me and politely urges me to have some more coffee. It is very early, he remarks. I must be tired from my long trip. Have I consulted on many forensic matters before?

I look sideways at him from the corner of my eye and mumble that I have done quite a few legal reports. Is he just being friendly, or is he fishing for information? Is this a friend or a dangerous foe here? His face is smooth and a bit bland, and I see no suspicion or guile on his features. There is a trace of professional curiosity and perhaps a tepid desire to make friends. As he chats, I realize that he sees me as someone much like himself, an upper-class and light-skinned professional. He doesn't ask whether or not I have any relationship to Everardo. Indeed, this doesn't seem to have entered his head. On this issue I am protected by the traditional and impenetrable wall of race realities here in Guatemala—apartheid, more or less. A few years later, when I tell them the truth about our marriage, Everardo, and present them with court documents, they will cry out that it is impossible. A white woman from Harvard could never have married an *indio*, so dark and thick-lipped, so uncultured. They will shout it at me at Las Cabañas as they stand on your grave.

I ramble on to Leonel about some trips to the morgue and he assumes I am talking about some sort of strange legal procedures in the United States. In fact, I am remembering the cadavers of La Verbena in Guatemala City. For a while we get along quite well and chat back and forth about cases we have worked on and various cities in Europe we have visited.

As the sun begins to rise, the fierce climate of the coastal lowlands strikes me in the face, hot and clammy. I feel as if I am breathing through a warm, wet towel wrapped around my nose and mouth. Leonel cheerfully offers me a packet of saltines, but it is impossible to eat. The coffee has set my nerves on edge and I already feel sick and dizzy. He looks at me quizzically and smiles. Perhaps I am on a diet? I nod yes and he shakes his head with disapproval. Women are too thin these days; I really must eat something. He hands me an orange and I make a show of taking it apart and placing the sections one by one in my mouth.

After a while he grows bored with the long drive and our talk turns once again to his work, which he clearly loves. He asks what tests I think should be done on the body out in Retalhuleu. I shrug and ask wanly for his opinion. With this invitation, he happily goes into his analysis. We should do the basic build and height estimates, of course, and break open the pelvic bone for an age range, since we won't be able to guess that from the face anymore. March, April, and now it's May. The body will be badly decomposed; it will be quite a messy job.

If they've buried the man in a plastic bag it will be even worse, since that retards the rotting. Better if they've just tossed him into an open grave, since that would give us clean bone or close by now, but that's unlikely. There may be some hair intact still, to give us more clues, dark or light, straight or curly. I suggest photographs of the face no matter what, and of course a dental chart, assuring him that the URNG will have all confirming details. We must simply send the information to Mexico City. The identification is up to them.

He nods at this and enthusiastically comes up with more ideas. Perhaps the URNG will have fingerprints. Have I heard of the new technique for getting prints off a cadaver even at this late stage? We should clip off some of the fingers—he has the clippers with him in his bag—then place them in bottles of formaldehyde and wait for them to swell. Prints have been retrieved this way even in cases of severe decomposition. I grit my teeth and recommend a complete dental chart, adding that I want to help with it, in fact. Everardo, if he cuts off a single finger I will lay him dead in his grave right next to yours.

After an interminable drive we arrive in Retalhuleu and find our way through the narrow streets to the town cemetery. It is filled with carved tombstones, brightly painted stucco mausoleums, and the catacomb graves of the poor. My heart sinks as we pull up to a crude morgue with open windows, surrounded by muddy uneven earth hacked free of all foliage. Ominous mounds and depressions crowd the small area, and a rectangular shape in the back is marked off with a yellow string. We have come to the graves of the unidentified, the graves of the XX. Two ragged men stand with shovels, ready to start digging. It's time now and I must get a grip on myself. Sparks fly through my head. Whose face will they pull from this mud? Everardo's? I struggle not to vomit right here in the car.

The other vehicle arrives and Jim, Sissy, and Tony climb out, forming a protective circle around me as we move toward the marked-off grave. The judge is here with his books and papers and his pretty assistant. Leonel talks with them briefly, gesturing with his hands and opening his neat leather portfolio. Someone hisses that there is a body in the morgue and a bloody pile of clothes folded up neatly in the corner, but I barely hear. Flies drone about in the heat. Finally the judge nods and signals for the grave diggers to get to work. The metal shovels bite into the soft earth, hurting my ears. I want to beg the men to dig more gently, but I can say nothing. I must show nothing. If they find out I am Everardo's wife, it will all come to an end and I will lose this chance to save his life—that is, if he is still alive. I press my lips together and force myself to breathe normally. I must show nothing. I will show nothing.

I stand toward the middle of the grave as they dig, not wanting to seem too eager, but needing to figure out which side of the rectangle the head will be on. I have to see the teeth, to look for that gap in the bright white half circle of the lower jaw. Once again the image of Everardo laughing as we lie together on the sofa comes to mind with a jolt. I will know immediately if it is him, but I may not get much of a chance to look. I don't, after all, have much of an excuse to get too close. Just one good clear look is all I need. Everything depends on it, everything in the world.

As I stand there, the sound of the clods begins to break my heart. Tony gently touches my arm, suggesting that I stand in the shade, but I give him a fierce look of silent refusal. I must see the face of this dead man, see the teeth, and I will only have a few seconds before Leonel takes over with his assistant. I must stay where I am. Tony shakes his head and moves back to the protective branches of a small tree. Sissy stands tall and serene, her calm aura giving me strength. Slowly, I begin to recover my equilibrium. It is either Everardo or it isn't. If it's someone else, I will have something to go on, something to fight with, something concrete. If it is Everardo, at least there will be no more thoughts of torture to horrify me, only death itself. I will bury him. It will be over forever. I remember what Chayo told me to expect of the face—mold and liquid, eyeless and lipless. This no longer frightens me. I will know in a flash if it is you, Everardo. If it is, I will lay you in your casket and hold your hands and tell you goodbye. I am no longer afraid.

The grave diggers reach the edges of a heavy plastic bag and Leonel nods his head and starts laying out his instruments on a neatly folded tarpaulin. Scissors, knives, forceps, a magnifying glass, and small bottles line up in a row. He pulls on rubber gloves like a surgeon heading for the operating room, nodding to me that we will soon begin. The grave diggers wrap scarves across their faces and bend to free the body bag, vanishing entirely into the pit of the grave.

A group of National Police arrive, dressed in blue uniforms and carrying rifles in their arms. The grave diggers hesitate and for a moment both Leonel and the judge look fearful. Now what? The police circle us quietly, looking us over but saying nothing. Are they here to arrest us? They make no move to do so. Instead an officer steps forward and says that they, too, have come to observe the exhumation, and that the army will soon be arriving as well. There is a long, tense silence. I speak up, answering that this is fine with us, that everyone is welcome as far as we're concerned. The digging continues, the judge standing by nervously, Jim and Sissy and Tony exchanging wary glances. We know that something is about to happen, and that it will probably not be good. The police say nothing and watch us in silence, their rifles slung over their shoulders or at ease at their sides. The officer is stifling a leer.

A shiny car screeches to a halt in front of the morgue and the policemen look up expectantly. A fat man in an expensive suit leaps out, crimson-faced and screaming at us. From the distance we cannot make out the words, and he races toward us, waving his arms and trampling the unmarked graves beneath his feet. He introduces himself as Asisclo Valladares, the *procurador nacional*—"attorney general for the nation." I exchange glances with Jim and he raises an eyebrow in amazement. What is the national attorney general doing out here and why did he leave home at 5:00 A.M. to get here? Asisclo is yelling so loudly and so fast that it is difficult to make out what he is saying in Spanish. The judge is clearly terrified and is shrinking back in silence, but Leonel seems calm enough.

Jim and I crowd closer to hear. We end up shoulder-to-shoulder with the police. Asisclo is saying that the exhumation proceeding must be stopped, that the papers are no good because they have not been preapproved by his office. Leonel is answering stubbornly that this is an international human rights case and that everything has been arranged for months by the ombudsman's office, including courtesy military approval. He hauls out a sheaf of papers and hands them to Asisclo, waiting for him to read them. The police crowd more tightly around us, listening to the heated argument. I watch their faces and am reminded of a cat playing with a trapped mouse, about to come in for the kill. A deep cramp starts up in my stomach. What about Sissy, and Jim and Tony? Perhaps I should have come here alone. This was not part of the agreement.

Asisclo shrieks louder and orders the grave diggers out of the grave, but Leonel quietly gestures for them to stay where they are until the discussion is finished. They remain in the pit, looking unhappily around them at the police and the fancy car, their dark eyes studiously blank. A creaking sound comes from beneath their feet and I wonder if those are Everardo's bones, cracking beneath their weight. I force myself to turn my attention back to Asisclo, to understand everything that he is saying. If I think about the creaking sound, I will start to scream. I crowd closer next to Jim and together we strain to hear what is being said.

Asisclo is now saying that the exhumation must be canceled in any event because foreigners are present and this cannot be allowed. Leonel's patrician calm is beginning to crack and he starts to argue, visibly irritated. My heart sinks. This is what they warned me about, the presence of foreigners raising the stakes too high. Are we the real problem here? I cut in and tell Asisclo that if our presence is a problem, we will gladly go over to the parking lot and wait. He turns a darker shade of red. This will not be good enough at all. Someone from the URNG must come in person to identify the body. Are any of us from the URNG? The police crowd a bit closer and Leonel's jaw drops open. The judge is white-faced and silent. A young man steps forward with a video and pans us carefully. Are any of us from the URNG? So this is it, I think to myself. They have come to arrest us. The camera lingers on me.

Leonel is openly angry now and points out that no URNG member can come forward publicly without being immediately arrested. Asisclo agrees with this but insists that someone must come anyway. He pulls out the URNG letters requesting the exhumation. They are signed by the public spokesperson in Mexico, Francisco Villalgran.

There! Asisclo points to the signature. This man Francisco has signed the letters. He must come to Guatemala and present himself for the exhumation. Leonel is darkening; his brows knit close together over his languid blue eyes. Villalgran cannot come here without being immediately arrested. He and Asisclo are shouting at one another again, and the police are circled tightly around us. Should I speak up, tell them I am Everardo's wife but not a URNG member? There was no time to stop at the embassy last night—who trusts them anyway?—and I have no lawyer with me. If I speak up, I will probably be arrested, since they don't seem to be in the mood for splitting hairs. And Jimmy and Sissy and Tony? They will probably be arrested, too, thanks to me. The air is electric. If I speak, there will be an explosion; if I don't, I could lose Everardo.

Asisclo and Leonel seem to be reaching a compromise position. They will postpone the exhumation for a day or two and rewrite the papers. Then we can come right back. It will only be a short delay. The grave diggers are climbing out of the grave, looking very relieved. My heart sinks. We can't leave. I can't at least. Asisclo is asking if any family members are present as he shepherds us firmly away toward the cars. Should I answer? What for, if we are already being forced to leave? If I answer, there will be a terrible uproar and scandal. Perhaps then we will never get back here, ever. The door could close permanently. I open and close my lips, hesitant, then decide to wait until the others are safely out of the country and I have contacted the embassy and a lawyer. Two days shouldn't kill me, though it might. We must do this right or it will all fall apart and there will be no way to fix it. We reach the cars in a jumble of civilians and police and rifles. Leonel is clearly frightened and signals for his assistant not to leave our side for even a moment. There are too many police, too many guns, and too many signs of military rage over this matter. In the end, no mere civilian is safe in Guatemala and Leonel knows this well enough. No one crosses the army here. He looks over his shoulder, as if expecting an assassin's bullet. The sound of clods falling into the grave behind us hits me like a slap.

And so they made me leave you, Everardo. You were still alive then, and chained to a bed in an army base not far away. When I learned that for certain, it was already too late. That night de León Carpio raged in his office, behind his heavy security doors with the multiple locks. He said it was all an outrage, that God only knew what the army was hiding, and that we had every right to be suspicious. He told us to leave the country for a few days while he made the new arrangements, to let things cool off just a bit while he dealt with Asisclo Valladares. This is Guatemala, he explained. People cannot lose face; official egos must be smoothed. We must give him a few days. I returned to Mexico and waited for the new exhumation date. De León Carpio and the judge came under heavy death threats and our frantic calls remained unanswered forever. And so the door closed.

The Last Letter
Mexico, May 1992

I FLY TO DALLAS WITH SISSY AND JIM AND TONY AND THEN SEE them off in the airport. They are grim-faced and anxious and promise to return with me to Guatemala as soon as matters are rearranged. We all know that it may take some time, since the first date took months to schedule, and we all know that there is no time left. We talk some over a cup of coffee, trying to figure out what exactly happened back there in Retalhuleu, puzzling over the wild events. The police had said that the army was coming and then Asisclo Valladares showed up instead, in near hysterics. Was he sent by the army? He must have been, for normally the national attorney general would not get out of bed at 4:00 A.M. to rush to the other side of the country and personally interfere with an ongoing exhumation on technical grounds. And why the screaming voice and red face? Was he frightened or was he hiding something, and if so, what? What was the army hiding back there? Was that Everardo in the black plastic bag in the grave, so badly mutilated that they did not want foreigners to see? Or was it someone else? If it was someone else, what chance is there that Everardo is still alive? Jim and Sissy look at each other and then back at me and we say nothing. We all know the answer and don't want to think about it.

They catch their connecting flights and I return to Mexico City to report in to Emilio and Gaspar. They are horrified by the story and hurry me off to an underground house, worried that the army, like a maddened rattlesnake, will now search for me even here. In my room I stow my clothes into a small cupboard and set out my papers while they pace up and down, evaluating every word I say. My own mind is reeling about in circles so tight that I am dizzy. I should have stayed, Everardo. I should have spoken up when they asked. I tell Gaspar and Emilio that I want to return immediately, and that this time I will go back as his wife. The discreet approach clearly did not work. They look at me as if I was offering to return to a burning building once the roof has already crashed in. They tell me to give them a few days; they will see to things at once. As they leave I see that their eyes are filled with tears.

I fuss about for a bit, fixing a cup of tea and trying not to think about anything. After a while I notice a small packet of things they have left behind on the rickety table, letters of support that the other *compañeros* have sent me, a few more things of Everardo's, a faded shirt and a small envelope. I open the envelope and find the notes I once left for Everardo back at our small apartment, short, silly notes, telling him when I would be coming home for dinner and that I loved him. He had saved each and every one and left them safely stashed at the border before he headed back to his volcano. Inside there is a smaller envelope too, addressed to Eva, and for a moment I think there is a mistake, that it belongs to someone else. Then I remember that Eva is my own code name for underground mail here in Mexico City and that this note was written to me.

Curious, I open it and find two sheets of paper filled with Everardo's small, sloping handwriting. My heart jolts painfully against my ribs. You? You are writing me now? From where? There is a flash of preposterous hope and then I see the date at the top, January 1992, and I am filled with fear. You must have written this to me just as you left, tucking it inside your other things. Somehow in all the uproar it was overlooked until now. I hesitate, knowing somehow that this letter could destroy me; then I smooth out the pages and begin to read:

To the love of my life . . . Eva,

It is just a few hours now till I cross into Guatemala, and I want to write you this letter. But before I begin, I wish you well in your work and in all the other parts of your life. You don't know how you have helped me with your love, your affection, and your deep commitment during the happy times that we have been together. I would have liked very much to have you with me, for you to have accompanied me on this trip to the *frente*, but the work has made this impossible. I would like to tell you so many things, what I feel for you, what I think during each moment of our love, during the times we have shared and lived together. I want to tell you much, but it is dawn and there is so little time before I must leave. I catch my flight at nine in the morning. . . .

About your trip to the *frente*:

1. I brought it up with Emilio and we talked it over—your staying with the *frente* is acceptable to him and he has no problems with your coming up. But first you must finish all your work, and of course you are doing that. If you can do this before or by May, it would be wonderful. . . . Before you come up though, you must set aside time to learn some kind of specific work you could do up there, and this you must discuss with Emilio. Quite apart from that is the physical preparation—it is important that you let me know so we can take it all into account. Also, not too many others should know that you will be coming. . . . Only those who must know should be told.

2. I want to tell you that these first three months of the year will be very decisive for our struggle. I also think they will be very important for our *frente* . . . these three months. So much depends on the results we are able to win, for these will open up new possibilities and allow us to advance

onward to an even more important trimester. These are the two goals that have been weighing on me—the next three months, the next six months . . . and even more from there. But we are not looking at an indefinite situation. This moment, the process, the developments demand so much effort, capacity, and sacrifice. So often we have a lot of good intentions and willingness, but without the other three qualities these are of no use. You can imagine what it is like, walking so many kilometers, for so many hours, days, and even years—across the Sierra Madre, climbing upward . . . descending downward. It is worth it all if you produce results, reach your goals, cast light on new possibilities and perspectives for the triumph of our struggle. I think that— since we have known in the *frente* so many diverse difficulties . . . and resolved so many problems for so many years—all that is left for us to do is to give our very lives to reach our goals.

Many times I lament that, unfortunately, one doesn't respond in the same way after five years, ten years, etc. . . . Given this, it is necessary to search for new ways, other means, to give more . . . and give better. I think this has been one of our inadequacies— deficiencies in achieving better development, improved results, and a greater dynamic. These are the ideas that have come to me during my reflections these last days, and so now I express them here in writing.

Well then, my love, I wanted to say these things and share with you what I am feeling and thinking. I have hopes of learning at least a little English so that I can communicate with you and say beautiful things to you in different words and ways. What I will not forget, and have carefully recorded, is the following: "I love you." I love you very much.

I hope and wish for you to come soon and find this letter. It is a little long, what I have written, but in writing these pages I feel as if I were talking to you, as if you were sitting here listening.

Very well my love, I must say good-bye. A lasting and

eternal kiss. Take care. I hope we see each other soon . . . who knows where?

Affectionately, Everardo

I finish reading and the memory of the crude black pit in the cemetery and the ominous edges of plastic wrapping loom before my eyes, the thin layer of mud hiding what from me? Your face? This letter, Everardo—what have you done? Now the churning ocean of tears breaks loose from the dam I have so fiercely constructed and sends me to my knees before I can even bolt and lock the door. Everardo, your name echoes like a scream through my mind. I am destroyed.

The Curse
Mexico, August 1992

NINETEEN NINETY-TWO SWEEPS RELENTLESSLY ONWARD LIKE SOME evil gothic curse. Happy Birthday, conquistadors, your spirit is all too alive and well, unfortunately for the *compañeros*. I sit in my small room, hoping for news of Everardo and watching in horror as one by one my friends find death, leaving the rest of us behind forever. A terrible silence begins to fill Mexico City as the others wipe away tears, divide up the extra work, and somehow carry on.

Jeremias is lost so quickly. I see him one last time as he leaves for the mountains and I offer him a small, lightweight cooking pot with an insulated handle and fitted lid. I have known him only briefly here in Mexico City, for he was called down urgently for special training after Everardo disappeared. Tiny and quick-witted, he is a villager who survived the long ago and dreaded earthquake, then starvation, then many years in the mountains with ORPA's forces. Many hope that he will soon take Everardo's place, for he has the brains and the experience, as well as a similar serenity under the crush of responsibility. I like him instantly, for he is very warm with a quick elfin laugh, and he takes me under his wing to comfort even though I am so very different. He is younger than Everardo, more mischievous, but he has the same old-man's eyes, the same habit of thinking things through to the bottom, the same relentless grip on matters of principle. I am sad when he leaves, yet also happy, for I know they need him up there in the mountains and I know he wants to go back. Within a few short weeks he takes a bullet through the head during a routine battle.

Oliverio is recovering from a badly torn foot and a bullet wound to the back of his skull that somehow managed to do little damage. He is an officer from the other *frente*, Javier Tambriz, and we meet in the underground clinic and become fast friends. Brash and impudent, sometimes outrageous, he makes me laugh out loud and fills me with strength. With the news of Jeremias's death, he straps his pack onto his sturdy frame and begins hiking daily up a nearby mountainside, willing his foot to recover, to grow new muscle and tendons. After a few months he is astoundingly strong again and he leaves for the mountains to take Jeremias's place. I hold him close, but this time I am afraid to say good-bye. I have learned to dread the words.

Capitán Ana, a legendary combatant and strategist, is down from the volcano after fifteen long years to have her child. A university graduate and once a city professional, she works tirelessly throughout her pregnancy, arranging for international supplies and support for her beloved *compañeros.* After her child is born she keeps up her work, but the little boy is clearly the joy of her life. She takes him with her everywhere she can, fitting in time to teach and play with him, worrying about how on earth to give him a normal child's life. The other *compañeros* pitch in as well, caring for the child when she must be away, showering him with time and affection. Soon he grows into a husky, fearless, questioning little rascal, loved by all and approaching his second birthday. Ana never arrives at the party, for she is stabbed in the back in a city parking lot by an infiltrator sent from Guatemala.

David, a quiet villager I met years ago in a safe house, takes several bullets in the leg up in combat. The *compañeros* rush him to an evacuation point and give him the best first aid they can, but the route is blocked for days and finally they have to drag him through the mountains to a different meeting place. By then his fever has risen dangerously and gangrene has set into some of the wounds. He dies very slowly in a secret clinic, his Mayan eyes wide open, no regrets and no second thoughts. His people were worth it, he tells us. As death approaches he quietly divides up his belongings, telling his friends not to grieve for him, that it was simply his turn. I grieve for him anyway, and so do the others.

There is a bad accident and several high-level *compañeros* are wounded, delaying their return to the mountains as they wait for their injuries to heal. They are in despair, for no more absences can be borne, but there is nothing to be done. An enormous arsenal goes down, looted by the army.

Then Antonio, the youngest and my favorite, is blown to bits in a bombing. I sit in shock, remembering his sweet face and good-natured manners during that long night climb into the volcano. The others are deadly pale as they tell of his death, for they could barely find the body parts to pull together for burial. It is a long time before Antonio's name is mentioned again, for it provokes fits of weeping that cannot be stopped. Late at night I remember him so clearly, the long talks we had, how he surprised me with his keen awareness of what he was doing and why, his good-natured resolve to give his life if necessary. His words and thoughts were so contradictory to the round and rosy eighteen-year-old face and his playful manners. Yet he was like the others, young in years and yet so very old. He had grown up, after all, in the time of the massacres. His family and his village had fought hard and lost many members and kept right on fighting hard, everyone giving whatever they could. This was the world he knew and he was quite comfortable with the choices he had made. Someday he would like a wife and child and some more schooling. But first things first; there was work to be done.

Up in Tajumulco volcano the Voz Popular continues to broadcast, much to the army's consternation. Despite the years of bombings and paratroopers and prisoners tortured for their information, it cannot be silenced. Yet the toll is heavy indeed. Emma is carried out of the peaks on a makeshift stretcher, her sturdy leg blown half off. She arrives in an underground clinic, in despair at being forced from the *frente*, for she had been determined to fight till the very end of the war. After all, she had been with ORPA since the very beginning. The doctors operate and threaten to amputate, but she backs them off as only Emma can. They tell her she will never walk again and she tells them that she will. When I see her, the leg is wrapped in heavy plaster from toes to hip, with blood seeping through the white wrappings at the heel. There are tears in her eyes from the pain, but she is fiercely lifting hand weights, determined to remain strong and healthy. The thought of failure does not enter her mind.

Soon her *compañero* Rodo arrives, together with Felipe, both from the radio post. They are badly injured and nearly blind and deaf from an explosion that almost took their heads off. They, too, have been carried down from the wild peaks, and Felipe is nearly captured even as he arrives within a few miles of the safe house. Disoriented, he misses a contact. A Salvadoran woman fleeing the violence of her own homeland takes a guess at what and who he must be, and takes him by the hand and leads him to safety. Emma takes one look at Rodo and Felipe and sets about caring for them. She has learned a lot about emergency medicine in the mountains and has cleaned out many a wound with a sterilized knife and tended the sick and the dying. Now she nurses them both, even as she wills her own leg to heal.

More friends die, and I am aghast and appalled. The *compañeros* only look at me with their dark and beautiful Mayan eyes. The conquistadors wiped out 90 percent of the hemisphere within a few short years of their arrival. Did I expect this five hundredth anniversary to be fun? Those guys were mean as hell the first time around. The *compas* shake their heads stoically, telling wry jokes, rolling up their sleeves and getting back to work. At night we sit together and they weep unashamedly for the dead, lighting candles and taking turns telling stories about the friends they will never see again. Bit by bit I understand and learn that by remembering, they stay close forever.

Emma begins to call and insist that I come for lengthy visits to the underground clinic. She and Rodo and Felipe and the others are all there, passing the time with books and exercises and small projects. They pull their chairs together in the salon and learn to repair backpacks and sew uniforms. They look for all the world to me as if they were back in the mountains at the evening campfire. Those who are too ill to work sit in the circle anyway, teasing and talking and sharing everything, holding hands and wrapping their arms about one another. Their bonds are so close that I feel sometimes as if they were all interconnected by an invisible umbilical cord, sharing their love, their physical strength, and their sheer collective will.

The months go by and they begin to heal one another as best they can. Marianna's shattered pelvis is finally released from its cast, only to reshatter, for her bones were left too frail from childhood malnutrition to ever heal properly. The doctors add in screws and metal plates, leaving her in tears from pain and frustration. The others massage her swollen feet and ankles and help her up and down the stairs, tempting her with special foods and cajoling her to stay with her exercises. She is a pretty villager who once worked as a maid in the City. She joined the *compañeros* and sneaked about to secret meetings, only to come face-to-face with her own aging mistress, who had also joined, together with her upper-class son. This strikes an old memory in my mind and we chat for a bit and find that we are both talking about Doña Trina, a feisty gray-haired friend from my long ago days in the City.

Emma is told that her own bones are none too strong, and she begins calcium treatments that make her gag with nausea. She takes them anyway and moves on to lifting heavier weights to keep her arms and back strong. She hands them to me and tells me to get to work, that if she can do it, so can I. Felipe and Rodo begin to recover, and they sit around the television at night with us as someone explains what the blurred shapes and shadows on the screen are doing. Slowly their eyes and ears are healing, to the delight of the others.

As for me, I don't get off the hook so easily. Emma and the others slowly but surely gather me in, pulling me closer and closer, insisting that I stay in the real world here with them. They have all lost someone. Emma's first *compañero* died in combat, the army leaving only his bloody brain intact on the soft earth of the cornfield for her to find. Her second *compañero* vanished forever in the streets of a small town. They spoke on the radio one day; his work was going well and he was to be back in the mountains soon. The army found him instead. Rodo will not speak of his first love. Marianna's brothers have all been dead for many years now. The *compas* all know how it is. They, too, have drifted off toward the outer edges of their sanity, trying to escape from memories that make them wish for death. Now they rein me in gently, insisting on the late-night game of checkers, asking me to help them read or bring them books and newspapers, teaching me to cook, talking late into the night and sharing their own wounds with me. When I curl up alone near the window, Felipe moves to sit silently at my side, a warm hand curled about my ankle. When I stare too long at the empty walls, Emma gently combs my hair.

When we are together at night she tells me stories again, as she did in the mountains so long ago. Sometimes she makes me laugh at the stories of the wicked squirrel she raised and how it ended up stealing all their food. Sometimes she leaves me inspired. During the hardest times, though, she does not try to comfort me. Instead she pulls the blankets close around me and tells me about you, Everardo, about the times when the two of you were young and green and full of hope, in the earliest days of the war.

The Last Visit
Mexico, September 1992

THE WEEKS SLIP INTO MONTHS AND THERE IS STILL NO WORD FROM Guatemala about a new exhumation date. De León Carpio has been receiving threats ever since the first attempt, and now he does not answer his calls at all. The *compas* work desperately to gather any bits of information they can, scouring the area where Everardo disappeared, talking with the villagers, sending message after message to their intelligence networks. But there is only the same terrible silence in response, the sad looks, the tired shake of the head in answer to all of the inquiries. Someone was taken from the combat site, wrapped up in a canvas bag. No one knows who the person was or if he was alive or dead, and no one could see the face. A helicopter came. They can find out nothing else. And yet I cannot leave Mexico City or even think of returning to Texas, for I am convinced that sooner or later something will happen, some news will come. I sit grimly in my small rented room, working on the book and waiting for the phone to ring and the voice to tell me sorry, still no trace, we'll be in touch.

I know that I am unwell, for my weight plummets and I cannot sleep. I turn the story over and over again in my mind, looking for some unnoticed nuance, some clue or hint that I have not seen before. But there is nothing left to find. Perhaps he died in combat; perhaps he was taken alive and tortured. Either way he must surely be dead by now, but this I cannot accept no matter how many times I hear it. I cannot just presume him dead and leave him in the past. My eyes grow bloodshot and my hair begins to break unevenly as I brush it, falling out in thick strands across my shoulders. I do not even care and pin it back flat and limp with barrettes. I wait for the telephone calls and the patient voice that has become my lifeline. There is nothing else to live for.

For months now Everardo has come to me in strange hours of the day and night, his sad face motionless and his disembodied voice telling me that he is cold, his image vanishing even as I hear the words. I cannot bear this message, and I jolt back to reality in despair every time, trying to decipher the strange image and repeated words. Tell me where you are, Everardo, tell me what to do. I will come and get you out of there no matter what it takes, but I do not understand your message. Please, tell me again, tell me more clearly, no matter how hard it makes me cry. But come back and tell me where you are.

After a while his visits stop, and though I try my best to summon him he never returns. I dream of him and remember him, but gone are the visions that brought him to me body and soul even as I sat wide awake on a chair or walked down the street. What does it mean? Where has he gone? Why doesn't he answer my calls? I grow more and more desperate and begin to play his favorite music and read poems from his worn books aloud, but he does not answer. Suddenly, I am excruciatingly alone.

One night I think of throwing myself from the rooftop. I am not hysterical, only terribly tired, and I want the screams inside my head to cease at last. My life has been full and good and I have no regrets, but I see no future that I care to deal with. I think about it for a while, but then I worry that Everardo could still be alive despite the silence, that he might need my help someday. I must wait still, at least until I know for certain what has become of him. With that thought I push myself away from the railing and return to my room. I must wait.

Back inside I sit down, feeling old and drained. Absently, I light the candles and wrap a blanket around my shoulders to keep from shivering. I play his music again and again and close my eyes, imagining as always, that he is listening with me. I know that this is unwholesome but I cannot help myself, for I long for those strange, sad apparitions. I do not know how they happen or what they are, whether messages hurled across the distance by his remarkable mind or only the echo of my own desperate psyche. Either way, I don't care. I need his presence.

And then it happens again, but not like the other times, not like the other visits. This time he does not come to me; I go to him, unbidden and uninvited. It is suddenly dark, but he is not there. I am swimming through a vast soft blackness, gentle enough, and yet I weep because there are strange pinpoints of light that I cannot really see, even though I know they exist. This confuses and frightens me, but I go down on my knees and reach out to explore, hoping to find you, Everardo, hoping against hope that you will come back to me just one more time. And then in a flood of relief I hear you, that light catlike step of yours, the familiar sound of a small foot laced in a boot. I recognize it at once, even though I can see nothing. Then you are holding me, cradling me against your chest and stroking my hair while I cry inconsolably. You are still in your uniform, and I hang on to the soft green cloth of your sleeves. You say nothing, but just hold me ever so gently, waiting for me to stop crying so that I will understand what you need to tell me.

Finally I am quiet, and you hold me for a few moments more. Then you grip my shoulder in your small hand, calling wordlessly for my attention. You wish to tell me something important and you are waiting for me to listen. I cannot see your face but your dark hair is soft against my cheek and I cling to you as if to life itself. Don't make me leave, Everardo, please don't make me leave. You push me gently to my feet. Ya, you tell me in that quiet voice. Ya. There, it is done. There, it is over. Words of comfort and yet also of finality. Then he is gone and I am in my small living room again, staring at the burnt-out candle.

I pace up and down, confused and agitated. Everardo, I didn't really understand what you were telling me, please come back. I can already imagine the look of bemused chagrin on your face as I start up my racket again. After all, you only just left. A Mayan would have understood you perfectly, I know. But I am not one of you, and your unspoken language does not flow in my veins. Come back and speak to me again. Please come back.

I wait for months, but he never does return. That was the last visit, or should I say crash entry? He has told me clearly enough that it is over and that I must go on with my life. But in what way is it over? Does he mean that it is hopeless and that I must go on without him? Does he want me to stop wishing for the impossible escape or rescue? Or is he dead? To him, it is clearly one and the same. It is done; it is over. Don't look back. He has set me free and he will not let me follow him again.

That night I think about his words for a long time. I know I am drifting dangerously and that for the sake of us both I must get a better grip on myself. The next morning I rise early, take a cold shower and drink some hot coffee, and then take off in search of Emma and some lessons in survival.

Tapachula
Mexico, Fall 1992

IT'S TIME TO GET OUT OF THE CITY, FOR I AM GROWING GOOD AND sick of myself. Enough of this disintegration. I gather up all of the yellow candles and pack them away with Everardo's music and books in a small box. I wrap them carefully and tie a double knot in the twine, as if fearful that they could somehow escape their cardboard confines and come back to haunt me. Then I scrub my small room from top to bottom and pull myself together, cutting my broken hair into a straight bob and ironing all of my shirts. From now on I will miss you and remember you every day of my life, Everardo, but I will not let myself lose my mind. Thanks for the warning.

I pack a small suitcase and head for the border town of Tapachula, hoping to talk with some of the *compañeros* myself. Amílcar is there, I know, recovering from the nasty bullet wound he received at the Ix-cucua River and answering questions again and again about Everardo's last moments with the *frente*. The two of them had been talking that morning when the hail of bullets began, and together they threw themselves toward the cover of the sheltering brush nearby. In that split-second dash, Amílcar felt a stab of pain at his back and the wet heat of his own blood splashing through his shirt. Darkness flooded across his eyes and he saw Everardo on the ground nearby. He seemed to be pushing himself up with one arm. Had he fallen, or had he thrown himself down flat to better dodge the bullets? Was he trying to cover the others as they reached the shelter of the foliage? Amílcar doesn't know. He remembers nothing more except that he woke up later, encircled by the desperate *compañeros*. Everardo was simply gone.

I know there is little to be gained from this trip, but I want to see Amílcar and hear the story for myself, and I want to get out of the city. I take the night bus to the border because the wild hairpin turns of the mountains scare me to death in broad daylight. What I can't see can't hurt me, I figure, and sure enough, I arrive at dawn rumpled and grouchy but quite alive. I leave my bag at a small pension and call in from the rickety phone at the corner store, and soon enough I find myself at the safe house with the *compas* of Luis Ixmata.

It is wonderful to see them again, Amílcar and Jorge and Juan Carlos and the others from the volcano. They are all down for training, debriefing, and medical care. It feels almost like home at last, for they all remind me so of Everardo. They pull me into the living room and swing me off my feet and whirl me around, asking me about Emma and Rodo and Felipe and calling me their sister. Then they sit me down on the most comfortable chair and hurry to bring me coffee and a rich soup. I am looking thin. Haven't I been taking care of myself? This will never do. Bits of chocolate appear out of nowhere as does a stack of steaming corn tortillas. Then they gather around me and chatter lightly while I eat, knowing full well what I have come for and trying to help me brace. I chew quietly and study their vivid faces—so bright-eyed and battered and full of beans, these *compañeros.* Already they are teasing and smoothing my hair and pulling out pictures of new babies, who seem somehow to belong to everyone at once. I take a deep breath, hoping to inhale the wild and irrepressible life force that seems to emanate from their very fingertips. These people are good for me.

When I finish eating they bring more coffee, and magically a small stool arrives next to me and Amílcar sits down, looking unhappy but determined. The others crowd tightly around us as he begins to speak, rubbing his shoulders and helping him gently through the hard parts. So stoical, this Amílcar; how many times now has he taken a bullet, only to return yet again to the volcanoes? He squares his small shoulders and keeps his voice carefully under control, telling me everything about that last morning—the villager who came to warn them, the rush to pack their maps and their lifeline, the radio. He shakes his head as he remembers the bullet that took him down, and the others hasten to pull up his shirt and show me the ugly gash across his back. As I look into his eyes, I see the same choking pain that has been dragging me down, the pain of self-doubt. Somehow he should have done more, stayed conscious, been stronger? I understand only too well, and take his hand in my own. The others fill in, telling the rest— about the villagers nearby and what they said, about the canvas bag and the helicopter, all the details I have heard before but could never quite absorb. And yet it is different now, hearing it from them in their straightforward, gentle words. I will never ask for this story again. Now it is profoundly real and there is nothing more to be said.

When the story finishes we are quiet for a while, holding hands and thoughtful in the comfortable silence. Soon it is time for me to leave and they hurry to push tiny cards and handmade gifts into my satchel, wishing me well and telling me to take care of myself. At the door I cling to each of them, for like them I have learned the hard way to take nothing for granted. I climb into the car then, and take one last look back as we pull away from the house. The *compas* are standing in a tight huddle at the gate, arms wrapped about one another's shoulders, small brown hands waving good-bye in a joint flurry.

It is not quite sundown when I reach the hotel, and so I wander a bit through the streets, musing. It is so tropical here, steamy and vivid green like Guatemala, just over there across the border. I am but a stone's throw from your hometown, Everardo. I follow the muddy roadway out past the last of the small houses and into the open countryside, reveling in the sight of the thick twisting vines and wild palm trees and rich, fertile earth. I walk farther and farther, stretching my legs and breathing in the clean wet air; then on sudden whim, I leave the pavement and cut across an open field. My feet sink to the ankles in the soft mud and I pull off my shoes and keep on hiking, now straight up a sharp incline. I reach the top after a battle with the intervening brambles and tangled shrubs, out of breath but happy. Let's see now . . . there's the sun setting in the west, so just over there is Guatemala.

I sit down on a small rock and stare to the east, toward the volcanoes and small villages of San Marcos. What are the *compañeros* doing now? I wonder to myself. Perhaps finishing up their tasks, returning to their base after a long day's march, maybe even preparing for combat or tending the wounded. In the valleys to the north, the soft mists must be gathering as the villagers haul firewood to cook the evening meal. Your homeland, Everardo, I can see it from here so clearly.

Out of nowhere three ragged *campesinos* have appeared behind me, and I start slightly as one of them coughs. How long have they been standing there in silence? I smile to them and they shyly step forward, asking me why I am here, do I not know these places are dangerous? They speak quietly in the lilting accents of Guatemala, their dark eyes tilted upward in their smooth faces. As they speak I realize they are refugees perhaps, or have come here to look for work at the coffee plantations. I nod my head and explain that I am here to remember someone, someone from the other side. They look quickly at one another, evaluating what I have just said and thinking over their response. The older one cocks his head to one side. Dead? He asks me quietly. Disappeared, I answer.

He nods, and the three of them cast fearful glances toward the border. It is dangerous here, they repeat patiently, trying to make me understand. Sometimes the army comes to this side, looking. I know I should get up and leave now, appease them by moving on back to the road. Yet I cannot quite. I need just a few more moments of this bracing calm, the peace that I am only beginning to find here. I will go soon, I tell them. Go ahead; I will not be long. They look dubiously at one another and quickly consult in an ancient language I cannot begin to understand. The older one pulls off his battered straw hat, looking worried, then takes a step forward. It is dangerous here; they will wait over there by the trees. They will wait for me. His voice trails off and his eyes ask me to understand; they mean no disrespect, but they cannot leave me here alone. It would not be right. I start to protest, but they have already planted themselves in a small cluster nearby, silent and watchful.

I turn back for one last look and feel the peace I crave growing within me. So beautiful, your homeland, in the evening light, Everardo. And your *paisanos* just over there, decent to the bone and clean of soul, taking the time to keep a total stranger from harm. As I stand my mind is quiet at last, and I smile to the others and thank them. They nod gravely in response, their open villager faces sad and understanding. Without a word, we acknowledge what we share. As we start down the steep hillside, the older one wraps a twist of grass around two sticks and bends to plant a small cross in the earth.

Christmas
Mexico, 1992

NINETEEN NINETY-TWO IS FINALLY CAREENING TO AN END, MUCH TO our collective relief. It is December and Rigoberta Menchú, a fierce and tireless Mayan spokeswoman, receives the Nobel Peace Prize for her human rights work and becomes the youngest laureate ever. Now she and Miguel Angel Asturias, the father of Gaspar Ilom, are Guatemala's two Nobel winners, an ironic fact that makes the army roar with outrage and pressure in vain to have the prize revoked. Even as we celebrate, my friends call in jubilantly from Texas with the news that my book, *Bridge of Courage*, has been accepted for publication by Common Courage Press. I hurry to tell the *compañeros* and they are shocked and moved to tears, for never before has anyone been willing to tell their story.

We spend an evening toasting the coming New Year, 1993, and I try to put on a cheerful face. It is difficult though, for the thought of Christmas celebrations quite frightens me. It has been exactly a year now since Everardo and I spent our last few days together, hanging on to the little time we had left. I remember Christmas Eve, the children, the festive dinner, and our long talks all with excruciating clarity and I do not want to be reminded. Slowly but surely I have been gluing myself back together, piece by piece, but I don't feel ready yet to deal with those particular memories. The thought of going away, perhaps to the coast to be alone, appeals greatly to me, but Emma will have none of it. She knows perfectly well what the problem is and she puts her foot down, taking me in hand. I am going nowhere at all. I am spending Christmas right there at the house where I belong, with her and Rodo and Felipe and Marianna and the others. Needless to say, when Emma puts her foot down . . . well, that's pretty much that.

And so I pack a small overnight bag and, by popular request, a bottle of good rum and meet my contact at the designated spot. I have the routine down by heart now and climb into the car and wait while the curtains are pulled. For a while I chat with the doctor in the front seat and then, on cue, keep my eyes on the floor, for the address of this house must remain top secret. Lives depend on it, including Emma's life, and I adhere strictly to these security rules. Once we are safely inside the covered garage, I bound into the house through the side door and find everyone gathered in the large kitchen. They hurry to hug me and exclaim over my health, Emma and Marianna on crutches, Rodo and Felipe following the sound of my voice, and then they take my bag and sit me down at the crowded table.

They are making tamales, the traditional Christmas dish in Guatemala, and the entire room is topsy-turvy and filled with delicious cooking odors. Marianna has put the others to work grinding the cornmeal to a perfect texture, smooth as silk, and she herself is busily separating out strips of the husk to use as ties later on. Emma is in charge of the sauce and has laid out whole onions, cloves of garlic, and small ripe tomatoes to roast together on the stove top, adding in curling sticks of cinnamon to add to the savory mixture. She tells me to pull up a chair and pay close attention, for this is a very special dish and I should learn how to make it too. Felipe is watching over small chunks of meat cooking in a broth, careful not to let them scorch, and tasting some for the flavor. He offers me a bit, wrapped in a hot corn tortilla, and I eat it with relish.

Finally all the components are ready and we line them up on the table in a neat row—cornmeal, meat, olives, sauce. I work with the others, copying them, my awkward movements making them laugh. It's not so easy, this routine. The cornmeal is slippery and you have to shape it into a neat small disk with an indentation in the center. The bits of meat go in there, with an olive and a dollop of sauce, and then you have to fold over a flap of the dough and seal the edges flat. If done right, it leaves a perfect sphere of clean cornmeal. If not, it falls apart into a soggy mess. I flunk out on the first few tries, but they call out advice and encouragement and after a while I get the hang of it. Then we wrap the spheres in flat banana leaves and tie them shut with strands of the corn husks. The tidy packets are placed into a giant steamer and put on the stove to cook slowly and gently for the rest of the afternoon.

Meanwhile we prepare plates of grapes and walnuts, also traditional, and set a huge table with plates and forks and spoons and candles. A special punch of spicy fruit cider has been prepared and they carefully hoist the large bowl onto a side table and set out their variety of donated mugs, cups, and glasses. Felipe and Rodo set about vacuuming the rugs while Emma and I dust and fluff up the pillows on the chairs. The others clean up the kitchen, carrying out the trash and washing the dishes, until everything is immaculate. Then we set to work on the tree, hanging tiny ornaments they have made themselves from scraps of colored papers and brightly woven threads. They bring me some sheets of red and yellow paper and ask me to make the small origami figures that I showed them long ago, back in Taju-mulco. My repertoire is limited to a bird of sorts, an owl that makes them shriek with laughter, and a tiny folding purse, but at least my contributions show up on the tree and we are all content.

Before we know it, the food is ready and we sit down at the table and have a veritable feast, passing the huge steaming platters of tamales and pouring out the cider. The grapes are sweet and delicious with the smooth cornmeal and the spicy sauce and soon we are too full for another bite. Compliments are passed all around, thanks to Felipe and Rodo for the excellent grinding job, to Marianna for the stuffing, to Emma for the sauce, to the others for the fruit drink. *Buen provecho. Muchas gracias.* As the dishes are cleared and taken to the kitchen, a small tray of brimming wineglasses appears with a steam-ing pot of coffee.

The mood is softer now, and thoughtful, as we all drink a toast to the future and to the *compañeros*. As if on cue everyone links hands around the table, forming a tight and intimate circle, and one by one they give a small speech, sharing their memories and gently honoring the dead. Pablo, blind and missing both hands, opens with a slow, soft tribute to the early days of the war, to those who fought when there was no food, no boots, no medicine, not even decent guns or enough bullets to get them through combat alive. They fought anyway, keep-ing the *frentes* going until new supply networks were worked out, until conditions changed. They did not survive to see it all, but they gave their lives to make it happen. As I listen I am reminded of my old friend, long dead now, who said that it was for him and his *compañeros* to lie down and die one by one until their bodies formed a bridge to the new Guatemala for the next generation. I named my book after you, I think to myself. *Bridge of Courage* is named after all of you.

The others add quiet stories, bittersweet and affectionate. Emma remembers her first *compañero*, all his hard work in the early years, how he respected her and helped her to grow up in the mountains when she first arrived, so very young. She grows silent and I know she is fighting off the memory of that terrible cornfield and the small cross where she had buried his brain. Rodo remembers the early days of the *Voz Popular*, their first broadcasts, and those who went down in its defense. They remember the old couple who took in the wounded and hid them until the evacuation team could arrive. *Los abuelos*, they call them, "the grandparents." They were taken in the night long ago, but now Felipe tells only of their kindness and courage. Next they speak of Teresa, a favorite of them all, how good and decent she was, how quick to learn, how affectionate, a real sister. She was braver than anyone else in combat, too, making more than one young man a bit rueful. I know this story and my heart goes out to them, for Teresa was hit by one of their own bullets in a tragic accident. She quickly bled to death as they held her despairingly in their arms. Yet as I look around I do not see tears, for they are speaking of these people as if they were here even now, at the dinner table with us. And in a sense indeed they are, just as you, Everardo, seem ever to be floating just behind my shoulder.

After a bit, the mood grows lighter and they tell hilarious stories that leave me laughing—about Emma's feisty puppy, which she somehow trained not to bark when the enemy was near; about the delicate equipment that fell off a cliff yet worked perfectly well after the horrified *compas* chased after it for miles and miles; about the stove that malfunctioned in a safe house and blew pots and pans about like flying saucers and sent the *compas* leaping instinctively for cover; about the top-secret code that a traumatized *compa* forgot, only to find that his four-year-old daughter knew it by heart; about the upper-class white-haired housewife who could pass through the checkpoints with ease because who, after all, would ever suspect such a grandma of anything at all. They laugh especially over this last one, remembering the grandma's rather shocking vocabulary and sassy manners.

Emma decides that we have spent enough time talking, so she turns on the music, telling us it is time to dance. We move on into the living room and the salsa rhythms ring out from the small tape recorder, as Emma starts tapping her crutches on the ground, smiling. You, she says, pointing at me. You are the guest, so you pick the first partner. I almost laugh, and we exchange knowing glances from across the room, both of us remembering that long-ago dance in the mountains when I first asked Everardo to be my partner.

For a split second I hesitate, for the men in this room are all either on crutches or cannot see. Then again, I realize, the same goes for the women here. So I ask Pablo, since he is the closest and perhaps also the quietest. Badly burned in an explosion ten long years ago, his eyes are destroyed and he is missing half of one arm and most of the other hand. His village was massacred years back. Yet he has learned to function remarkably well and maintains at all times a disciplined serenity that I find remarkable. Now he quickly accepts my invitation and rises, smiling and offering me his plastic hand without the slightest hesitation. Soon he is swinging me about the room, utterly at ease, and I quickly lose my fear that somehow I will hurt him, pull too hard at the stump of his arm or twist the remaining fingers on his other hand. After a few rounds, he is pulling me through pirouettes and the others are clapping and laughing. Emma is dancing away on her crutches with Rodo, and Marianna is dancing in place, braced by her cane, while Elder, a recent arrival from the *frente*, gently gives her support with his one good arm, the other withered and held in a sling. Maria turns up her hearing aids and steps out with tiny Edgar, on medical leave from intelligence, who moves quite gracefully on his wooden leg.

After several hot and flirty rounds, the *compas* break out the bottles of rum and we knock off several toasts and then get back to the dance floor, changing partners every few rounds. The alcohol goes immediately to my head, making me feel as if I am floating through the room from partner to partner. I dance with Elder, who teaches me a complex loop, and then with Rodo, who does an excellent waltz, and then with Felipe and Edgar and Pablo again. Drinks go around again and I protest that I have had enough, but no one is taking no for an answer. We drink to life and dance some more. By one o'clock I protest that I am getting old and should go to bed, but they answer in concert that this is not allowed, that they have a party only at Christmas, that Christmas comes once a year, and that this party is not over till tomorrow morning. No one leaves. We dance through three more tapes of music. Here among us everyone is whole.

Finally Emma flops onto the sofa, her leg throbbing with pain and she drinks some fruit punch, offering me a glass. It is cool and delicious and half-revives me. We sit for a while and chat, watching the others and applauding. Now Maria teaches Pablo a fancy double loop and he stumbles, but the others pick him up off the floor and urge him to try again. Gamely, he gives it another shot, and the others cheer, yelling "John Travolta" from across the room. Felipe lifts Marianna into his arms so that she can waltz, weightless, just one time.

I dance again and again and soon enough Emma returns to the floor. When Rodo takes time out, she is missing a partner and turns to me, teaching me quite a fancy tango and looping me across the floor through the complex movements as if I were a lightweight rag doll. Soon we are dancing dramatically up and down while the others cheer and I choke with laughter. As we take turns twirling, we almost crash into each other and Emma's cigar comes close to lighting my hair afire. By the end of the song we collapse back onto the sofa, out of breath and giggling hysterically. The others decide we win the dance prize.

By six in the morning all is well, and we fumble about in the kitchen for some soft drinks and cookies, then stumble off to bed at last. As we exchange hugs and jokes upstairs, I realize that the dreaded holiday has come and gone and that they have pulled me through with them, refusing to leave me behind.

Santiago
Mexico City, January 1993

WITHIN MINUTES I KNOW THAT HE IS TELLING ME THE TRUTH. HE sits in a straight wooden chair, hands folded primly on the cheap hotel table, telling me his story and trying not to choke. He is a vil-

lager, very Mayan, with huge dark eyes and a sculpted face. Perhaps
he is in his mid-twenties, no older certainly, and he is very slender and
lithe in his movements. As he speaks, his tone of voice changes from
angry and determined to a flat, cracking monotone as he struggles to
explain, to be clear with me. His eyes never leave my face and they
plead mutely with me to please, please believe him. Those eyes tor-
ment me, for they glow with barely suppressed tears and a remembered horror that he knows will destroy him should it ever burst free
of his control. As he speaks he blinks convulsively, his long lashes
fluttering as he takes a deep breath and plunges onward. I have heard
that choking monotone before and have seen those half-dead eyes. I
remember them from the torture victims hidden out in the church
basements. I remember them from the terrified survivors in the
morgues. This man has suffered.

His name is Santiago Cabrera Lopez, but he calls himself Carlos.
He was Carlos for years in the mountains under your command, Everardo. He was one of the best and the brightest, a member of a special combat unit and ever so promising for his intelligence and
leadership skills. I remember when you told me he had been lost, captured alive with Karina in 1991. You were so sad about it then; you
grieved over the loss of them both, so young and talented and committed. You loved them and like everyone else you assumed that they
were dead, for no one had ever come back alive. And yet here sits Santiago, very much alive, nearly two years later. And he has seen you,
Everardo, he has seen you.

Santiago starts at the beginning, speaking slowly and carefully,
placing every detail in order, intent on making us understand. He and
Karina were out on the road together on a routine supply mission. It
was routine but, as always, very dangerous. They were dressed in civilian clothes and their work was almost finished; the other *compañeros*
were deep inside the trees, carrying away the last of the bundles. A vehicle suddenly approached, and the last thing Santiago remembers is
the heavy blow to his head, a start of fear, and then the darkness of
lost consciousness. When he awoke he was tied up on the floor of the
vehicle, a gun barrel stuffed into his mouth. The blood was choking
him and he moved his head slightly to spit it out. As he stirred, he re-

alized that he was lying on the body of another young man, who was horribly battered and bleeding to death.

After a while they arrived at a military base and the soldiers dragged Santiago inside, questioned him, then beat him mercilessly until he again lost consciousness. Later Karina appeared and for the first time he realized that she, too, had been captured alive. The military officers were furious, screaming that Santiago and Karina had told differing stories and that they had better start telling the truth. They tied Santiago and beat him again, this time with cement blocks. He remembers waking up with Karina bending over him, sobbing hysterically. She was pleading with the soldiers to kill her first, to leave Santiago alone, he was too young, to please kill her first since she was the older of the two. Then they were dragged back inside, where the officer's desk was pulled back to reveal a trap door in the floor underneath the carpet. The soldiers opened it and tossed Santiago and Karina into a dark pit and left them there. Some food arrived later on, but Karina would not eat. She wanted to die.

They stayed in the pit all night long and into the next day. Then they were hauled out and separated once again, and for a while Santiago did not know whether Karina had survived or not. He himself began a hellish session of abuse that lasted for nearly five months. The officers screamed at him and battered him, he was beaten across the feet so badly that his toenails fell out, he was buried in another pit in a hillside, he was hung by his arms from a rifle rack, he was chained to a bed for months without a blanket. From time to time he would be taken to different bases and forced to give information or else be tortured again. He was terrified, but he tried to give things that would not get any of the other *compañeros* killed or caught. He did not want anyone else to suffer as he was suffering. So he would give up old codes, identify old caches of arms that no one was likely to return to, or point out meeting places that were no longer used.

To break his spirit, they dragged him to the morgues and he would identify the blood-spattered bodies of his friends, glad that they were safely dead in combat instead of alive as he was. From time to time the officers would bring in a terrified and bleeding villager and Santiago's heart would go out to the new prisoner. He would tell the soldiers that he did not know the person, that this was no combatant, no *compañero*, but the villagers were always killed anyway. They were killed so that they could not tell of what they had seen, so they could not tell that Santiago was still alive. Once, an officer became enraged and accused Santiago of holding back on these identities. He ordered Santiago tied to a chair and given electrical shocks to the legs and testicles, leaving him to scream until he fainted.

Slowly Santiago recognized other prisoners like himself. They were dressed in army uniforms and forbidden to tell even the other soldiers that they were prisoners. Instead, everyone assumed they were specialists in the G-2, or intelligence division. In a sense they were, since they were all giving bits and pieces of information to avoid more torture. Like Santiago, all had suffered months of abuse, which had left them pale and hollow-eyed. They weren't allowed to leave the army, nor would they try to escape, for they were told that if they tried, their families would be killed. None had ever been reported to the Red Cross as a prisoner of war. Outside of the military, no one knew that they were still alive.

Santiago thought about it all for a very long time. Slowly he learned that there was a new army experiment going on. Instead of killing all prisoners immediately, a few with useful information were selected out for special treatment. These were subjected to long-term torture in order to break them psychologically, until they became docile enough to begin work as a secret cadre of informants for G-2. This was where Santiago found himself, selected out for survival of sorts.

He began to plan. His family had long ago gone to another country as refugees, and two brothers had already died in combat. There were no relatives left in Guatemala to kill if he ran, but he would have to earn the chance to escape; he would have to earn the army's trust. As his five months of torture ended, he began to pretend that he had snapped. He became a model prisoner, polishing his boots and jumping to attention, hurrying to be the most helpful of them all. The officers were pleased and began to treat him better, respecting his work and liking his humble manner. As time passed, Santiago began to hope that he might survive and even escape someday.

He was lonely and wanted to befriend the other prisoners, but they were frightening to him. Karina began to drink heavily, and though he saw her from time to time, he barely recognized her. Gone were the bright lights and bold, witty humor. She looked like the walking dead and sounded like it, too. The others were the same, gruff and wary, working closely with the G-2 officers. Were they really broken? Were they pretending, as he was? He could not tell and could not risk trusting anyone. In turn, the others distrusted him, wounding him deeply. By the time he escaped some two years later, he had counted thirty-five of the others, but who was who, who wanted out, who really wanted to stay, he could not say. He knew only that the others would die in silence before they would attempt to escape at the cost of their relatives' lives.

After a year, he was issued papers so that he could be moved more easily from base to base. They began to test him, leaving him without a guard to see if he would try to run. He made no move, knowing he would not get far. Then they issued him a gun, but without bullets. Again, he made no move. Finally he was armed, but remained under strict security. As he still made no attempt to leave, they began to take him for granted and his hope began to grow. He became watchful.

It was then, on March 12, 1992 that he saw you, Everardo. You were chained to a bed in the Santa Ana Berlin base, in the same room where Santiago had been chained himself for so long. Simeon Cum Chuta, a G-2 specialist, dragged him and the other prisoners in to identify you. Santiago couldn't believe his eyes, didn't want to believe his eyes, for he knew what it meant for the *compañeros* that a *comandante* had gone down. He knew what it meant for the war. It was you, Everardo, in olive green, lashed to that bed. You were disheveled and dirty, as if you had just been dragged from the fields of combat. You spoke not a word.

Santiago saw you there for nearly twenty days. He wanted to talk with you alone, but you were under such a heavy guard that it was never possible. The officers pushed the other prisoners to tell you to give up, that it was all over, that the struggle had been wrong. They told you to save yourself by switching sides, by talking. They wanted to break your spirit by setting your own people against you. They talked about you to one another, laughing about how the outside world believed that you lay dead in the Retalhuleu grave.

They abused you, Everardo. Santiago saw Maj. Mario Sosa Orellana screaming at you and telling you that you did not deserve to live, pressing his gun to your head and asking how you wanted to die. You said nothing. You only stared back at him with those ancient black eyes. Later it grew much worse, but still you said nothing. You never spoke at all.

After a while, Santiago saw them take you away in a helicopter bound for the capital. At the end of May, Maj. Sosa Orellana called all of the prisoners together and told them that you had attempted to escape and had been shot and killed. They were never to speak of you again, not to anybody. Santiago's heart sank but he kept a carefully neutral face, for the officers were watching the prisoners intently, searching for any hints that someone might still side with the resistance. This was not the time for tears or sighs or for any reaction at all.

For a long time Santiago believed that Everardo was dead, and he grieved in silence. Then to his amazement he saw him again, very much alive at the end of July, this time at the base in San Marcos. At this part of the story, I sit up straight, baffled. Why were the officers faking his death for a second time? The dates make me stop and think. Asisclo Valladares had just dragged us from the cemetery in Retalhuleu in late May. The army knew then that we suspected them of taking Everardo alive. Was that why they lied about his death to the prisoners? Were they trying to conceal all clues, erase all trails, even with Santiago and the others?

Col. Julio Roberto Alpírez was in San Marcos too, with Maj. Mario Sosa Orellana. They became furious when Santiago saw Everardo and they ordered him to keep the matter top secret. Then they sent Everardo to be locked up in the nearby infirmary and placed under heavy guard. The other prisoners were forbidden to go near the building or to attempt to speak with him. They were never to speak of him to anyone at all.

The next day Sosa Orellana sent a special agent to town for medical equipment. Santiago's heart sank as the man returned with a gas tank, greenish in color and with metal valves attached, and carried it off to the infirmary where Everardo was being held. He heard the men say that the equipment had arrived and that a doctor was on the way. Santiago knew what this meant—that Everardo was being tortured. He passed the night in misery, trying not to think, trying not to remember.

The following day Special Agent Simeon Cum Chuta ordered Santiago to pick up the typewriter in the infirmary. Santiago protested, reminding him that he was under orders to go nowhere near the place, but Simeon insisted. Terrified, Santiago approached the infirmary door and explained to the three guards that he had been ordered to enter. They let him in easily enough, obedient to any commands from the powerful Simeon. Santiago entered quietly and bent to pick up the typewriter, trying desperately to be discreet. As he did so, his eyes focused on a sight that he would never forget. His voice begins to crack as he tries to tell us and his eyes blink despairingly. My heart goes out to him, for I know it is killing him to tell this story, that it is bringing all the horror back to him. It is killing me to listen. And yet I must hear it, all of it. He straightens his shoulders resolutely and continues.

There in the infirmary, he saw Everardo strapped to a small cot, the gas tank sitting next to him. He was stripped to his underwear and his entire body was grotesquely swollen. Santiago shakes his head at the memory, as if to exorcise a demon. He had never seen anything like that before. Everardo's entire body was so swollen that it seemed deformed. One arm and one leg were heavily bandaged. He was speaking in a strange voice, as if drugged, raving almost. Maj. Soto and Jimenez Rosales were in the room. Col. Julio Alpírez was bending over the torture table. He looked up when Santiago entered and roared for him to leave at once, saying that he had defied orders and that he knew very well what would happen if he ever spoke of what he had seen.

Santiago knew well enough indeed. He fled the room in horror and remained silent, telling the others nothing. He saw Everardo one last time before he escaped to Mexico. You were pale and tired, Everardo, and perhaps ill. Santiago couldn't say much to you, and your arm and leg were covered up with your uniform. But the swelling had gone down and your voice was normal when he heard you respond to the officers' questions. They had kept you alive. They wanted you alive and talking. That's why they called for a doctor to stand by even as they tortured you. They wanted you alive.

After this Santiago waited and waited. The officers trusted him so now that he hadn't long to wait. They let him go off on short trips without a guard, but never far enough away to escape. He didn't try, and came trotting docilely back to the base. They let him out a bit farther and he returned again. Then over Christmas they let him out for a bit too long and he ran for his life through the trees and across the mountains into Mexico and back to the *compañeros*, who could not believe their eyes.

Santiago is quiet now and he sips at a glass of water, waiting patiently for me to question him. Yet I have little to ask, for he has said it all. Instead I stare at him, trying to pinpoint his age. This youth with the lean face and haunted eyes cannot be a day over twenty-five, if he is that. He is clearly a villager, uncertain of himself here in this city hotel, his manners straightforward, no clutter of sophistication. If I remember correctly, he has had three years of schooling. And for two years now he has managed, all alone, to outwit the entire intelligence division of the Guatemalan army.

The Decision
Mexico, January 1993

AFTER THE MEETING WITH SANTIAGO, I GO BACK TO MY ROOM AND sit motionless in the small wooden chair for hours. I feel so blank, like a freshly erased blackboard wiped clean by unseen hands, no bits of information or tatty graffiti left anywhere to read. There is no more pain or desperation or even anger, just the void of utter shock. Outside my window are the city streets of Mexico, the bustling cars and honking trucks and buses, the students with their armloads of books, the businessmen in dark suits, the raggedy children begging for a few centavos for food there at the corner. I watch them mindlessly until the room fills with shadows and the streetlights appear in the dusk. Finally a telephone rings down the hall, the sudden sharp trill rousing me like a grim and unwelcome alarm.

I must think. I must shake off this stupor and begin to think, to plan, to come up with some kind of an idea. I pull off my clothes and step into the shower, turning the cold water on full blast and gasping as it hits my face and body. Wake-up call, girl. Get it together. I resist the urge to warm it up, and wash my hair in the icy water, rinsing it clean and letting it drip down my neck. Awake now, kid? Okay, okay. I let myself out of the shower stall and towel-dry, bundling back up in my jeans and a heavy sweater. Next I put a kettle of water on the stove to boil. I need some strong black Mexican coffee, maybe two cups in fact. I pull out the small jar of ground coffee, the paper filters, and the heavy mug I bought at the street vendor's next door. While I wait for the water to boil I fix a plate of bread, cheese, and a bit of fruit. I set the food down on my small table, turn on the study lamp, and get out some pens and paper. Now it's time to get to work.

Get to work. My mind drags itself back to Santiago's story and I see Everardo strapped to the table, hideously swollen, raving, blindfolded. The image gags me and I struggle against the anesthetizing stupor that floods back to my rescue. More than anything I want to put this aside, to go to sleep for just a little while, to think about it all later. I have no more will to fight. Is this how it feels to drown? I wonder. I shake my head and force myself to drink the mug of coffee, then pour another, softening it with powdered milk. I am not going to sleep; I am going to think. There is no time to lose. I go back to Santiago's story and suddenly it roars into my mind like a poisonous gas.

So they took you alive, Everardo, just as we feared. But it is so much worse than anything we ever imagined. Torture, yes, we knew about that, and we knew what you must be suffering if you were not lying dead in that lonely grave. We all knew about army torture, just as you did, for we had all seen the bodies tossed like broken dolls into the streets, or laid out like waxen figurines on the metal morgue trays. We have all seen them, with their slashed arms and legs, the amputated hands, the mud-filled sockets of their eyes. This we knew, and the thought of what you might have suffered has driven us all to madness for many months now. But this new experiment, this new program? They have kept you alive so that you could suffer these things for months or even years, destroying you in slow motion, body and soul, until only a broken husk remained to do their bidding? I would rather see you dead, Everardo, as much as I love you. And you would fight to find a way to die. This much I know about you.

Unbidden, the story of Father Pellecer comes to my mind. A liberal priest working with the poor, he was kidnapped by the army and "disappeared" for many months. His friends knew that he was being tortured, for word leaked out, and a dentist called to repair his broken teeth was later shot to death. Then suddenly Pellecer reappeared on television, surrounded by soldiers and talking vacantly about his brothers in the army. His old church friends rushed to see him, to rescue him, but they found that it was far too late. The good man they had known was gone forever. His body had survived, but with someone else inside. The real Pellecer was quite dead.

Too much coffee. Now I cannot sit still, and pace furiously about the tiny room. Everardo could have drawn a map of Mexico City, with bright red circles around the houses of all the *comandantes*. But he didn't do it, for they are still here safe and sound. He knew every arsenal and every supply line in the villages, every safe house. They are all still there, untouched. Santiago said Alpírez was torturing Everardo that day to make him tell about the *Voz Popular* radio station, how to reach it, which trails to take, how to shut it down. Yet I just heard it broadcasting last night, clear as ever. No one has gone down because of you, Everardo. You never spoke.

Are you still alive? For army intelligence you are the goose that laid the golden egg, a treasure trove of information. There is nothing you do not know about, after those seventeen long years. You were there from the earliest days of the war, one of the few survivors, and you sat as a *comandante* at the most secret meeting tables. What did Santiago say? They had called for a doctor to stand by as they tortured you. They did not want to kill you accidentally. They were not about to let you slip through their fingers so easily.

And if you are still alive, Everardo, I cannot think about what you are going through, how they must be raging over your refusal to talk, to give them what they want. How they must be working to break you, to smash you, for once and for all. They will never break your mind or your will, Everardo, for you are not like the rest of us. That much Gaspar knew even those first few days when he refused to flee to another house, as the security rules demanded. He knew you would never speak a word, and he was right.

But what has it cost you to keep your silence? How many months of torture have you already known, and how many more await you? Or have they already destroyed you in a foolish rage? I think not, I fear not, for they are barbaric but not stupid, and you are their greatest intelligence treasure in many years.

I sit back down and close my eyes, feeling dizzy. The most logical situation, given all the new information and circumstances, is that Everardo is still alive and suffering terribly, and that he may suffer for a long time yet to come. But not forever. They will not wait for him forever.

Now then, what to do with all of this? What on earth can I do? The army will never admit they have him, and they will say Santiago is a subversive and a liar, that he has made the whole thing up for propaganda purposes. I can fight this, but what proof do I have? Who will believe me? The human rights groups, perhaps, for they know the truth of Guatemala all too well, but they will be afraid to back me. The McCarthy-like atmosphere of the Bush and Reagan years has taken its toll—the church people jailed for their sanctuary work, the solidarity networks harassed and threatened by the FBI, different groups faced with loss of funding if they stress very real but disfavored political issues. Everardo has many rights under the Geneva Conventions and international law. But will anyone dare to say so? Everyone knows about the army's grim record on prisoners of war, yet it is rarely mentioned. The URNG is almost a forbidden topic, something to be tiptoed around in public and referred to almost obliquely.

Yet I must fight. The discreet style of last spring's exhumation attempt failed miserably. We have only lost valuable time. But if I push publicly for him, will the army panic and shoot him? Will they tor-

ture him all the more to punish me? Will I provoke his death by trying to save his life?

I think about it for a long while, making cup after cup of black
coffee and watching the people on the streets below. If I do nothing,
they will kill him. The army has never released anyone alive in all these
thirty years of war. They may try to use him for a while, but they will
never let him live to tell of what he has gone through. If I fight
openly, there is a very slender chance of saving him. Clinton has just
come into office, and the Cold War is officially over. There is a very
slender chance if I fight, but otherwise there is none at all.

A child is crying outside, just below my window, and I get up to
take a look. It is a little boy, tired and hungry, sitting next to his
mother as she tries to sell small packets of Chiclets to the people hurrying toward the metro. I return to my chair and try to think again,
remembering the women of the GAM, fighting for the disappeared
in Guatemala. I knew them in those grim and very early days when
they were all alone, shouting and weeping in front of the National
Palace, begging and demanding the return of their loved ones. No
one ever returned, but they fought on anyway, university professors
hand in hand with barefooted women from the villages. First Hector
was dragged away and killed with a blowtorch, but they fought even
harder. Then beautiful Rosario was killed with her younger brother
and her two-year-old son, the child's fingernails torn out and his baby
neck broken with a heavy metal bar. The women still would not be
stopped. Tiny Nineth and quiet Isabel wept as they worked through
the nights with the little old ladies and the frantic teenagers, Magic
Markers in hand, preparing posters and banners for yet another
march, yet another protest. No one ever came back alive, but they
never gave up and they never gave in. They fought as only women can
fight, against ridiculous odds, with a few coins and some fading
Magic Markers, using their very lives as weapons.

I think for a very long time. This will be quite a battle. It will be
slow and painful and dangerous and expensive. Maybe I will end up
with nothing, but it doesn't matter. I must fight now too. There is no
other way.

I pack my bags and leave the next morning. My first stop is Texas, where I close down our house, Everardo, and sell everything I own except for your shoes and your sweater and the books and scraps of poetry that you left behind. From these I will not be parted.

Takeoff
United States, February 1993

NOW THAT I'VE MADE UP MY MIND, THINGS START TO TAKE ON A LIFE of their own, accelerating wildly and leaving me a little out of breath. In Texas I fax a habeas corpus petition to the Guatemalan Supreme Court, demanding that Everardo be brought before a judge and given all proper protections required by law. I put my name, address, and passport number at the bottom and send courtesy copies to President Serrano of Guatemala as well as to the minister of defense. After the pages finish whirring through the machine, I feel a preliminary attack of panic. Am I quite out of my mind? I just told the Guatemalan army that I am a URNG commander's wife and used my real name and address to boot. Then I think about Everardo and fight off the temptation to add the footnote "And proud of it, you swine." If this is going to work at all, I must remain coldly professional—no hysterics, no theatrics, no pleas for special favors. I must ask for the law and for nothing else.

Next I pack my small suitcase and a cardboard box full of photos and documents and catch a flight for Washington, D.C. I have decided to file suit with the Inter-American Commission on Human Rights of the Organization of American States (OAS) and to give my testimony to the current panel. They can investigate the case, make findings of fact, and even give protective orders if they see fit. They can also send up the case to the Inter-American Court for an international trial. This last I hardly expect, since almost no Guatemalan cases have ever gone to trial. But meanwhile OAS can embarrass the hell out of the army internationally. Since the military is frantically trying to avoid trade sanctions and convince the outside world that really, after all, they aren't so bad, such pressure might at least make them think twice about shooting Everardo. I don't want the generals to burn their bridges behind them in a panic, since their bridges happen to be my own bridges as well. Like vampires, they cringe away from bright lights, so I need to shine the largest, hottest spotlight on Everardo that I possibly can while I get things started up. These first few months are going to be very dangerous.

Thinking about it all, my head begins to ache and I long to speak with Emma and the others. Yet from now on, I will see them only rarely. Since I have gone public, there is too much risk that I will be followed to their doorways or that my phone calls will be traced to their safe houses. I must avoid contact now and try to manage alone as much as I can.

I have the name and phone number of a lawyer who will help. His name is Jose Pertierra, and he is a Cuban-American married to a woman from Guatemala. From the airport I take a taxi to his downtown address, finding myself but a few blocks from the White House. There is still some snow on the ground, a problem I had not foreseen after my dozen years in southern Texas, and I make a mental note to myself to buy a heavier jacket. Hearing so much English in the streets is strange too, and I feel oddly like a foreigner here in my own capital. I brush the thought aside and hurry to the sixth-floor office. There I find Jose, a kindly man with bold brown eyes, a feisty grin, and a cigar permanently clenched between his teeth. He doesn't know much about my case, so we sit down together and as I tell my story, his eyes begin to sparkle with wicked glee. I like him immediately and when he bursts out laughing and invites me home for dinner, I know that I have come to the right place. This man is not afraid of the unconventional or the outrageous at all. In fact, he seems to thrive on it. He is more than up for this challenge and he is definitely on my side.

As it turns out he's also quite a chef, for that evening he prepares an Italian feast, telling me wild Cuban and Guatemalan jokes as he pours wine from his own collection and bends to test the pasta. His wife,

America, is quiet and very beautiful. Older now, she is a bit round, with perfect lips and dark eyes with long lashes and a telltale Guatemalan tilt. She speaks little, but in her face I see unfathomable pain. Watching her, I know without asking that she left Guatemala on the run.

The next day Jose and I get to work, madly writing up the papers for our afternoon presentation. We work well as a team, and he takes care of all the court documents while I get going on my testimony. As I type away on his word processor, my nervousness returns. No one has ever done this before. How will the panel react? How much should I say? I am so trained now to say nothing at all about the guerrillas that it seems almost blasphemous to go so public. If I do this, will I make things worse? Will the military torture him even more to punish me, or kill him in a fit of panic? Grimly, I push the thoughts from my mind, for if I do nothing, he is dead for certain. As for torture, I have already heard more than enough from Santiago. I take a deep breath and go back to typing. I am going to tell everything, damn it. That way there is nothing to hide and there is nothing to hold over my head. As I write, my sense of calm returns and I clench my jaw. Human rights apply to everyone, not just to the people my own government happens to favor these days.

That afternoon the session goes well. Jose makes a flawless opening statement, summarizing both my situation and Santiago's testimony. We have not been able to work out visas for him to come in person and so we offer a video of his testimony. The members of the panel are very quiet as Jose speaks, and they eye me cautiously, as they would a small package making an odd ticking sound. For the most part they seem kindly enough, except for an Argentine who positively glowers at me from across the room. Soon it is my turn and I grasp the microphone, suddenly feeling both confident and desperate. This is my chance, our chance, and I must not waste it. I begin to tell my story, about my time in Guatemala nearly a decade ago, my dead friends, the work on the book, the volcano, then Everardo. I tell them about March 12, 1992, his disappearance, the letter from de León Carpio giving the perfect description, and Asisclo Valladares screaming and red-faced in the Retalhuleu graveyard. Eyebrows begin to rise and the panel members are leaning forward, listening intently, utterly silent. The Argentine looks as if he would like to throw poison darts, but his glare gives me strength. I am going to tell this story, and you, Piggy Face, are not going to stop me.

I tell them about Santiago, how he was tortured, what he saw happening to Everardo, how the officers were talking about the fake grave in Retalhuleu. I ask them for help. I ask them to save his life. When I finish, I look around the circle and see kindness, horror, caution, and what I think is belief. Jose and I leave feeling hopeful, congratulating each other and making wicked cracks about the Argentine. As we leave I recognize Helen Mack standing in the hallway. Quiet and studious, she is the sister of Myrna Mack, a young anthropologist stabbed twenty-six times by an army agent because of her work with massacre survivors. Helen is battling the case through the courts and has become very famous for her courage and for her brilliant mind. I have long admired her, and stop to shake her hand, for her very presence gives me strength.

The next day I hurry to the Human Rights Watch office to see an old friend. She immediately offers to connect me to Congressman Moakley, a fierce critic of human rights violations in El Salvador. She quickly makes the phone calls and scribbles down an address, and soon I am off to the Hill in search of a legislative aide named Jim McGovern. McGovern is a good man, very Irish Bostonian, with many years of experience with the Salvadorans. On his wall hang the photographs of the four Jesuit priests murdered there in the city by the rampaging army. He listens to me very seriously, asking a few questions and nodding his head. By the end of the afternoon he has drafted a letter of support, and I am taking it door-to-door through the halls of Congress for signatures. There is so little time, and this is not an easy job, Everardo. I tell everyone the truth and the whole truth, for it is the only way, but it frightens some of them. They ask if signing the letter will not be taken as support for the guerrillas. I answer that not signing it will be support for torture. They sign. Day after day I canvass the offices, presenting drafts, answering questions, begging for help, returning again and again. I skip lunch, since that turns out to be a good hour for finding aides at their desks. I stay till far past five for the same reason. I drop off copies of Santiago's testimony and answer the same questions over and over again. I don't care how many times I have to do this as long as I get more signatures. My feet swell painfully and I am exhausted, but I still hike up and down the interminable corridors each and every day until all the doors are closed for the night. A few weeks later I have thirty-two signatures, a respectable number for any letter, and a shocking first for the Guatemalan embassy. I have already tried a chat with the ambassador, and he told me that Everardo got what he deserved. So take that, Mr. Ambassador, I think to myself. Take that.

I approach the human rights groups one by one, for I want more letters of protest. I must keep that light very, very bright indeed, Everardo, for your sake as well as for my own. Soon I will have to go to Guatemala and open the grave in Retalhuleu. There is simply no other way, for the army is insisting that Santiago is a liar and that you are buried right where they told me last year. They think I will not dare come back, now that I have admitted I am your wife. They have made one serious miscalculation there. When they took you away they took my very life, so I have little left to lose. I'll be back, and this time they are not going to throw me out of the cemetery. This time I am going back with a spotlight so bright they will not even dare to try. And so I go door-to-door in Washington and up and down on the Amtrak to New York City, turning over copies of my fact summaries and documents and explaining Santiago's testimony. The Lawyers Committee on Human Rights writes, as well as the Kennedy Center, the Human Rights Watch, Amnesty International, the World Council of Churches, and the Lawyers Guild. The smaller groups are more difficult, for they lack the protection of the others. They could lose funding, be singled out as nonneutral, and receive a few visits from the FBI, just as they have in the past. These people listen with sympathy and promise to think it over, but I know even as we shake hands that they are not going to write.

Then I go to the Guatemalan Human Rights Commission for a presentation to the staff there. They have already helped Jose on a number of issues, including preparing this case for the OAS hearing, and they have put me in their bulletin without even waiting to be asked. I have heard of the director, Sister Alice, for many years now and am curious about her. She is now nearly seventy and has been running her office since the early eighties, despite FBI harassment and scarce funding. Her newsletter is unique. When I arrive in her office, she hurries to sit me down and bring me coffee and make me feel at home. I look around me as she fiddles with the coffee machine, and I immediately like the place. It is simple and tidy, the walls covered with drawings, posters, and thank-you weavings from the people of Guatemala. Huge file cabinets crowd about everywhere, jammed with some fifteen years of clippings, bulletins, and correspondence. This is a place, I can see, of very hard work.

Alice calls the other staff members in and we all sit down together at the small table. They are an interesting array. Alice herself is a sturdy, apple-cheeked woman with the calm, commonsense blue eyes of a mid-western farm woman. Around her is a cluster of younger women, most of them students. One is very pretty and shy, and introduces herself as Pat Davis. They seem so eager to hear me out that I take a gulp of coffee and start to tell my story for the hundredth time. As I talk, I glance up and see that Pat and Alice are both on the verge of tears and I look quickly away, unnerved. I have learned that the only way I can tell this story and survive is to present it as a legal matter, clinically, repressing my own feelings. Now those feelings begin to surface with a vengeance and I have to close my eyes, focus on the pretty weavings on the wall, fight for my equilibrium. I finish as quickly as I can and Alice throws her arms around me, promising her help and support and urging me to come to her for anything at all. I know then that I have found a true friend. What I do not realize is that it will be Pat and Alice and Jose who will later save my life.

I think for a long, long time before I contact the State Department. I have hated them ever since my two years in Guatemala and am quite convinced that their only role in life is to lie about what is really happening down there. But then I stop and think about it for a while. Perhaps I should not be so hasty. After all, that was under Reagan, during the full-fledged Contra wars and the all-out FBI assault on anyone anywhere doing solidarity work. Now that era is ending, the Cold War is supposedly over, and Clinton, a man of my own generation, is President of the United States. Could things be different? Maybe, maybe not.

They certainly couldn't be any worse, and I might have something to gain by asking for help. The worst that could happen is a little harassment, maybe even a lot. Big deal. Why not give it a shot? Things might be different now.

And so I go by the State Department for a visit to the Guatemala desk officer. He is polite enough, a bit starchy perhaps, and motions for me to take a seat and tell him what the problem is. I start by explaining that my husband is missing in Guatemala, and he looks up in alarm. Then I explain that Everardo is not a U.S. citizen, and his expression changes to one of polite boredom. When I go on to explain that he is a URNG commander, he puts his pencil down and stares at me, as if to ask if I am serious. I tell him I am and give him all of my documents and information. He says he will make inquiries. I remind him I am a U.S. citizen and have a right to embassy assistance, and he nods a bit grudgingly and suggests that I also call a Mr. Jeff Moon at the embassy in Guatemala City. I take him up on this and call, sending down a fax with all of the information. Soon enough, a response comes back. The army says they do not have him. He died in combat and is buried in Retalhuleu.

Liars! I rage to myself and grit my teeth at night, knowing that it's time to go back to the jungle cemetery. I will damn well open that grave and prove who is lying and who is not. First though, I need a brief stopover in Texas. It's time to ask the courts for confirmation of my marriage and to do a fund-raiser. I am flat out of money now and my old friends there are all volunteering to help. I fly home on someone's frequent flyer ticket and have a glorious and affectionate reunion.

It is so easy to get things moving here, for I have known these people for years. First I gather together copies of all the protest letters we have so far and make sure the Guatemalan embassy receives a full courtesy packet. We even have a letter from Jimmy Carter now, and the folder is impressively jammed. Word will certainly reach the military that the human rights community and the U.S. Congress are watching out for this case. Still, my friends decide a little extra pressure can't hurt and so we rig up a Monday-morning "Call the Embassy" routine, with all of my friends and all of their friends and all of the friends' friends calling the Guatemalan embassy every Monday to tell them to do something about this case. The Guatemalan staff, hardly used to freedom of speech from the general public, reacts with total panic, their answers alternately snide and insulting then cajoling, and sometimes outright hostile. Whatever, we know that cables are going south every single Monday afternoon.

Next we set to work to plan a hasty fund-raiser, for I will need to hire a forensic specialist and pay for transportation, hotels, and other expenses. It will not be easy. But then Tish Hinojosa, a local singer well on the way to becoming a national star, agrees to sing for us at a local hangout. Friends volunteer to sell a certain number of tickets apiece, and bright yellow posters with Everardo's photograph suddenly appear all over the city. We need food, but several hundred people could show up and the thought of buying so many groceries and preparing so many dishes becomes a staggering concept. Then someone tells me to ask for help from trendy local restaurants. Most are willing to supply some entrées in return for a public thank you as good publicity. And so I take off in a friend's truck and scavenge about and find nearly a dozen good-hearted shop owners who pledge enchiladas, salads, vegetables, ice cream, and coffee for free.

The big day comes and I am feeling more and more confident. I have the court papers now on my marriage and I have contacted a Guatemalan lawyer and a U.S. forensic specialist who has worked for years with MIA groups. I have arranged for volunteers to stay with me in Guatemala and accompany me everywhere so that no army agent can catch me alone in some dark corner. I have gone to the library and read half a dozen forensic books and I know what tests can be run, and that we have enough photographs and records. I have also watched, over and over again, a video of the exhumation of a mass grave in Panama. At first it left me so horrified I could barely breathe, but I forced myself to keep playing it until the sights no longer shocked me, until I was prepared. I am ready now, Everardo, I know I am.

As we prepare for the evening bash the news comes in over the radio and television. President Serrano has decided to pull his own coup d'état, Fujimori-style. The airport is closed and the Guatemalan Congress and Supreme Court are surrounded. De León Carpio is under house arrest. Clinton has cut off all aid in an emergency measure. I snap off the TV. I cannot watch, knowing full well that as I stand there, people are dying in Guatemala. And Everardo? I push away the thought and hurry to pick up the food trays and deliver them to the restaurant. I must not think about Everardo. I must get myself to Retalhuleu and get there very fast.

Soon the restaurant is filled with old friends flocking to help me in any way they can, and their hugs and sympathy move me to tears. I give a talk about Guatemala and we all eat together in the flower-filled courtyard, listening to Tish Hinojosa's extraordinary voice as she sings the fierce protest songs of the women of Latin America.

A few short days later, the coup in Guatemala ends and de León Carpio becomes president through an emergency congressional election. The people in the streets grow wild with hope and Clinton resumes U.S. aid. Then Carpio Nicolle, a prominent newspaper editor and politician, who also just happens to be the new president's cousin, is shot dead on a rural road very near a military base. More than twenty masked men carrying military-style rifles attack the car, screaming, "Get Carpio! Get Carpio!" and nothing is stolen. The army declares the killing a mere matter of common crime by a local gang, and the embassy hastens to agree. In the next few months, de León Carpio will reverse every human rights position he has ever held as ombudsman and the archbishop's office will announce that human rights violations are on the rise.

In the midst of this uproar, I board a plane and head for Guatemala, where I will meet with Pat Davis and the Guatemalan Jurists Association, then head for Retalhuleu.

Preparations
Guatemala City, July 1993

GUATEMALA CITY IS EERILY STILL WHEN I ARRIVE. I WALK THROUGH customs at the Aurora National Airport, glancing upward at the balconies above, apprehensive. I remember all too well the police informants and the armed men who used to stand there, hidden in the crowds of waiting relatives, watching for suspected leftists. I would not be the first person to vanish here in the shadowy halls of the airport or on the remote stretch of road leading into town. I shake my head briskly and banish the memories. I am here now, I have my packet of support letters, and I am not going to let anything happen. Everardo needs me and that is that. I hand over my passport at the desk and the immigration officer looks up blandly, granting me a ninety-day visa and motioning me on through to the outside. I pass through the swinging doors and the strong sunlight of late afternoon hits me in the face, momentarily blinding me. The bright warmth is steadying though, as is the uproar of reunited families all around me. I find Pat Davis standing to one side, her soft red hair blowing about in the wind as she anxiously scans the crowd to see if I am allowed through. We are both relieved to find each other and break into grins as we embrace. So far so good— we are both here safe and sound. Then we bundle our luggage into a waiting taxicab and head toward our hotel.

I have heard about the Spring Hotel before, although I have never stayed there. It is a favorite of human rights delegations, visiting philanthropists, and travel-worn journalists, and I have selected it for this reason. I know the army well enough to know they won't drag me kicking and screaming out of my hotel room in front of a hundred international activists. We will be safe at the Spring. As it turns out we are happy too, for though the rooms are a bit bare, there is plenty of hot water, a kindly staff, and several walled gardens filled with luxuriant clinging vines and tropical plants. Here it is quiet, and we can sip our hot coffee and milk in the mornings and read the papers in peace.

Our first stop is the jurists' office, and Pat and I go to several meetings with a sympathetic group of lawyers who agree to draw up the exhumation papers for us. They are all in their forties now, more or less my own age, and they have all survived the extermination campaign of the early eighties here in the City. Most of them have spent some time in exile, and all of them have lost friends and family members to the death squads. Their faces are firm, a bit bemused and a bit frightened, and they have the sad, remote expressions of people who would rather not remember the past. As I listen to them explaining the legal procedures, I am filled with affection for them, since even signing these papers for me could well call down the army's wrath. Any imagined link to the URNG still carries a death penalty here. We talk about their safety for a while, but they only shrug and smile. I should not use their individual names too often, they suggest. If there is trouble, maybe I will be able to help with emergency visas or place a call to the OAS for them. Meanwhile, I should stay off the streets as much as possible myself, no? This case they will do—for my sake, for everyone's sake. Here in Guatemala, we must all stay together.

As they work on the documents and begin carefully clearing the preliminary red tape, Pat and I make the rounds of friendly embassies. I grow stir-crazy in the hotel, and in any event I know that the quiet visits are being watched and noted by army spies and that they are creating a margin of safety for both of us. The military would prefer to wait until we are lost in the shadows before they arrange for some tragic accident for us. Meanwhile I for one, have no intention of ever leaving the blinding spotlight I am working so hard to create. We visit the Canadian embassy, and the British, and the French. The Spanish ambassador is warm and friendly, and he writes his home telephone number down on his card in case we ever meet with an emergency. His quiet security guard, Juan, walks us to the door and stays with us till our cab arrives. He was here when the army burned the embassy in 1981; most of his friends were inside. The Argentine ambassador is also kindly, a torture survivor of the Dirty War himself. The Venezuelan ambassador quickly becomes a favorite as well, with his eye patch and bold humor. They all receive us generously, read our documents, and hear us out, and I know that behind the scenes they will keep their promises and quietly pressure the army.

Pat quickly becomes my most trusted adviser and companion. She is young, but I am very impressed with her comments and observations and I trust her instincts completely. We stay up late into the night, giggling over our own mistakes, past and mangled love matters, and our current ridiculous situation. Though a bit shy, she has a keen eye for the absurd, and her wicked swipes fit my own gallows humor perfectly.

We also make the inevitable rounds at the U.S. embassy. We meet with Mary Grandfield, who is friendly enough, and with various human rights officials, who immediately infuriate me. As always, they brush off all of the current murders and obvious acts of political violence as "mysterious," or merely matters of street crime. One, a skinny young man whom I secretly nickname "Needle Nose," repeatedly assures me that the guerrillas also kill all their prisoners of war. I tell him that this is ridiculous, that most of the *compañeros* have brothers who were forcibly recruited into the army and that they routinely release all their prisoners unharmed, minus their weapons and ammunition, of course. I urge him to talk with Bishop Ramazzini, who once retrieved a young prisoner from the Luis Ixmata *frente*. The army had refused to take the soldier back, claiming that he was a deserter and should be shot, and the Red Cross could not help either. After twelve months, the *compañeros* returned him to his home village and handed him over to the bishop for protection. The public meeting is on film. I also hand Needle Nose a sheaf of papers giving the names, dates, and places of capture of scores of different prisoners who were released unharmed, and suggest he look into things a bit more. He smiles blandly and promises that he will, but weeks later he is still mumbling about URNG killings of prisoners. I ask point-blank if he has interviewed Bishop Ramazzini, but he averts his eyes and says he has not yet had time. Late that night, Pat and I spend hours performing savage imitations of Needle Nose and laughing into our pillows. Still, I am furious. It is ten years later, Clinton is president, and nothing has changed, nothing at all.

At times I am wistful for all of my old friends here, but I dare not call or visit them or even wave when I see them in the streets. Word has traveled fast, as it always does in Guatemala, and they know why I am here. They hesitate as we pass on the sidewalk, their eyes meeting mine, waiting for a signal. I shake my head no and they continue onward, faces blank, their hands brushing momentarily against my own or flashing a tiny victory sign for me to see. At the law offices one day I see Nineth for the first time in many years. She is still young and very beautiful, and the fiery pain in her eyes is unchanged. Yet when I throw my arms around her, I sense a new serenity forged by the long years. She hurries to wish me well and offer support; then she turns to the other unionists and human rights activists, telling them to help me too. This quiet meeting warms me, but I still dare not approach their offices. My passport and my packet of congressional letters will keep me safe for a bit longer, but I have long since learned that the Guatemalans have no protection at all. The army knows full well they can kill their own with utter impunity. And they will.

Pat and I take to cutting out newspaper clippings each night, appalled by what we are reading. Two villagers are found dead near Sololá, their bodies showing signs of torture. A judge receives death threats. A university couple is shot to death. Nine bodies are found in a Petén secret grave. Four more are found in a cave, all showing signs of torture and the coup de grace. A schoolteacher flees the country with his family because of numerous death threats. A Catholic priest is shot at and there is a drive-by shooting at a local welfare office. A Coca-Cola unionist is kidnapped and interrogated about political issues by heavily armed men. Two women unionists are dragged away in Jeep Cherokees with tinted windows. One is released, the other beaten unconscious and left in the street with two broken ribs. A civil rights lawyer is shot at. The new human rights *procurador* is receiving death threats. A lawyer is being harassed; an undertaker is sent every so often to his office to take his measurements. In Colotenango, the army-backed civil patrollers open fire on unarmed villagers protesting human rights abuses. Several are killed. The U.S. government considers resuming military aid. By the end of July, Pat and I stare at each other over the pile of clippings and shake our heads grimly. So much for the new government under de León Carpio. He may once have been a human rights ombudsman, but as president, he clearly has no power whatsoever.

A few days later as we sit in the waiting room at the Jurists Association, two union activists walk in. The woman, bright-eyed and bold-looking, has a swollen face and walks with a limp. The young man looks wan and frightened, and he has a badly cut lip and a bruise at his hairline. They sit and talk with us for a while, feeling safe in the shelter of the office walls. The woman explains that she was dragged out of a City restaurant just a few days ago. The armed men simply burst into the dining room and hauled her out. She struggled and they knocked her down onto the pavement and beat her across the back with their rifle butts. They also struck her across the face. Then they held her without a lawyer at the police station for days. They discussed killing her, but she had managed to scream her name out the window of the vehicle, and they were worried about being caught. Finally they decided to let her go, but they warned her about what would happen if she kept up her activities. She seems quite unruffled, though, and has a sheaf of pamphlets in her hands even as she speaks. I immediately like her bold manners and am filled with admiration.

The frail young man at her side tells us his story, as well. He was seized by a group of armed men on the street a few nights ago and badly beaten. Since he survived, he was not too worried, but last night the same men climbed up on the roof of his house while he was away and threatened his wife and children. Now his family wants to move, but he has no place to take them. At this, his composure cracks and he begins to weep, his shoulders heaving with dry, exhausted sobs.

Pat and I are appalled and pull together some small bills to offer him toward a new apartment. He pockets them and thanks us, but he continues crying quietly, too tired to hold back. Pat is writing furious notes and offers to wire back to Washington for support letters. The woman smiles and accepts for them both. Pat reaches into her purse and pulls out cards from the Human Rights Commission, stuffing them into the woman's hands and urging her and all the others to call at once if anything else happens. The woman nods and smiles again. This she will do. It had never occurred to her or her friend to denounce either of these events. After all, they were released alive, were they not?

The Files
Guatemala, August 1993

THE JUDGE DOES NOT LIKE THIS AT ALL. HE WAS PLACED UNDER heavy death threats after last year's graveyard scandal, together with de León Carpio and the local human rights workers. He does not mention this of course, but I have heard all about it from the others. As we talk it over I feel sad, for he is a good and decent man with a kind face. He cannot be forty yet, and no doubt he has a family to worry about should he meet with a "tragic accident," Guatemala-style. Watching him, I wish there was some way to leave him out of all of this, but there isn't. I can't open the grave without a court order, and I can't get a court order without a judge.

He leafs through my stack of documents with their triple stamps and seals of authentication, nodding quietly and taking small notes. After a while he looks up and gives a half smile, a bit rueful, and says that I do have the legal right to an exhumation order. He will assign us a date for next week. At this, he leans over and circles a day on his calendar in red ink. My heart skips a beat and I look up sideways at Pat. As usual, I see my own feelings precisely reflected on her perfect features. She looks grimly pleased but also horrified. That's exactly how I feel, Everardo, that sense of triumph colliding head-on with a cold wash of fear. I've prepared and prepared for this day, but will I be strong enough, if that really is you lying dead out there in the mud, to come face-to-face with you at last? I push the thought from my mind. I will have to be strong enough, for there is no other way out of all this. I will make myself strong enough.

The thick legal folder lies on the desk and I ask the judge if I may read through it. It is normally sealed, secure from public scrutiny, but my marriage papers act as a key. As a family member, I now have the right to see what is there, what was really reported last year when that body was brought in from the battlefield. The judge hesitates for a moment and then, having no grounds for refusal, hands me the file.

I am not sure what I expect to find—perhaps nothing at all, perhaps something interesting. The first few pages are purely bureaucratic, the opening of a routine case about the discovery of an unidentified cadaver. One more XX, almost a daily matter here. I scan, noting that the place and dates are correct: March 12, 1992, the Rio Ixcucua, near Montufar, Nuevo San Carlos. So far so good. I flip through some more forms and find the report of the justice of the peace who retrieved the body from the muddy riverbank. My chest constricts and I begin to read word for word what he has written about that day. As I read I become terrified, for he is describing Everardo, lying dead with his brains scattered around him from a bullet to the head. It is like the letter from de León Carpio last year, a perfect description—eyes, nose, lips, shape of face, hair, brows, coloring, height, and approximate age. Even the wording is the same. With this terrible image, the pain comes back to me in a rush. Could I have been wrong all this time? Could Santiago possibly have been lying to me? I think it over, trying to regain my composure. No. He was telling the truth, I know it as I know myself.

I clench my teeth and read on. The report describes the olive green uniform, the number of bullets in each bullet bag, the cans of sardines from El Salvador, and the underpants with blue stripes. The next part stops me dead in my tracks. "Scars: none," says the report. Scars, none. I remember Everardo's battered body, the faded gash in the upper lip, the bright white circle over the heart, the thick pink scar on the upper arm, the tiny pale scars across the shoulders, the deep pockmarks and ragged holes covering his legs from shrapnel wounds. Seventeen years in combat, Everardo—you were a walking war museum. This justice of the peace says he looked so carefully that he knew your sardines came from El Salvador, that you had two bullet clips with twenty-eight bullets apiece and a pouch with seventy-two bullets more, and that your underwear was white with horizontal blue lines. He says he knew your eyebrows, eyes, forehead, lips, hair, lack of mustache, and that you were in your thirties and about one meter sixty. Yet he saw not one single scar of all those that were right there for him to see?

Rage pours over me now, making my fingers tingle with heat. This justice of the peace never saw Everardo dead and bloody at the river last year. He never saw Everardo at all. Liar! He is lying right here in his official report. Why? I close my eyes and think back to the press clippings and remember the photograph of a man standing over a crumpled form on the ground, clipboard in hand and surrounded by soldiers. The image hits me full in the face like a slap. That's it. He was surrounded by soldiers, so that's what happened. He was given a prepared description to report to the courts and, not being a fool, he obeyed the army. After all, they were the ones with the guns. Now I understand exactly what happened. Exactly.

I say nothing and grimly continue to turn the pages. I flip through another form and come to the autopsy report. Guatemalan law, in cases like this of the unidentified dead, requires an autopsy and burial within twenty-four hours. I am sweating in the heat and push the sticky strands of hair out of my face so that I can see clearly. This document I will read word for word as well.

The report begins by giving the date, March 13, 1992, and describing a body just brought in, dressed in olive green. It is the one from the Rio Ixcucua. No surprise there, since no other *compañero* was killed or missing that week. I read on, then stop with the first few words of the preliminary description, shocked. This is not Everardo at all; it is someone entirely different. The victim is a man, but not in his thirties. He is in his twenties. He is not one meter sixty; he is one meter fifty-five. He is not clean-shaven like Everardo, he has a mustache. His eyes are different too—"Chinese-shaped," not almond like Everardo's eyes, and his coloring is lighter. On his hand there is a scar that Everardo does not have.

My skin begins to crawl. This is it. This is the proof. They lied, Everardo. They lied about finding you dead. Santiago was telling the truth. It was all a military hoax and now I am going to prove it. I read on, trying to show nothing although I know very well that Pat, hovering at my shoulder, is thinking everything that I am thinking. Like me, she is deadly quiet, her blue eyes round and intent as she reads.

I go back to the page before me, growing ill as I continue. This poor young man did not die in combat and he did not kill himself. He lay dead on the autopsy slab, his boots missing and his fingertips black with printing ink. So they had taken prints and lied about that, too. His ankles had been tied with a sock so tightly it had etched the weaving print in his skin. He had been shot and stabbed and battered, leaving gravel embedded in his face. There was a strangulation gash of two centimeters around his throat. His skull was smashed in, not from a bullet but from heavy blows. Cause of death: asphyxiation and severe contusions to the head and thorax.

I close my eyes and take a deep breath, trying not to be too obvious in front of the gawking court clerks. Who was this pathetic young man and where did he come from? He was not a *compañero* originally, so the army brought him in from someplace else, a human sacrifice to help cover up for Everardo's capture and torture. Did they take him out there dead, tossing him from a burlap bag onto the slippery riverbank? Or did they drag him there alive, bound and gagged and dressed in someone else's uniform, and then destroy him there in the mud? In the back of my mind I can hear him scream, and I shake my head sharply to stop the sound. I want to start crying, but I know I must not make a scene or attract attention in any way. It is just beginning to dawn on me how very dangerous this document could be.

By law we cannot take a Xerox copy, but we can copy the report word for word and we begin to do so, my lawyer neatly taking it down on his yellow legal pad as I read aloud. Later he will give it the proper stamps and seals. It takes a very long time to write it all out, but I insist fiercely, remembering the vanished files at de León Carpio's office back in the City. This report could disappear overnight, and we will need some way to prove that it ever existed at all.

Finally we are finished and start our long drive back through the heat and dust to the capital. Pat dozes as we thread our way through the black clouds of exhaust and blaring horns of the trucks and cars and buses. I want to sleep but I am too worried. What Pandora's box is this that we have opened now? We cannot say anything about this discovery or else the exhumation will never happen; it will come crashing down around our heads just as it did last year. I would never survive that twice, I know. But if we say nothing? What if the army figures out that we have found this report? To their way of thinking, won't they have to kill us? These long, hot drives, how easy to go off the road, to be stopped and raped and robbed and shot by *delincuentes*—"common thieves." How very tragic. I look at Pat and choke at the thought of anything ever happening to her.

We talk it over until late that night and finally decide to make several copies and have a friend hand-carry them back to Washington to Jose and Alice. We include a note in the packet, telling them that if anything happens to us, it will be no accident. It is now only a few days till the exhumation. Until then, we will be very watchful and alert, and we will not stray far from the friendly shelter of our hotel.

The nightmares return, Everardo, and I cannot sleep. What if they have killed you in these recent months and buried you out there for me to find next week? I could not bear it, for despite myself, the hope of saving your life is growing stronger and stronger. I know I should not hope, Everardo—you warned me about that clearly enough—but I cannot help it. I have hope. Are you alive? I don't know which is worse. Who was that poor young man in the morgue, Everardo? And if that's what they did to him, what in God's name are they doing to you?

The Exhumation
Retalhuleu, August 1993

I WAKE EARLY AND WITH A SENSE OF GREAT CAUTION. I FEAR THAT if I move about too quickly the migraine of the night before will roar back with full force, so I lie still for a bit, trying to remember the layout of the strange hotel room. Pat and Janet, my journalist friend from Boston, sleep restlessly in their small beds nearby, their faces flushed from the tropical heat. Their familiarity steadies me. I listen to their rhythmic breathing while the dim morning light filters in through the window; then I rise for a cool shower in the tiled bathroom. As I stand beneath the stream of water, I go through my mental checklist for the day: what to ask, what to look for—the gap between Everardo's front teeth, the old extraction in his lower jaw. Once again I see him laughing, the missing tooth marking a clean space in the curve of his bright white teeth, but I quickly push the memory away. This is no day for nostalgia or for love.

I dry off with a thin hotel towel and pull on my clothes while Pat and Janet climb out of bed, rubbing their eyes and exchanging looks of apprehension. I dress in the cheap clothes I bought for the occasion: a sheer cotton blouse in a bright color, dark pants, and low-heeled shoes. I bought them just for today, knowing that I will throw them into a trash bin by nightfall. I will survive the next twelve hours somehow, and will either confirm or deny the identity of the body in the grave. Today I will find Everardo dead, or I'll prove that he was taken alive, as Santiago said. I will move one step closer to discovering the truth. Either way, I have no intention of bringing any grim reminders with me into the future. I will find out who is really buried in that shallow pit behind the morgue and then I will move on without ever looking back.

The three of us have breakfast together, Pat and Janet picking miserably at their food. I eat stubbornly, the familiar rage giving me strength. Memories come flooding back of the last time I was here, when the authorities threw us out of the cemetery just as we reached the flimsy body bag at the bottom of the grave. I missed my chance the last time, but no one will stop me today. If I have to seize the shovel and fight or dig with my bare hands I will, but I am not leaving again without seeing the face of the dead man. They will have to shoot me there, in that miserable stretch of untended cemetery, if they want to stop me. I will not leave, I will not cry, I will not faint, I will not fail. It is my only chance to save Everardo if he is still alive. So I chew my eggs and tortillas and swallow my black coffee, my mind clear and deadly calm. I look up and see tears in Pat's eyes, her oval face reflecting the pain that I cannot allow myself, and I feel a flash of love soften my fierce mood.

We drive in caravan to the cemetery and gather at the clearing behind the makeshift morgue. Already it is very hot. My lawyers are there, giving last-minute instructions to the team of anxious young forensic specialists who have volunteered to help. My forensic specialist, Dr. Charney, is calm and white-haired. He seats himself on the uneven ground, checking the equipment in his medical bag. At eighty-two his age does not show, but he is saving his strength, waiting for the grim task ahead. There are vague outlines of unmarked graves all around us, pathetic borders around the bodies of the unidentified dead. I note with a shudder, that the four recently dug graves that lay open and empty the day before are now filled and covered over with fresh earth. I wonder vaguely who lies buried there, and if their families know where to look for them.

The judge arrives with his secretary, fresh from another round of police threats, his handsome face furrowed with anxiety, a large sheaf of court records clutched in his arms. I introduce him to Mary, from the U.S. embassy, in the hopes of giving him some protection. Next come the cemetery administrator with his maps and the funeral home employees in their raggedy clothes, ready to begin the digging. The funeral director approaches me gingerly, tapping me on the arm and asking where to leave the plain wooden coffin I purchased the night before. Round and dark, with one dead eye, he stands close to me for a while, trying discreetly to show me support. An unmarked helicopter arrives and begins to drone in slow, endless circles overhead. Its pulsing blades seem to echo the heavy beating of my heart. A fat man in a tight polyester suit introduces himself and holds out his hand, but before he even speaks, I know he is from the attorney general's office and that he has come to try, once again, to throw us out. We both stand for a few moments, sweating in the heat and eyeing each other like wrestlers approaching a match. When I look away, I see that the area has filled with journalists and heavily armed members of the police force. Carrying his book of regulations, the health administrator arrives late, together with a crowd of curious onlookers. It is time to begin.

We sign a lengthy legal document, which the judge first reads aloud over the grave site. It has been carefully marked with a bit of twine by the cemetery administrator. Then the grave diggers begin to swing their picks and shovels, hacking at the earth as if they are about to build a road. Clumps of dirt and tangled roots fly through the air, and the sounds strike me like the blows of a club. I can only think that perhaps Everardo lies below that rough surface and I want to scream at them to have at it more gently. The irrational fear comes to me that if they do not slow down, I will soon see his hand or foot fly through the air, hacked loose by a careless shovel. I know without the slightest doubt that if that happens, I will drop stone-dead where I stand. Mercifully, the forensic team takes over quickly and begins to dig with tiny spades and brushes with surgical care and skill.

I try to take a few steps back, but I find myself hemmed in by the crowd of police, journalists, and gawkers. Instead I kneel down at the edge of the grave, my arms crossed over my chest, reminding myself that I cannot faint or even cry. The authorities are all too desperate to say that the cadaver we are about to uncover is indeed Everardo's and that at this stage of decomposition, I cannot possibly know otherwise. They need to say that Santiago is lying. They need me to become hysterical. They need my theatrics. They are not going to get them from me. I half-close my eyes and in the innermost part of my mind I begin to play classical music to myself, listening carefully to all the chords. When I look up again, a blackened skeleton lies fully exposed at the bottom of the pit in front of me.

I suppose it is the body of a man, given the short curly hair that still clings to the skull. It is his position that hurts me. He has been tossed into the grave and has landed on his side, with one arm thrown up across his head, as if to shelter himself, too late, from a fatal blow. Though he is mostly bone now, the smell of death begins to fill the air, and the onlookers pull scarves and masks around their faces to block the stench. The forensic team consults briefly with the local forensic physician. He performed the autopsy the year before on the body brought in from the river, and this is the wrong cadaver. He is quite insistent, waving his autopsy report in the hot air. The young man brought in after the combat was dressed in olive green fatigues and had a skull smashed in from terrible blows to the head. This person is dressed in civilian clothes and the skull is intact, although a large crack is visible. We have opened the wrong grave. The unidentified dead are buried almost on top of one another, and the uneven, overgrown ground is difficult to measure with accuracy. The correct grave lies but a few inches away, but this is not the one. We have lost almost three hours.

The fat man in the suit then huddles with my lawyers and the judge and it is decided that I must, all the same, rule out the possibility that this person is my husband. After more bickering, it is decided that in order to save time, only the head will be brought out of the grave. Curly-haired Andrés of the forensic team is sitting at the bottom of the pit, and he obligingly wrenches the skull loose from the spine and the muck of hair and clay. It gives way with a sucking sound, and thuds into a red plastic bowl. The bowl goes first to Dr. Charney, and I heave a sigh of relief as he bends his white head over the skull. But then it is passed, in a whirl of camera flashes and clicking shutters, to me. One of the officials looks at me carefully, gauging my reaction.

Well, Mrs. Bámaca, he asks coolly, Is this your husband?

I look at the head in the bowl in front of me. The hair is matted but clearly wavy, not like Everardo's straight jet black hair. The bones of the face are still smeared with blackened bits of flesh, and the jaws hang open as if in a scream. Mixed with the desire to weep for this pathetic man, I feel a momentary lurch of panic. I know without a doubt that this is not Everardo, from the hair and the shape of the face, but this is not enough. I have but moments to give a rational explanation. Then, through the mud crusting the teeth, I see the bright gold cap. Everardo grew up starving on a plantation. He has no gold caps on his teeth. I hand back the red bowl with the man's head, shaking my head and pointing at the tooth. Andrés places the skull gently back in the grave, pulling the plastic over it like a sheet from a morgue. Then the hacking sounds start again, just a few inches to the right.

For a moment, I feel a wave of relief. It was not Everardo. I did not faint. I was able to find a solid basis for ruling out the dead man. But then I want desperately to weep, for the man in the grave and the cruel death he met, for the indignity we had just inflicted upon him, and for Everardo, wherever he is. Is he also dead, a pile of blackened bones tossed like trash into a shallow pit? Will I find him here, today, in this terrible cemetery? I try to listen for his voice, some echo in my mind to tell me that he is still alive, but I can hear nothing but the hacking of the earth at the second grave.

As the grave diggers uncover the body, a groan goes up from the crowd. We have opened the grave just to the right of the first one, but once again we have found a civilian with an intact skull, and the forensic doctor is vehemently shaking his head. The correct grave must lie just to the left of the first one and we have again opened the wrong grave. A second human head is pulled from the earth, placed in the red plastic bowl, and handed to Dr. Charney. This time he asks to take it into the morgue for a better look, and I am swept along with him by the crowd into the tiny building. The electricity is out, so they hook up some lights with the help of a truck engine while Dr. Charney rinses off the skull in the plugged-up sink, the mucky water splashing onto me. An old veteran, he handles the skull matter-of-factly, cleaning off the teeth with a brush and noting the bullet still lodged in the side of the head. Under the running water the hair comes off in his hands, and when he sets the head on the tabletop, bits of muck jar loose from the eye sockets. Again, I want to weep, to beg them not to pull off the man's hair, to be more careful of his eyes. He isn't alive, but he was once a human being. It could have been Everardo. They could all have been Everardo.

It isn't him though. Dr. Charney knows it even before he calls me over for a closer look. The skull is now clean and white in his hands, the teeth clearly visible. Again, the cameras whir and the police and the government lawyers wait for my answer, their smug faces making me grit my teeth. At first I see nothing to judge by, but then I notice the missing front tooth and the bone grown tightly closed across the space, leaving a smooth surface. I have read the forensic books long before coming here. After a tooth is pulled, the jawbone closes with time. If the bone still shows a gaping hole, then the tooth was knocked out near the time of death. Everardo was not missing a front tooth. I consult briefly with Dr. Charney, trying to avoid the microphones and tape recorders held too close to my lips. He confirms that the dead man had lost this tooth years ago. This man is not Everardo.

With this a pitched battle breaks out between the judge and all of the lawyers. The fat man from the attorney general's office wants us thrown out. He is waving his arms and shouting that we have had our chance and that Everardo is buried there somewhere, and that it is time for us all to go home. My lawyers shout back that there is still plenty of daylight left and that no one is going anywhere. The judge looks distraught, his kindly face furrowed with both pity and fear. The police and gawkers form a tight circle around us, commenting and fighting for space. It is all too much like last year, and the rage snaps through my brain like a high-voltage line gone amok. If they want to throw me out again, they are going to carry me out dead. I take the judge by the arm, rudely turning my back on the lawyer from the attorney general's office, and point out that if we leave today, the authorities will simply force me to come back again until I find the correct grave. They will not consider my evidence complete until we find the body, so we might as well get it over with now. The very threat of my return is quite enough, and the judge shrugs his shoulders in despair, ordering the last two graves in the block to be opened simultaneously. The hacking noises start once again.

I feel dizzy from the heat and try to lean back, but the people are pressed so tightly up against me that they are almost pushing me into the open grave. I shove them roughly away and walk to a low tree stump to sit with Dr. Charney. He puts a grandfatherly arm around me and offers some water, then launches into a series of ribald forensic jokes that leave me laughing shamelessly into the cameras. Janet sits there with us, giving me a back rub and roaring with me at the crazy stories, while Pat glides back and forth, listening in on the conversations and bringing me reports. To my amazement, she is even able to snap a photograph of the autopsy report in the hands of the forensic physician without getting caught. I am still afraid it will disappear. Now there is no need to worry, and I give her a silent smile of gratitude. Meanwhile a police spy is caught taking photos of the people in the crowd, and he is ordered to remove his film from the camera. He does so sullenly, pulling the film out and exposing it in the sunlight as the crowd cheers with approval. Then Andrés calls out from the bottom of a grave, flinging an olive green shirt out onto the ground above him, and abruptly we all fall silent.

I stumble tiredly back to the edge of the grave where Andrés is at work with his brush and tiny shovel, and bend to look at the shirt. There is no doubt. It is part of the guerilla uniform, with its heavy pockets and snap buttons, made of a fabric so waterproof that it has not rotted during its long year in the earth. It does not look like Everardo's, for it is far too small, cut for a slightly built young *campesino*. All the same it forces hot tears into my eyes, making me blink furiously. So who is it, then, that lies there under the shroud of emerging black plastic? Looking at the shirt, I remember the volcano and think of impish eighteen-year-old Ariel, now dead, with his head of bright black curls, and shy Antonio with his dimples and good-natured smile. A grenade took his life not long ago. I loved them both as younger brothers, and either one of them could have worn this shirt. It makes their deaths too real, too hard. A slender pair of pants flies out of the grave, along with bits of a familiar-looking first-aid kit. I no longer want to watch. Whoever lies below was once a friend, and I do not want to find him there. The helicopter overhead drones on ruthlessly, winding my nerves tighter and tighter with its circling blades.

Finally the body lies exposed, the plastic sheet pulled back from the smashed head. The forensic doctor nods that this is, at last, the right grave, and all eyes turn uneasily toward me. A makeshift stretcher is brought to the edge of the pit and with a concerted heave, the dead man is dragged from the grave in his black plastic wrapper and hauled into the morgue. Dr. Charney goes in first, then comes out quickly, warning me that it is very bad and asking me if I am going to make it. I nod yes, then lean up against the morgue wall for a moment, wondering if I have been wrong, if the crumpled shirt and pants had indeed belonged to Everardo. Is that him, now, laid out upon the rough concrete slab inside, waiting for me to come and analyze his teeth? I close my eyes, remembering him so clearly that my head aches with the year and a half of pent-up grief. If that is Everardo inside, then nothing could keep me from him. I will have his bones back; they are mine. I will bury them far up in the green peaks he loved and say good-bye at last. I start to go inside. Dr. Charney warns me once again that it is very bad, but I shake him off. Everardo could never be dreadful to me.

I hurry inside, shoving through the crowds of people with their heavy cloths wrapped around their noses and mouths. An electric bulb hangs over the table, and I hear the sound of the truck engine grinding outside. The body lies flat, the black plastic slit open to the pelvis to show blackened bones encased in a thick mud of rotted flesh. The head is at an odd angle, confusing me for a moment, until I realize that the crown is smashed flat over the face. Dr. Charney tries to reposition it, then pushes back the broken clumps of skull and hair and lifts out the lower part of the face. While I watch, he scrapes the muck from the jaws to reveal the dead man's teeth. They are small and straight and pressed close together in an even row, two gold caps glinting in the upper jaw. They are nothing like Everardo's crooked teeth, with the gap in the front and the overcrowded sides. I shake my head and point at the gold caps, and the crowd sighs with relief. Dr. Charney bends for a look at the pelvic bone and holds it up to the light. The dead man was perhaps eighteen years old. Everardo was thirty-four when he disappeared. It isn't Everardo, but where is he then? And who is this pathetic child?

As if on cue, a clap of thunder roars outside, bringing with it the afternoon downpour of tropical rain. The crowd at the door shrieks and begins to disperse, people running toward the cars and nearby trees for shelter. I stand between the judge and the one-eyed funeral director while the journalists fire their last-minute questions at me and ask me to point one more time—for the cameras—at the jawbone perched on the tabletop. When they finish, a man taps me on the shoulder and murmurs into my ear that the civil war has been cruel indeed, pitting brother against brother, and that the human being there on the slab was a true Guatemalan brother. Then he turns and walks into the rain, leaving me to stare after him in surprise.

Two men come into the morgue then, out of breath and dragging the plain wooden coffin between them, banging it down on the wet floor. Gingerly, the funeral director asks me what they should do, and I tell him to bury the young man in it. I watch grimly while they lay the pieces of skull back into the plastic bag, then half-lift, half-pour the remains into the coffin and neatly fold the white winding-sheet over the terrible head. They hammer the lid shut with quick, sharp blows. An official wanders in aimlessly and mumbles that since the man is still unidentified, I cannot bury him in the plot I had purchased on the other side of the cemetery, where the graves are marked with crosses and angels and the grass is well tended. I must rebury him there where I found him, behind the morgue, beneath the weeds. The thought makes me choke, but a man from the funeral parlor clutches my hand, whispering promises to give me a tombstone engraved with any words that I might choose. Looking down at him, I realize he is quite serious.

Promise me, I ask, to put on it the words "Still with Us in the Struggle." These are the guerrillas' sober words of toast at Christmas and other celebrations, shouted aloud to keep their dead alive and with them always. I expect an immediate refusal to this dangerous request, but he only smiles his acceptance, his dark eyes reflecting fierce approval. He follows me outside and waits with me in the pouring rain while the coffin is lowered hastily into the ground and the muddy clods of earth are thrown back over it. The cool rain on my face helps to clear my mind, and I leave then with Janet and Pat, to search for the priest.

It is not hard to find him, for in Guatemala there is always a town square and in the town square there is always a church. Retalhuleu is no different. I find the church easily enough, and in the church I find the priest, Father Javier from Spain. I have heard about him before, for he is a brave man who speaks out fiercely against the repression, and he often comes under death threats himself. He stands quickly to greet me as I walk through the door, explaining with a sardonic smile that he has just been watching my exploits on the evening news and that I am always welcome in his parish. He is a tall, slender man with snow-white hair and the beautiful uncorrupted face of a child. When I explain what I want, he packs up a small leather bag and follows me out the door without a word.

We drive back to the cemetery in his Jeep, Pat and Janet sitting silent and exhausted in the backseat. The rain has subsided and it is growing cooler, the harsh sunlight dimmed to a muted twilight. A crowd gathers to watch as we go back through the painted plaster arches, but this time no one follows, and we shuffle down the muddy path to the morgue in silence. The four graves have been filled up again, but they lie hacked and uneven, the rude marks of our interference visible everywhere. The priest draws a Bible out of his bag and reads aloud for a few moments, then sprinkles holy water across the graves of the unknown. As he begins to pray, I close my eyes and listen to his beautiful voice speak of hope, of love, of justice, and of defiance, and I know that he is praying for the souls of us all. I think of

Everardo then, as I saw him in the old dreams, trapped in a small dark space, his black eyes so wistful for the life that had been snatched from us, his faint voice telling me that he is cold. The dream has always tormented me so. Was he speaking from a shallow grave, like the pitiful ones surrounding us here? Or was he trying to call out to me from some terrible cell? Perhaps I will never learn the truth; perhaps all days will end like this one, with horror and unanswered questions. But as I stand there in the mud, surrounded by the battered dead, I know beyond certainty that I will love you, Everardo, until the end of my days and that I will never, never give you up.

Busted
Guatemala City, September 1993

YOU GUYS ARE BUSTED. YOU THERE BEHIND THOSE STONE WALLS and the rows of cannons, you in the camouflage uniforms and the dark glasses, with the big guns. I've caught you now, and I can prove it at last and I am coming after you. You'd better get ready, because you are going to give me Everardo back or I am going to take you down.

My friends laugh good-naturedly at my attitude, pointing out that the army is, after all, a tad bigger and better armed than I am and that they are not exactly shaking in their boots at my approach. In fact, they seem to have barely noticed me at all. This observation has no effect on my mood, for a mad and white-hot rage is flowing through my veins, burning out any ability to weigh the odds, to protect myself. To hell with the odds, I think. They will give me Everardo back or I am taking them down. There is simply nothing else to discuss. The others give up trying to reason with me and shake their heads, baffled by my stubborn refusal to see the obvious. *¡Obstinante! ¡Pero obstinante, vos!*

There is uproar in the City as I return from Retalhuleu, for the exhumation has been covered on national television and the case is creating a scandal. A guerrilla commander? Hush, don't say those words out loud, are you mad? His wife is a gringa lawyer. A what? What was that she said in public about the army? One of the newspapers trumpets across the front page that I have admitted that the body in the grave is indeed Everardo's. I call them and suggest they watch their own nightly news a bit more carefully. The man in the grave is fifteen years too young, five centimeters too short, and has quite different dental patterns. I demand a correction and get one of sorts. The next day the journalist writes that I have abruptly changed my story. I roar complaints to my Guatemalan friends, but they only laugh at my indignation. Who did I think controlled the press? Haven't I noticed how many journalists have been killed by death squads or run out of the country during all these years? Hadn't I ever heard of the *faferos* — "bribe takers"?

Pat and I both assume we will have to leave the hotel. After all, it is a small place and the owners will be too terrified to shelter me. But where on earth will we go? We walk hesitantly through the front door, worn-out and expecting the worst. I am sad to think about leaving, for the staff has been very kind to us. They know I am looking for a missing husband, just as the man at the front desk is searching for his missing brother, and they give me much advice and support. Now what will they say? The receptionist looks up as we walk in and gives us a wan smile, then hurries to get the key to our room. Señora. Señora! You are back! Are you well? His voice drops lower and he puts a comforting hand on my shoulder. Very tense, señora, very tense. You told me you were looking for your husband, but you never said what husband it was that you were looking for! I wait for the ax to drop and for him to tell us that the owners want us out. To my surprise he gives us both a hug instead and welcomes us back, hurrying to help us with our bags. Later the small metal room number disappears from above our door, taken down for "cleaning," although really to make it harder for anyone to sneak up on us unannounced. Then a special metal security gate is added, complete with an electronic buzzer. While it is being installed, two huge heavy tables are set up like battering rams against the outside doors each night. Amazed, I ask if this is all because of me. They tell me no, certainly not. Why would I think such a thing? Then they hire an armed guard.

Journalists begin to flock to the hotel, wanting to hear the whole story yet too terrified to print it. I give them all the facts in writing, but only garbled scraps of information make it into their stories. Just one has the courage to really write the truth, a woman named Mayra from *Prensa Libre*. She writes it up for the Sunday magazine and the cover story runs with the headline WHERE IS EVERARDO? printed against the ghostly backdrop of his photograph. The story stirs up mayhem. Pacifica radio calls from New York City and I shout the story point-blank across the telephone lines, knowing full well the army is listening. The next day, some fifteen government telephone company cars, all with black glass windows, surround the hotel for the entire day. Okay, okay, message received, you donkeys. But don't dream that you can scare me off so easily, for you have taken my very life from me and I have nothing left to lose. You will never scare me away, and this battle has only just begun. Get ready, because I am coming to take you down.

The next stop is the U.S. embassy for a visit with Ambassador Marilyn MacAfee. So far she has been kindly enough during our brief meetings and I have promised to fill her in on the details of the exhumation. Janet Hawkins comes with me, for her story for the *Harvard Magazine* has begun taking on a life of its own. I am glad for her company, even though I know that the embassy staff will insist on everything being off the record. At least this way I will have a witness. We catch the bus together and get through the front gates, checking in with the outside security guards, and then through the inside check, where Janet has to leave her camera and we are issued visitor cards. Then at last, we are ushered upstairs.

Marilyn MacAfee comes out of her office right away and greets us warmly. She is, as always, splendidly dressed and good-naturedly charming and she hurries us into her sumptuous chambers. Small china cups of excellent coffee appear as we settle onto the comfortable sofa. Needle Nose is with her and I brace for a fight.

I start out by telling MacAfee about the exhumation. She has already heard about it from Mary Grandfield, but I fill her in on the various officials, which forensic doctors were present, and why and how we were able to certify that the body in the grave was not Everardo's. She listens very carefully, leaning forward in her chair and nodding as I explain the test for age approximations and the many differences in the teeth. I wince slightly as I tell her about this, for it brings back the vivid image of the pathetic youth on the morgue table. For a moment I choke on pent-up tears, then grit my teeth and continue. A softer look passes over the ambassador's face as I speak. Sympathy perhaps? I don't know, but I certainly think so. As I finish, she shakes her head, agreeing that this issue, at least, has been resolved for good.

Needle Nose is quite unhappy. He sits up in his chair and chirps that the guerrillas, too, have always killed all of their prisoners of war. My patience snaps and I ask him loudly if he has ever bothered to contact Bishop Ramazzini or to research the list of returned prisoners I gave him long ago. He looks embarrassed and shakes his head, muttering that he has been rather busy. I pull out a copy of the list from my briefcase and hand the sheaf of papers to Marilyn MacAfee, explaining that I have given this information to Needle Nose quite some time ago. She lifts a polite eyebrow and takes the papers, promising to look them over and assuring me that the matter seems rather clear. Needle Nose lapses into silence, sensing that I am now circling like a maddened shark.

I tell the ambassador that I remember her earlier concern, that it would be one thing to show that the body in the grave is not Everardo's, and yet quite another to prove that the army ever had him in the first place. Well, I can cover that, I tell her. I put Everardo's photograph down on the polished table and tell her to look carefully at it while I read a certain document aloud. Then I pull out de León Carpio's letter from the year before, giving the description of the body the army claimed to have found at the combat site. Holding it in my hands, I remember how the letter made me weep back in Mexico a year ago and my rage begins to build. MacAfee looks at the picture while I read aloud. The letter says that a man was wounded and then shot himself through the mouth to avoid being captured alive.

He had a round face, broad forehead, full lips, dark eyes, dark skin, a turned-down Mayan nose, heavy eyebrows, and straight black hair. He was about a meter sixty and in his thirties. Well, that's Everardo all right, every feature in his face, the age and height correct. MacAfee nods again, waiting for me to get to the punch line. I deliver it, asking where, if the army never had Everardo in the first place, did they get such a perfect description of him? Surely they didn't happen to guess it, to pull it out of thin air? Moreover, why did they send Everardo's description when they were asked for a description of the body found by the riverside?

Janet's mouth has dropped open and she is staring at me, her hands stuffed into the pockets of her corduroy jumper. MacAfee is staring too, her face gone very pale. I continue, handing her a copy of de León Carpio's letter for her files. I pull out the autopsy report and hand that to her as well. Here is what the young man who was brought in from the combat site really looked like. The forensic doctor examined the body the same day it arrived. He estimated the man had been in his twenties, not his thirties, when he died. Moreover, the dead man was five centimeters shorter than Everardo and had a scar on his hand that Everardo did not have. The facial features were very different. He did not die in combat; he was tied at the ankles, fingerprinted, shot, stabbed, strangled, beaten, and his skull had been smashed by heavy blows. Not a combat death and probably not a suicide. What happened, I tell MacAfee, is that the army took Everardo alive, just exactly as Santiago told us. To conceal this from the outside world, they took another young man to the battleground on the same day and beat him to death. Then they called the press and announced that they had "found" the cadaver of a guerrilla member out there and had sent the body to Retalhuleu for burial. When the URNG asked for a description, the army sent a perfect description of Everardo, not of the young man. This international hoax was carried out even as they were sitting at the peace table with the URNG and discussing the issue of human rights. Not good, I say. Not good.

There is a deafening silence in the room now. Needle Nose is appalled and says nothing at all. Janet is still staring, her warm brown eyes sparkling with tears. Marilyn MacAfee is pale and motionless.

Finally, she clears her throat. Would I please put this matter into writing immediately? She will make inquiries about this and get in touch with the military and the proper authorities at once. She will get back to me as soon as she can to let me know what she finds out, and will do everything possible to help. I feel a faint rush of relief, mixed with my old cynicism about the U.S. embassy. Help at last from someone with power. She seems different somehow, for real. The Reagan-Bush era is definitely over and so is the Cold War. She is going to help me. Or is she?

The Opening Shot
Guatemala, September 1993

IT IS TIME FOR PAT AND JANET TO RETURN TO THE STATES, AND I see them off at the airport with a heavy heart. They seem like sisters after all this time, and I have become quite dependent on their support and ideas and cannot imagine Guatemala without them. We spend our last night in a fancy restaurant drinking wine and sharing shameless gallows-humor jokes, plotting out future strategies, and evaluating Pat's numerous and desperate admirers. She has still not broken up with her current boyfriend, but I know without asking that she will soon enough. She has changed so over this long summer, come into her own. There is a new confidence to the set of her jaw. She has found her own strength yet retained her old compassion, and as I watch her I feel a combination of love and pride.

Susan Lee arrives from Texas the same day to take their place and accompany me through the streets of the City, for I dare not be alone. Assassinations and kidnappings fill the papers, and the scandal over the case is growing by the day, appearing even in the heavily censored Guatemalan press in bits and pieces. There is furious tension in the air, like static before a storm, but I cannot keep a low profile just now. This is my long-awaited chance and I must not waste it. I shout my story defiantly into long-distance phone lines to faraway press offices and fax summaries to every human rights group I can think of. I have proof now! I have proof about who has been lying and who has been telling the truth. I have proof that they took Everardo alive. Now it is time to call in my chips, demand help and protests from all of those with the "wait and see" attitude before. Now it is time for action, whether the army likes it or not, and they definitely don't like it.

Susan seems comfortable enough with the chaotic situation and my own wild-eyed attitude. She is my own age, tiny and slim, with a headful of thick graying curls, and she clearly likes a good fight herself. We sit up late at night while I fill her in on the background facts, and she laughs out loud at my wicked asides and plots for future mayhem if they don't turn over Everardo. When I tell her our first task in the morning is a visit to the minister of defense, she doesn't bat an eye. This woman is tough and street-smart and definitely on my side. I fall asleep feeling confident.

The next day we dress up, swapping jewelry and helping with hairpins as if we were backstage before a school play. After a while we are ready, in full somber business attire that makes both of us laugh out loud, aging former hippies that we are. Then we gulp down some black coffee in the central garden and hurry out to catch the bus at the corner. As we take off toward the Avenida de la Reforma, with its plush shops and embassy suites, we both try to hide the rush of anxiety that is catching up with us. Are we really going to go through with this? After all, this is the minister of defense we are talking about, not exactly Mr. Nice Guy or anything. Just who, exactly, do we think we are? We start discussing the weather and the arts to keep our minds away from these dangerous thoughts.

As we arrive at the Politécnica, we both are a little quiet, the adrenaline flowing to bolster us up. As always, the building reminds me of the Wicked Witch of the West's castle in *The Wizard of Oz*, making me smile despite myself. It is an enormous gray palacelike structure, complete with turrets and arches, and it is painted a stone gray color with white trim. In the towers the uniformed guards linger with their sub-machine guns, watching the streets below, and a neat row of iron cannons lines the manicured lawn. *Do not enter,* is the clear message I get from this building. *Go back the way you came.* I feel a stab of pain as I look at the heavily guarded entry, for Everardo may well be inside. The Politécnica has long been reported a center of secret torture cells for special prisoners like him. As I stare I remember the story of the Bastille and promise myself that someday I will be back to tear this place down brick by brick. I will, that is, if I can squeeze in someplace between all the Guatemalans who get there first.

We go to the official residence around the corner and bang on the door. A guard lets us in, slinging his rifle over one shoulder and ushering us to a small and elegant sitting room. Susan and I glance at each other like schoolgirls sent in for a word with the headmistress. We are a bit nervous, but also defiant. A young soldier comes in and offers us coffee on a small silver tray, and we accept it gratefully, fiddling with the china cups and spooning out the sugar. Then a side door opens abruptly.

General Enríquez makes a good entry, his boots clicking neatly on the polished floor, his uniform immaculate and perfectly pressed. He has a shock of silvery hair and vivid blue eyes and his features are taut, watchful, as if he was walking into a dangerous ambush. He eyes me carefully as he crosses the room, his lips smiling politely, his mind registering every detail. This man is no fool, I think to myself, and he is as nervous as I am. He holds out a tentative hand, and we shake, both of us all too aware of the absurdity of this encounter. I feel my lips twitch ever so slightly and I studiously avoid looking at Susan. I search Enríquez's face instead and find a mirrored hint of amusement in his eyes, mingled with something less pleasant. It is the amusement of a cat watching a cornered mouse.

We sit down and exchange pleasantries, inquiring after each other's health and claiming to be pleased to meet each other. I cross my ankles and he sits very straight and there is a bit of a pause, each one hoping that the other will make the first move. I take the plunge, telling him that I am here to ask for his help on the case of my husband, Efraín Bámaca Velásquez. He nods politely and begins to comment that this man was a subversive, so I make a preemptive strike, cutting him off and saying that my husband was also known as Comandante Everardo and was one of the founders of ORPA. The unthinkable having been said, Enríquez is now a bit speechless, and he sits back and waits for my next move. I tell him about Everardo's disappearance, the army's reports that a body had been found, de León Carpio's letter with the perfect description, and Santiago's escape and his story of Everardo's imprisonment and torture. Then I tell him about the exhumation. My anger returns now, steadying my nerves and making me bold. So you see, I tell him, the army took Everardo alive and carried out an international hoax, faking his death so that he could be tortured in secret for his information. I want him released to the courts for a fair trial, together with all the other prisoners. Otherwise, I am going to make one hell of a racket.

Enríquez keeps a studiously blank and courteous expression on his face, wincing only when I suggest he talk with Colonel Alpírez and Major Sosa Orellana. Susan has not moved a muscle. There is a long pause and then the general breaks into a smile, ready to make his move. Well, he says, this is all very tragic indeed, and he would be delighted to help me. But I must understand that the army never had my husband at all; this is just a terrible misunderstanding. They found a body. I myself say the body is not my husband's—so they never had him. Who knows where he is? If I would just tell him where I think Everardo might be hiding out, Enríquez himself will be glad to escort me in person to the place in his own helicopter.

Donkey! You have walked right into the trap, I think to myself, and hurry to bolt shut the escape route. Well, the problem is, last year the army gave a description of the body that matched Everardo feature by feature and to the centimeter. If they never had Everardo in the first place, where did they get the description and why did they send it? The body in the grave is completely different.

Enríquez thinks this over, a sour glint in his eyes, then smiles again. I feel as if we are playing a bizarre form of Ping-Pong and that he is a sore loser returning to the table for vengeance. Well, he says, clearing his throat, the *subversivos* must have switched the body in the grave to make us look bad. They do things like that, you know.

Susan's eyes are wide and she remains motionless in her chair. I take a swing at the Ping-Pong ball and tell him that we have the autopsy report from last year, done the same day the body was brought in from the river and before it was buried. The body brought in from the combat site was never Everardo in the first place; it was someone five centimeters too short, a decade too young, who was tied up and beaten to death. Moreover, the body in the grave matches the description in the autopsy report. No switch has been made. I cross my arms. His move.

He is angry now but fighting not to show it. The glimmer in his eyes frightens me, but I won't lay off. I tell him again to release Everardo to the courts, along with the other prisoner. This is the new administration of Ramiro de León Carpio, former human rights ombudsman. This is the army's chance to turn over a new leaf, to show they are serious about human rights. It would be a milestone in Guatemalan history to turn over the first prisoners of war ever in thirty years to the courts. He would receive international applause for this. There is no need for us to work against each other like this, bashing heads, causing scandal. This doesn't do anyone any good.

He agrees that scandal is bad, nodding emphatically. But they don't have my husband; I must get this through my head. Perhaps he is hiding out in the jungle on a secret mission and forgot to let me know. Perhaps he is off with another woman. It is not the army's problem. For many years now, the military has been accused of having secret prisons and secret prisoners. But even de León Carpio says there is no such thing. Haven't I heard? He gives a smug smile.

Now I am furious. It is true that de León Carpio has said exactly that. After his cousin was assassinated on that lonely road, he reversed every human rights position that he ever held. Now he won't even help his own family investigate. God only knows what threats the army is holding over his head. Now I hate this uniformed man sitting across from me.

Well if there's no such thing, how do you explain the case of Sister Dianna Ortiz? Dianna is a young and beautiful Ursuline nun who was kidnapped from a convent garden in Guatemala, placed in a police car, and taken to the Politécnica. There she was gang-raped, left with more than one hundred cigarette burns on her back, and lowered into a pit filled with rats and humans, most of them dead, some of them dying. She was a U.S. citizen, and at the end of the day a mysterious North American came into the room and took her away. De León Carpio himself had denounced her case back when he was ombudsman.

Enríquez stiffens as the Ping-Pong ball hits him between the eyes, and his lips take on an irritated twist. Susan sits rigidly in her chair, gripping the sides with her small white hands. I want to throw my coffee cup in this man's face. He clearly wants to strangle me. I suspect this meeting is coming to an end.

Enríquez mumbles that he understands my position and then we all rise to shake hands again. He sees us courteously to the door and across the courtyard filled with gaping soldiers. Then the guard slides the black iron gate open and we are outside again, safe and sound in the bright sunlight. Susan and I hug each other, breaking into fits of nervous giggles, and spend the rest of the day treating ourselves to chocolates and beer and special bubble baths back in the safety of our hotel. It is only noon, but we are calling it a day.

Twister
Guatemala, September 1993

AT LAST I KNOW HOW TORNADOES FORM. I REMEMBER THEM FROM my early days in the Texas Panhandle, when they roared across the dusty flatlands as if they owned the world. So feisty for a mere twist of hot air, they left me both bemused and very respectful, especially after a windstorm neatly removed the office roof. Now I feel a mad and inexplicable vortex growing within me as well, fueled by the growing hope that Everardo might still be alive, and the wild rage stoked white-hot by Retalhuleu and Enríquez. No obstacle exists that could survive the witchcraft exploding through my mind. I will not be stopped.

I have already plotted out my next few steps. I will start by sending a very loud message to the army and also the outside world. They need a clear warning that I will not stand for this, that I am to be reckoned with, that the tornado is coming in their direction. Everardo, I will not let you be torn apart and tossed aside like some rag doll without value. I am not the helpless heroine of some bad movie, to stand by weeping and wringing my hands as you die, bit by bit, in some unnamed cell. I demand the rights of the law for you—a trial, decent treatment, a doctor if you need one. I demand what is due to you as a human being and I am going to take action to get it.

My first stop is with the OAS, for the Inter-American Commission is in town for the week and they want to hear about the new evidence I have discovered. I scramble through my files and gather together the letter from de León Carpio, my photograph of Everardo, the justice of the peace's report, and the autopsy findings. I add the exhumation results to the top of the stack, then outline my legal arguments in black ink on a pad of lined yellow paper, tools of my old trade. I could speak to the panel when I get back to Washington, but I cannot wait. I need them to understand me now, for I may need their help while I am still here in Guatemala. I have already decided on what I will do next.

I am taking on the Politécnica, that accursed gray Bastille out there with its secret torture cells. I am taking it, not with a gun, but with a seven-day hunger strike on their front lawn. Starting tomorrow, I am going to sit out there with your picture, Everardo, and scream to the heavens above that you have a right to a trial and that you are being tortured and that I want something done. I will not be stopped. If anyone even tries, they are going to find themselves scattered in bits and pieces across the Politécnica courtyard. The army is going to have to choose, Everardo, between your life and their own destruction.

I spend the evening at the elegant Princess Hotel, waiting my turn and sipping hot chocolate while I go over my notes. Some people in the hallway recognize me and stop to chat in hushed tones, asking how things are going and if I think I am safe here in Guatemala. They have seen me on the television and are afraid for me and wish me well. I thank them and tell them I am safe enough, and think to myself that they ain't seen nothing yet. Just wait until tomorrow. The army hates exposure and international focus on their human rights record, and tomorrow is The Emperor Has No Clothes Day. Tomorrow starts the scandal of their life. As I daydream, the kindly receptionist calls to tell me it is my turn to testify.

I enter the conference room and sit down before the circle of courteous, bespectacled faces, setting out my notes before me and handing the chairperson my fact summary for distribution. For a moment I am nervous, so desperate to convince them, to make them understand. Then I meet the gentle eyes of one of the women and my confidence comes back with a rush. After all, I am in the right and my demands are well within the law. Guerrilla or not, Everardo has the right to a fair trial. He cannot be tortured or held in a clandestine cell. All I have to do now is give the information to this waiting circle. All I need to do is make myself clear.

I sit up straight and begin to speak, starting out slowly, careful to use my best Spanish, to leave out nothing. This one is for you, Everardo. For the third time this week I tell my story. I remind them of the army's early claims of finding the body out at the combat site, and the official report sent by de León Carpio, which gave a description of the body that matched every feature in Everardo's face. I hold up his photograph and read the description, and they begin to nod intently, a hush falling over the room. Then I retell Santiago's story. I explain how the army denied everything, insisting that Everardo's body had been found and buried and that Santiago was a liar. I pull out the justice of the peace's report and underscore the line saying that the body had no scars or birthmarks; then I describe Everardo's numerous combat scars, the gash on his lip, the thick scar on his arm, the scattered pellet marks on his shoulders, the white circle over his heart, the shrapnel scars across his legs. That justice of the peace never saw Everardo lying dead out there. This report has been falsified. Once again the faces nod, the lips pressed tight in concentration. I pass out copies of the 1992 autopsy report. Here is the true description of the body, I tell them. A man far too young and too short, tied by the ankles, fingerprinted, shot, stabbed, strangled, battered. No suicide, no combat death. Just murder.

They are sitting up straighter now and I continue, telling them about the exhumation, the bodies in the grave, the frail remains of the young man in the olive green uniform, the glint of the metal caps on his teeth. There is a wild clarity in my own mind now and I tell the story as I have never told it before, as if I were telling it for the first time. I bring out all the army's excuses and destroy them one by one. I ask them who was lying and who was telling the truth, Santiago or the army? So far, every word of Santiago's story has been confirmed, and every word of the army's has been proven false. They took Everardo alive, and they have lied and lied again. Help me. Please, help us.

As I finish there is a hush, and I know that I have won. They understand now exactly what has happened. They understand completely. As I leave they pass by me one by one, giving a nod of the head, a crisp shake of the hand. They are professional and cautious and studiously neutral, but I know that I have won at last and that help is on the way.

In a rush of relief I career back to the hotel, where Susan is waiting for me with Anna Gallagher, a feisty Irish-American woman who has done human rights down here for two years now. I have singled her out as a new friend, for I trusted and liked her the first time we met and I know without asking that she understands Guatemala as few other foreigners. Now I need her help and she has come by to listen, no questions asked, making it clear that she is with me all the way. Now for the acid test.

I sit them both down and explain my plan: the Politécnica, tomorrow morning, a seven-day hunger strike. They both shriek in unison, but I continue. The OAS is in town. I have just finished talking to them and they will be here all week, so the army will have to be on its best behavior. Also, the U.S. embassy is just three blocks away and there's already a big fuss going on back home about all this. It's not the moment to be bumping me off, and in any event, I'll be sitting in front of their guard towers. If someone shoots me, they can't exactly say they didn't see what happened, right? They'll practically be forced to protect me. It's safe enough, and I'm betting my life on it.

Anna and Susan shriek again, but these are not shrieks of protest, but rather of resigned support. Their eyes are sparkling wildly and they are stifling hilarious, frightened giggles at the very thought. It is so right and so outrageous that we are drawn toward it inexorably. Soon they are hard at work painting black letters on bright yellow banners on the hotel floor and arranging for international journalists to be there at 8:00 A.M. on the dot, no questions asked. We are going over this waterfall together and there is no turning back.

The Politécnica
September 1993

I CAN'T BELIEVE I AM DOING THIS. THE GRIM WALLS OF THE Politécnica loom above me like some kind of indignant horse rearing back from the antics of a scampering mouse, namely myself. The guards in the towers are hurrying back and forth, submachine guns in hand, leaning from the turrets to see what the hell I am doing and calling reports back inside. Four bright yellow banners surround me, making me the dead center of the show, and also the bull's-eye. We have painted all night long in waterproof black ink, these fierce and less-than-subtle slogans. WHERE IS EVERARDO? HUMAN RIGHTS APPLY TO EVERYONE! PRESENT THE PRISONERS! IS THIS THE NEW HUMAN RIGHTS ARMY OR NOT? In short, Surrender Dorothy! I am simultaneously scared to death and furious and euphoric. Cars shriek to a halt as they pass us, the drivers staring out their windows in disbelief. Sirens howl, circling the block. This is going to be quite a day.

We got off to a rough start this morning, or at least I did. I woke up at dawn with a blast of adrenaline that left me feeling jolted and disoriented, as if I had fallen out of bed. A long, hot shower and some slow stretches helped, but I was still too nervous to eat much, even though I knew I wouldn't be touching food for the next seven days. Jim Schrider, a former Jesuit priest, arrived late last night, no questions asked, and after breakfast he and Susan and I piled our cement blocks, banners, and string into a rickety taxicab. The driver looked dubious when we asked for the Politécnica and downright frightened as we began to drag our things across the median strip to a front-and-center position. He barely waited to pocket his fare, then took off in a screech of old tires, leaving us alone out there. For a moment I thought that Anna and the others had not yet arrived, but as we lined up the cinder blocks, they came running toward us from across the street.

At first nothing seemed to work. We raised the banners, but a roguish wind came up and blew them down again and again. We tied them tighter and Susan slashed airholes between the letters, cutting her hand and dramatically adding bloodstains to her own artwork. Still, over they went again in an ignominious tangle as we performed a Laurel and Hardy act for the patient international journalists. The row of buildings on either side of the street formed a mean wind tunnel, so we finally had to content ourselves with laying the banners flat on the ground and holding them in place with the heavy blocks of cement. I tried to light the thirty-five candles then, one for each of the prisoners named by Santiago. They were hard to light and as soon as I managed to do it, a bus roared by and blew them all out. I tried again, but a truck finished me off. I threw my hands up in the air and told the journalists, good grief, I give up. Why don't I just read my statement. By then they were all laughing good-naturedly, and their smiles steadied my rattled nerves. Then I read my de facto declaration of war and announced my seven-day fast and they looked at me as if I had gone clean out of my mind.

So here I sit, cross-legged in my square of yellow banners, glowering at that accursed building across the street and wondering if Everardo might be inside. In the pit of my stomach is the old sickly fear that if he is still alive I am making it all so much worse for him, that they will torture him more to punish me. I push the thought aside. The beast has swallowed Everardo whole and I must jump down its throat now or lose him forever. This is no time for a ladylike, white-glove approach. I take a long drink of water and try to read a novel.

The buses rush by and the heads of the passengers swivel back and forth as they read my signs. Cars honk. The exhaust fumes are choking me to death. Susan is down the street at the embassy, breaking the news to Consular Services, and so I don't expect her back very soon. Jim sits a prim distance away, as befits an observer, reading a paper and holding his camera at the ready. Whatever happens, I told him, film it. Don't intervene; just live long enough to run and tell what happened. If you intervene, they will have grounds to deport you, and then I will be left all alone—hardly convenient, right?

The sirens have stopped and I look up to see a blue Jeep full of police and rifles jerk to a halt in front of me. I shriek for Jim and he comes closer, video whirring. Four policemen walk swiftly across the grass to me, eyeing the camera uneasily. I rise to greet them but stay put in the middle of the yellow square of banners. We shake hands; so far so good. Of course, it would be touchy to drag me off kicking and screaming in my carefully selected heels and nylons and prim lavender jacket. Caste—it means something here, and I see it reflected in the officers' wary eyes. I would normally reject it as a matter of principle, but today I cling to it like a life preserver.

The biggest of the officials clears his throat. Madam, what is the meaning of this? He holds out his hands in bewilderment, taking in the entire scene and waiting for an explanation. As I look at the incriminating banners all around me and Everardo's photograph in the position of honor, self-doubt attacks. A gnawing voice hisses in the back of my head. Yeah, kid. What *is* the meaning of all this? You'd better make it good.

I take a deep breath and pick up Everardo's picture. This is my husband, I tell them. He's an ORPA *comandante* and the army has him alive and under torture and I can prove it. Now that's just not legal. They can keep him as a prisoner, but they can't abuse him. That's the law. I won't be causing any kind of disturbance here. The officer's eyebrows rise to the top of his head, but I keep on going, feeling argumentative now that I have started. I won't cause any kind of disturbance, but I will go ahead and exercise my right to free expression, just like your constitution allows. I'll be quiet, and I won't break any windows or anything, okay? Here's my passport, why don't you write down the name and number so you can let the other guys know. Wouldn't want for there to be any misunderstanding. If you have any questions, you can check with General Enríquez across the street; he knows all about this. So does the embassy over there, and I just left all the information with OAS, too. They're just down the avenue at the Princess. I hand him my passport and sit down, smiling. Have a nice day, sir. I appreciate your checking on my safety.

The officer stares at me as if he has just seen a flying saucer. He fingers his rifle thoughtfully and decides not to bite this particular bait. He nods to the others and they hike down to the corner telephone booth, where I see him talking and gesticulating vehemently for quite some time. Finally he shrugs and they walk back toward me. Yes, he says, of course Guatemala is a democracy and you have the right to free expression? Despite himself, his voice makes it a question. He will, though, take down my passport number like I have said . . . to avoid any misunderstandings. They will be patrolling the block to be sure of my safety. I thank him profusely. He leaves. For the rest of the week they circle intermittently, staring. I wave. They wave. We understand our roles here.

After the Jeep vanishes down the street, Jim puts down the video and gives me a fatherly bear hug, chuckling loudly. My knees are weak all of a sudden, and I have never been so glad to hang on to anybody. Then I sit back down again, fighting the hunger pangs that are already starting up. Lord, it's only noon. If I'm hungry now, it's going to be one hellish week.

I smooth out the rumpled banners and pick up my book again, only to be overwhelmed by a rush of journalists with flashing cameras and microphones. Good. These guys I need. I need to stay dead center in the public eye for my own sake, and I need for the press to catch on to this story. The press creates public opinion and public opinion makes for votes and votes make for congressional action. Everardo and I both need the press desperately if we are going to stay alive. I talk all afternoon, telling them about the mountains and the letters and the falsified description and Santiago and the Retalhuleu graveyard. The Guatemalans studiously keep a straight face and take down every outrageous word, their eyes sparkling merrily. Every so often, they glance apprehensively across the street, as if expecting a barrage of cannon fire. I answer every question and then I answer them again. I hang on to Everardo's photograph and refuse to put it down. This story is about him, and my picture goes with his or it doesn't go at all. Eerily, in the evening papers, my image will appear pale and blurred in the sharp sunlight, while his stands out like an ink drawing, clear as a bell and larger than life.

By nightfall the Guatemalans have all heard the radio broadcasts and watched the evening news. A group of flight attendants arrives with a pot of black coffee, and a wealthy woman from a tower apartment comes down to offer the key to her home if I would like a hot shower. A car screeches up and a man in a business suit hands me a jug of orange juice. I explain that I cannot drink it and he comes back in five minutes with a gallon of water, which I gratefully accept. A garage mechanic stops by on the way from work and stays for hours. A young man in a T-shirt leans out his car window, his face registering shock; then he falls into his seat, screaming with laughter. After a moment he appears at the window again, wiping tears from his eyes. He thrusts his body halfway out of the car, raising victory signs in the air with both hands. *¡Bueno!* he screams. *¡Bueno!* Good one!

The next day I have a splitting headache and am ravenously hungry, and it is the same the next day and the next. The press is everywhere and a public official lists me as one of the top three destabilizing events in the country. First on the list are the massacre survivors in the central square, in town to protest the bombings of their villages. The army says they are not bombing. The survivors are dumping the shrapnel and bomb fragments they have brought with them as proof in front of the National Palace and are talking to OAS. Nineth and the other human rights leaders have seized the Congress, demanding justice. I read the papers and howl with delight. Down! You vultures are going down!

A bomb goes off at 3:00 A.M. in my lawyers' office, a thank-you note for the exhumation. It's costly to hit the damn gringa, so hit her Guatemalan friends instead. No one in Washington will care. It is a classic army move. Message received, I frantically send a friend to check on them and he finds my lawyers quietly sweeping the broken glass and rubble from the floor. They send back the message that they are okay, no problem, don't worry, just keep it up. I roar my protests to the press.

The embassy sends out a staff member each day to check on my situation. Marilyn MacAfee is in Washington, but she has been fully advised; measures have been taken. Take measures for Everardo, too, I ask. Please help him. They will do what they can; they are looking into it; they are trying. I appear on the front pages now of the local papers and my statements reverberate over the radio and TV throughout the days. One magazine makes me woman of the month. The journalists are terrified, but they are doing their best.

A pile of gifts begins to grow—bottles of water, blankets, and bouquets of flowers. Visitors come at all hours, defiant of the outraged Bastille across the street and the men in dark glasses who hover nearby with walkie-talkies in their hands and odd shapes stuffed beneath their jackets. The visitors come with flowers and hugs and children. They come to tell me of their own dead, the loved ones dragged away, the brothers found beaten to death in the streets. You are speaking for us, they tell me as they hold me close. Keep it up. We are with you. We love you. An old Mayan woman comes by every day at precisely noon, barefoot and wrapped in her woven güipil and ragged falda.* We do not speak each other's language, but she sees Everardo's photograph and she knows full well what I am saying. Each day she comes with tortillas, which I must later pass to the others for their lunch. Each day she strokes my hand. She does not miss a single day.

The air grows electric with official rage as I push the envelope. It's day five now and I am bleary-eyed and weak. Good God, how do people do these fast things, anyway? A doctor comes by and tells me I am dehydrating, that I need to drink far more water. I try, but it is so hard, it feels like I will die of a ruptured bladder or drown if I lie

---

*A güipil is an indigenous woman's traditional woven blouse. A falda is her skirt.

down. I dehydrate more and the fire department arrives in full crimson glory to check my vital signs. Okay already, I'll drink more water.

A bus drives slowly by, filled with students on their way to the university. As they pass me they roll down their windows in unison and raise clenched fists. Bámaca! They chant together all the way down the Reforma. Bámaca! Bámaca! Bámaca! My eyes fill with tears.

A good team has gathered to stay with me in shifts, day and night: Jo, the quiet carpenter from east Texas; Julie, a writer; Lisa, a photographer; and Susan, Raki, and Jim. We grow into a tightly knit family, battling through the days together, hanging on to one another for support. Jo and Julie slowly fall in love. A car drives by with a man hanging from the window screaming, "Down with the army." A soldier swivels his head about, trying to write down the license number.

By day six my mind is like a television set filled with static. I try to read, but my mind skips across the sentences and I have to read every page several times over to understand or begin to remember what it said. Conversations seem like a tremendous amount of work. The press keeps on coming and I pull myself together and shout out my story over and over again. You up there in the towers, you cannot hide this. The truth is coming out. I keep on talking to every journalist, counting each as a weapon in the battle for Everardo. The *San Francisco Chronicle* covers my story, and the *Miami Herald* and the Associated Press and the *Los Angeles Times*. They are starting to listen, Everardo. They are starting to listen.

On day seven, I am hoarse and sunburned and want nothing more than a long night's sleep in a bed with sheets. I want dry clothes and the shade of a roof and some silence. Food? I am no longer hungry, only numb and exhausted. A man drives up and quietly pulls three small children out of his car. He leads them to me and hands me a single rose. My brother was a unionist, he tells me. He died long long ago here in the City with so many others. I will not tell you how he died. My children never knew their uncle, but I want them to sit here now with you so that they will understand what it is all about, what it is that he lived and died for. He takes my hands and pulls his wide-eyed children close and we enter into a silent prayer, broken only by the sound of his hushed weeping.

The press gathers one last time for a final statement on the seventh night. I stagger to my feet and square my shoulders. This case is ordinary, I croak to them. Ordinary. There are two hundred thousand dead and disappeared here. How many more? Torture, kidnapping, secret prisons, murder. Two hundred thousand. How many more can Guatemala stand? No military officer has ever paid for these crimes in any way. If there are no consequences, there will be more deaths. Impunity must end. This is not a question of revenge; it is a question of protection of the next generation. Is the army sincere about human rights? If it is, let the prisoners be turned over to the courts for a fair trial. Turn over Everardo, I shout to the towers. You are being tested and you are failing the test. How many more deaths? In the crowd of nodding journalists, I see Anna blinking back tears.

The next morning my friends hurry me to the airport and bundle me on the next flight out. It is Army Day, time for the machine guns and Doberman pinschers and goose-stepping soldiers with their faces painted black. Time for me to be out of here. We drive right by the Politécnica on the way to the airport. I cannot take my eyes off the iron gates. Is Everardo in there? Does he even know I am looking for him?

You up there in the towers, I will be back. I will be back to fight you, not like a man, but like a woman. You don't stand a chance.

Grassroots, Washington, D.C.
September 1993

I LAND IN WASHINGTON WITH MIXED FEELINGS, EVERARDO, PART euphoria and part fear. We have come so far, and so much has changed. Now everyone knows the truth about your capture and the other unidentified man in the Retalhuleu graveyard. They know about the army's hoax and Santiago's story and they are all paying attention at last. Jose and Pat and Alice meet me at the airport with joyful hugs, congratulations, and messages of support and we laugh and chatter all the way back to the city. Yes it made the press here, and yes it was favorable. Senator so and so called, and congressman so and so. They want to hear from me right away. Yet beneath it all, I am already frightened. Where do I go from here? What should I do first? How do I push things from concern to action? There is so precious little time left, Everardo.

It is clear enough that I am going to be in Washington for a good while yet. The State Department and the White House are here, and the CIA and the Pentagon. OAS is here, and most of the international human rights networks. The United States Congress and Senate are here too, and in the eyes of the Guatemalan army, that means the great pocketbook in the sky. I already understand quite clearly that if I am going to get Everardo out alive, I must somehow reach the people with the purse strings, for the army cares about nothing else. That will mean spending months here in the city, maybe even longer.

I move into a small religious community of church folk who understand Guatemala all too well. Most have been there; others have survived the horrors of El Salvador, Peru, and Bolivia. They quickly welcome me, setting aside a small room with a bed and desk and helping me with my suitcases. I soon grow to love them, with their quiet ways and steady ethics, and before long they become close advisers and confidants.

Next, I roll up my sleeves and get to work on a revised case summary, mailing copies out by the dozen and making the rounds once again to the different human rights offices. The response is quick and very strong now, and a barrage of official protests is fired off to Guatemala City. The army turns a deaf ear and stubbornly insists that Everardo was never taken alive and that this is all a publicity stunt. The OAS commissioners are good as their word and issue stinging protective orders on our behalf, requiring the military to search for Everardo and the other prisoners forthwith and to file a status report within thirty days.

Months of sullen silence pass; then the army replies that there exists no war in Guatemala, only illegal sedition, and that therefore no prisoners of war exist and the OAS orders are unnecessary and inappropriate. Reading the churlish answer, I gloat a bit, happy that the army is showing its true colors. Yet I am also frightened. Are these madmen even capable of change? Is there any hope at all?

I head for the Hill and make the endless rounds from office to office, begging for help. The legislative aides are bright, well informed, and quick to give me advice and support. Another barrage of official letters goes south, and soon I hear that the case will be included in a House and Senate resolution on Guatemala. I am overjoyed, for at last Everardo's case will become one of several that must be resolved in order for U.S. funding to continue. The army will be hearing that I am reaching their purse strings, and I can only hope that the news will keep Everardo alive for just a bit longer. It is good, but it is still not enough.

I spend long hours seeking advice on what to do next and I hear the same thing again and again. I must get the word out to the voters. Congress answers to the voting public, and I must get the public to send a message to Congress. Only then will real action become possible. The advice sends me into a panic, for the task seems so impossible. I can organize places like Texas, where I lived for years and have many friends. But all of the United States? How do I keep the press interested now that I have left the Politécnica? How can I reach Middle America? How can I even pay the rent? The cash from last year's fundraiser is almost gone and there is no time to lose with a part-time job. Even now, I am putting in ten to twelve hours or more, writing and talking and sending out letters until I am too exhausted to move.

I am invited to a nearby church to speak and I accept. I talk for an hour and they give me a standing ovation and pass the hat. Five hundred dollars comes in and I am shocked. They promise to write, and they are true to their word. Within weeks, I get a letter from their senator. More invitations come in and I take to the road, turning no one down who is willing to listen. Local journalists begin to pick up a bit on my story here and there, and Pacifica radio broadcasts my situation from New York to California. Every month, I get down to my last thirty dollars, but every month another check comes in from somewhere. I learn not to worry.

My health holds out, but I am exhausted. Sometimes I speak five times a day, fighting off the despair that comes with remembering, but every speech is for Everardo. I want everyone on his side, our side, that I can possibly reach. There is so little to work with, but it is growing every day.

I stay up late at night, reading through Alice's files at the Human Rights Commission, searching for new ideas, new angles, new tools to use in this battle for Everardo's life. I gradually come upon the files of other Americans maimed or murdered by the Guatemalan army, and I read about the desperate struggles of their families to find out what became of them. I begin to call them, and slowly we band together and form Coalition Missing. I find Trish Ahern, whose younger sister was on the plane with Father William Woods when the army shot them down out of the sky. I find Dianna Ortiz, the young and beautiful nun kidnapped and tortured by members of the military, and Meredith Larsen, a human rights worker who was stabbed after her office was bombed. We begin to grow and gather in new members, and slowly but surely we become fast friends, for we share an all-consuming passion. We will never forget Guatemala or the Guatemalans, and we are determined to bring the repression to an end.

As Christmas draws closer, I fall into a deep depression. It has been two years now since I last saw Everardo, and almost a year since Santiago escaped with his terrible news. There is so little to show for it all—a few letters, some official protests, an army that ignores all warnings. A somber note begins to sound in my mind. Despite all the uproar in Guatemala over the case, there has been no effort to connect quietly with the URNG, to arrange discreetly for some negotiations and deals. Why won't they even try to work things out, to compromise? Are they so sure of themselves that they think nothing at all can ever touch them? Would they rather die than submit to a mere woman? Possibly, I admit to myself. Or is Everardo already dead, leaving nothing to discuss? I shake the thought off, for it cripples me, and there is no time now for an emotional cripple.

The holidays are brutal, for I am repelled by the cold snow and gawking commercials and the painful reminders that seem to be everywhere at once. The sand is sliding through the hourglass so quickly, Everardo. We are running out of time, if there is any left at all for us. I drift through the New Year's celebrations like a pale ghost and night by night I watch an old video of you, back in the mountains, speaking with Emilio. Gaspar found it in their internal training files and sent it to me. There is no sound to the tape, but this makes no difference. It is you there, sitting so straight on a tree stump, rifle across your knees, trying earnestly to find just the right answer to every question asked. Toward the end some joke or crack is made, for you break into that easy smile that makes me want to throw my arms around your shadowy image.

I buy a ticket to Guatemala and leave at once. It's time for another talk with General Enríquez.

Casa Crema
Guatemala, January 1994

HERE WE GO AGAIN, BACK IN GUATEMALA, BACK IN THE SPRING Hotel, and back in the center of the maelstrom. The sound of roaring jet planes and low-flying helicopters awakens me at dawn, reminding me that for better or worse I am home again and that I had best brace myself for battle. Today I will dress severely, preparing for a bizarre sort of power lunch, although what game rules will apply to this morning's meeting, I cannot imagine. At ten I have an appointment for coffee with the minister of defense at his official residence, a walled-off Gothic complex known as the Casa Crema. I will arrive armed with the recent uproar over the exhumation and the Politécnica fast, together with the cloud of anger slowly gathering over Washington, D.C., the army's eternal source of manna. On their side they have Everardo, and of course, rather a lot of guns. It should be an interesting tête-à-tête.

I decide to start with a cold shower, so I stumble down the hotel hallway to the communal baths, nodding to the young Swiss tourists struggling with their packs. It is still early, but we are downtown and squarely located on the main truck and bus route. Already the soft morning air is filling with the screech of brakes and the roar of un-muffled city traffic, complete with backfires, birthday rockets, and the shouts of street vendors, sounds so familiar they no longer make me tense, only tired. In the shower I let the cold water pour over me and I scrub from head to foot until I am completely awake. Then I dry off with a rough towel and comb out my hair, pinning it severely into place with small barrettes. No unruly curls today. By military stan-dards, this meeting had best be man-to-man.

Back in my room, I fidget with my clothes. Thanks to the thrift stores back home, I have a fine supply of tailored jackets and somber-colored dresses, all of which the Guatemalans consider to be terribly dowdy but which make me feel secure. I discard the dresses and select dark trousers, navy flats, pearls, and a fitted summer jacket from D.C.'s finest thrift shop. After a glance in the mirror, I add lipstick and mascara, hoping to mask the lines of exhaustion on my face, or at least to distract attention from them. The end result is severe and disciplined, no trace of vulnerability or flirtation. Dressed for success or dressed to kill, I have come a long way, baby, from my carefree days with the farmworkers. After a few last tugs and pats I am satisfied, and I prepare my notebooks and file folders for battle, tucking them into a small briefcase.

The downstairs patio with its huge green potted ferns is filled with the other hotel guests, busy with their breakfast plates and chattering about scenic routes and local politics. Quiet Alicia, as usual, is han-dling the entire crowd, moving swiftly about, taking orders, cooking food, and washing dishes all at the same time, without ever making the slightest mistake. Small, slim, and middle-aged, she is ever cheery and kind, and gives me an encouraging pat on the shoulder now as she plops down a large mug of coffee and hot milk on my table. She knows what I want without even asking, and pretty soon a small plat-ter of tropical fruit arrives, the sharp, sweet taste giving me instant en-ergy. After I finish eating I linger over more coffee, daydreaming and gathering strength. My arguments and strategy are long since prepared, and now is the time to listen, for a few quiet moments, to the classical music playing deep inside my own mind.

I catch the bus from the noisy street corner a few blocks away, trying not to breathe in the black exhaust that is already filling the air. The bus seats are jammed with businessmen and students and housemaids and mothers with babies and *campesinos* with baskets of fruits and bundles of handwoven cloth the colors of the rainbow. I hold on to a railing and the bus lurches off toward the Avenida de la Reforma, jolting through the traffic and swaying to one side as we pull around the tight corners of narrower streets. We drive through the commercial district first with its street stalls and open-air vegetable markets and then into the embassy district of luxury hotels and glass-walled shops selling imported European perfumes. When we reach the turreted gray walls of the Politécnica with its front lawn lined with cannons, I jerk the buzzer and get off with a number of uniformed men. They start slightly when they see my face, obviously recognizing me; then they quickly turn their heads, pretending they have not seen. Together we await a break in the traffic and dart across the street. They enter the fortresslike building and watch furtively from the entry arch as I walk past them to the Casa Crema next door.

Interesting, the name Casa Crema. Instead of Casa Blanca, or "white house," it means "cream-colored house," and it carries a similar ring of official clout. Supposedly de León Carpio, the former human rights ombudsman, is president now and civilian authority rules in Guatemala; yet as the name of this place discreetly suggests, the army de facto also rules. No surprises here, just a not-so-subtle reminder of what everyone already knows: that there is a brass-knuckled fist inside this velvet glove. I skirt the high walls topped with their spiked ornaments to the black metal side door, check my watch, and bang loudly, demanding entry into the mouth of the dragon. As I knock, an abrupt rush of rage clears my mind. They have taken Everardo and now they will damned well have to deal with me as well. Where he goes, I go. I bang on the door with my fist and fantasize about knocking it down altogether with a small battering ram.

A metal panel slides open from the sentry post and a soldier asks me what I want, peering down at me with a baffled look. I tell him I am Bámaca's wife and that I have come for my appointment with General Enríquez. He nods, still looking baffled, and disappears for a moment. I hear shouts from behind the metal door, and the sounds of heavy boots striding quickly across an inner courtyard. The gate flies open then and an officer greets me, bowing slightly and inviting me inside. I take a deep breath, and step over the threshold and into a small courtyard filled with heavily armed soldiers. As the officer escorts me toward the main building, their heads swivel toward me, brows lifted in both shock and confusion. By their norms, I should be taken prisoner immediately; indeed, I should be long dead. By my rules, they should all be in jail. We are playing an interesting game of chess here, but the rule book comes from Mars and none of us can read it. Instead we all try to pretend that everything is quite normal, business as usual.

The officer leaves me in an ornate sitting room, telling me that the general will be with me shortly. I settle onto the couch and look around, taking in the tasteful arrangement of tropical flowers in bracing colors, the immaculate tiled floor, and the well-polished wooden coffee tables. The large armchairs are upholstered in the same fabric as the sofa, a crisp heavy silk with stripes of cream, salmon, and gold with deep blue edgings. It is a good room, receptive and firmly attractive, yet it is a man's room altogether, no woman's touch even hinted at here. It is a room for military men, strong and large, with a sheer glaze of civilian niceties for the visitors.

As I muse on the surroundings, General Enríquez enters the room with an energetic stride, his boots cutting a quick staccato on the tiles. He is not very tall, but quite burly and fair, with his florid face, blue eyes, and a shock of white hair. No Mayan features here. When he sees me sitting on his sofa, he squints slightly, then bursts into a broad grin and throws out a hand for me to shake, playing the role of good-humored grandpa to my naughty, perhaps even comical, child. We are both remembering my last visit, and the scandal in front of the Politécnica, and he is struggling to find an acceptable tone for this meeting. Not bad, I think to myself, not a bad strategy at all, this grandpa mode.

Behind Enríquez comes another man—very dark, with quite an ugly face looming over a double chin. He, too, is in uniform and heavily armed, but he is not smiling at all and does not step forward. His small eyes are bulging with a sparkling rage and under his smooth brown skin his color is a dangerous purplish shade. He hesitates near the door, clearly wanting to observe me without being observed—or better yet to beat me with his fists. Enríquez frowns, then jerks a thumb toward one of the chairs. The man comes forward and is introduced as Colonel Mérida, the head of G-2, military intelligence. He stiffens slightly as we are introduced, a half bow, then sits down at an angle from us, separate but watching, shifting furiously in his seat.

Enríquez smiles broadly once again and clears his throat, signaling that our conversation will begin. He is warning Mérida with his eyes that they are now on display as good and decent men and to get with the program already. While Mérida squirms and glares, Enríquez speaks, telling me that he respects me very much. He says at first he thought I was merely a tool of the Marxist subversives but that during my fast he changed his mind and decided that I was a sincere and honorable woman, if perhaps a bit misguided. He tells me he even talked to his wife at night about coming on out to see me when I was camped out there, practically on his front lawn. Back then he felt really troubled about my health. He gives me a tolerant and charming smile. Mérida gives an outraged grunt.

A young soldier enters discreetly with a silver tray, watching Enríquez for his cue, then placing fine china cups and saucers in front of us and filling them with good Guatemalan coffee from a silver pot. With my permission, he pours a bit of milk into my cup without spilling a drop, and adds a neat spoonful of sugar, then vanishes with a click of his heels. Enríquez continues his speech, but his honeyed tones begin to harden a bit and he mentions reading my book, which, diplomatically enough, began appearing in bookstores as I sat in front of the Politécnica. After reading it he became greatly disappointed in such an intelligent woman as myself, for there at the end it explains how to donate money to the subversives for such matters as prosthetic limbs and the expenses of the peace talks. So perhaps I am indeed a subversive myself, or else a mere foolish tool. What is he to think of me, after all? What is he to do? He leans toward me now, as if catching me in a trap, watchful as a coiled snake about to strike. Mérida is going quite mad in his chair, gripping the armrests and snapping his lips open and shut without a sound.

I hold the coffee cup and saucer tightly in my hands, feeling the first pricklings of fear. These are Everardo's torturers here, and perhaps his murderers; we are looking one another full in the face. What are they thinking? Will they arrest me now on some trumped-up charge? What exactly did I write? Did I make a mistake in my research? I take a sip of coffee, then remember the last chapter clearly enough, together with a flood of other memories—of Rosario with her dead and tortured child, of the massacres, of the endless unmarked graves in the city cemetery—and suddenly I am angrier by far than that donkey Mérida or that grade-B Santa Claus Enríquez with his fake little bullying smile.

I rudely cut off one of Enríquez's run-on sentences and he sits up with a start. I explain to him that such donations in my country are quite legal and that he and Mérida can just get over it. Furthermore, I am not here to win their high opinion; I am here to discuss the immediate release of Everardo and the other thirty-five prisoners to the courts for a fair and public trial. Proof is proof, so let's get going. As I finish with this outburst, the prickles of fear wash back over me and I notice that the china cup is shaking in my unsteady hand. Then I look up at Enríquez and see that his face is covered with a fine layer of sweat and that he is also nervous. It seems that we are at a bit of a draw here. I plunge in again, promising that if Everardo is tried fairly and placed in a public prison with adequate safeguards, I will quiet down and even publicly recognize the army for reaching a milestone in Guatemalan human rights history. Discreetly but nastily, I am reminding them that despite thirty years of war, all prisoners taken by the army, civilian or combatant, have ended up mutilated and dead. Capture and arrest have always been terminal events.

With my admittedly snide insinuation, Mérida loses all control and pops out of his chair like an evil jack-in-the-box. He keeps his distance but bends from the waist, leaning toward me and growling that the army never had anything to do with Everardo and that it is all a subversive propaganda stunt, and that perhaps Everardo is away on a secret mission somewhere else and forgot to tell me or even ran off with another woman and that my marital problems are certainly not their fault. Enríquez rolls his eyes at this rather indelicate outburst and tries vainly to order Mérida back into his chair with discreet hand signals. It doesn't work. Finally, I tell Mérida I want to give him all of the evidence that I've already given to General Enríquez so that we can converse on the same footing and hopefully make some progress. Mérida likes this idea, pumping for information being his line of work, and he sits back down expectantly, as if waiting to be fed. Enríquez coughs loudly, a light vein in his temple beginning to beat a steady and visible pulse. He doesn't want to hear the facts again. Once was quite enough. I made things perfectly clear in front of the Politécnica.

I plunge in anyway, staring into Mérida's eyes, wanting his complete attention and concentration while I set his trap. Everardo vanished in combat on March 12, 1992, I explain, as if he didn't already know this. When the skirmish ended, Everardo was the only combatant missing. The next day the army announced they had found a body in olive green at the battle site. The URNG asked for a description of the cadaver and received one that matched Everardo's physical characteristics perfectly. Then Santiago escaped and told us he had seen Everardo alive and under torture. I returned to Guatemala and opened the grave and found a young man five centimeters too short, fifteen years too young, and with different dental patterns. Simple enough, no?

As I speak, Mérida finally sees what's coming and begins to look away, trying to feign boredom with my prattle. Enríquez looks as if he is developing a serious headache. I grow angrier and continue in a loud voice. In short, what the army did was capture Everardo alive and torture him for his information. To conceal this fact from the international community, they took another young man to the combat site on the same day and tied him up and beat him to death, reporting that they had "found" the cadaver and sent it to Retalhuleu for burial. All this was done while they were sitting at the peace table with the URNG discussing the issue of human rights. Not very good, I tell Mérida. Not very good.

I pull myself up straight, glowering, a feeling of grim yet almost joyous recklessness washing over me. I like this, telling them to their face, sitting on their sofa, drinking their damned coffee. I like it that they are circling me like hungry sharks but can't quite find an opening to bite and slash at me. Perhaps they will someday, but not today. I can see from their faces that it will not be today. A voice deep inside my mind says to let them eat cake, and I struggle not to say the words aloud. Enríquez looks as if he is choking silently, the pulse at his temple now throbbing so visibly that it looks as if it might burst. He sips at his coffee and gives Mérida a look over the rim of his cup, a controlled and murderous look, almost surgical in its rage.

There is nothing surgical or disciplined about Mérida's reaction. He begins to bark questions and excuses at me, alternately standing and sitting, his face mottled. I am truly a propaganda tool of the subversives and should not let myself be used in this way. I answer that I am not accepting any theories from the URNG. I am using the facts I just gave him. This makes him pause for a moment; then he explains that the army never had Everardo in the first place. They found a body out there at the river and buried it. Now I say it is not him, so what more can they do? What the hell do I want? I pull out the letter signed by de León Carpio, giving Everardo's precise description. If the army never had him in the first place, where did this description come from, and why did they send it instead of the description of the body they actually found? Eh?

Now Mérida grows sly and softens his voice a bit, weasling. Perhaps the guerrillas changed the body in the grave to make the army look bad. These things certainly happen. Perhaps I am being duped. Would I have any proof about all this? Enríquez shakes his head, knowing what is coming. I jerk the autopsy report out of my briefcase. I do have proof, and here it is. I flail the papers in his face. The Retalhuleu forensic doctor did an autopsy on the body when it first arrived from the combat site, before it was ever buried. The description of the person doesn't match Everardo at all, but it does match the body in the grave. It's the same body. More importantly, it was never Everardo.

Mérida is caught off guard and flushes visibly. He did not know I had these papers. He resorts to telling me once again that I should not allow myself to be used as a propaganda tool for the subversives. I tell him to have a chat with Colonel Alpírez and Major Soso Orellana, among others, and find out what they have done with Everardo. When I say these two names, both Enríquez and Mérida start forward in their seats, shooting each other swift glances of caution and alarm. Trying not to smirk, I tell them that we are all chained together at the neck. Everardo is chained to them, I am chained to him, and their pocketbook in D.C. is chained to me. We can all swim to shore together or we can all drown. Can't we find a way to work things out more smoothly?

Enríquez is nodding yes, but Mérida attacks like a maddened bull. He screams that he can prove that I am a subversive myself because the URNG commanders knew how to reach me when Everardo disappeared. They actually called me, knew where to find me, and that is all the proof he needs. How else would they know this? I am a subversive! He has the proof! Enríquez winces and tries to silence him, but Mérida shouts that as head of intelligence, he has the right to answers. I tell him that I will answer him and he sits back down, surprised. I tell him that I gave the URNG my telephone number when Everardo returned to the mountains because we were married and I was worried about him. My parents' telephone number is in the phone book, moreover. It is not a secret number. It is public. With this Mérida sits back in his chair, a bit deflated. For the first time he really looks at me, trying to figure me out, puzzled.

As if on cue we all clear our throats in unison and return to the rather civilized tone that the meeting began with. Enríquez, his grandfatherly smile a bit worse for wear, offers me more coffee and I accept. I take a few decorous sips then put the small cup and saucer down, for more adrenaline I certainly do not need. As it is my hands are shaking, and I tuck them deeply into the cushions of the sofa. I return then to my original suggestion—that perhaps we could work things out in a less confrontational manner. Perhaps things could be arranged more discreetly, less painfully for all parties involved. Enríquez nods his head cordially, murmuring that this would be quite advantageous to everyone and that he has always greatly respected me. He cocks his head to one side and listens sympathetically as I repeat, for the hundredth time, my basic demands: that the prisoners be turned over to the courts at once; that if found guilty of any crime, they be placed in public prisons; that they be free of torture; and that they be given access to family members, physicians, and human rights representatives. In return I will waive my right to prosecute, drop my OAS case, and, in so many words, shut the hell up.

Enríquez and Mérida are having a long conversation with their eyes while I speak. When I finish, Enríquez coughs and tells me that he understands everything I am telling him, that he understands quite well. Then he speaks more slowly, clearly, making careful eye contact. A message is about to be delivered. Cautiously, he explains that they never captured Everardo and have no idea what happened to him. If I know where he is, please tell Grandpa, and he will take me out there himself in a helicopter. I tell him to ask Alpírez, but he ignores me and continues smoothly, saying that perhaps something else happened that we have not thought about. Perhaps Everardo is someplace else and has not been able to reach me. Perhaps he will show up soon in Texas looking for me. With that, my control snaps. I tell him not to be ridiculous, that the facts are the facts; nobody at all is fooled anymore. Enríquez and Mérida shoot each other another look, and this time I can see that it is one of great disappointment, as if a trial balloon had just popped. They look at me, not angrily but sadly now, and I realize that I have missed something, some cue, some hint, something important. But what?

Enríquez repeats quietly that perhaps Everardo will show up in Texas or some other unexpected place soon. I stare at him, frustrated, but he offers no further explanation and the meeting fizzles out. After a few moments he shows me to the gate himself, smiling courteously and placing a friendly hand on my shoulder as his troops gape in amazement at us. As he says good-bye, he starts to say something, then stops himself, and I again sense a missed cue or hint. He watches with an expectant look on his face as I step out into the noisy streets, baffled. What was that fleeting thought that I did not hear or understand? What did I miss?

Anna's House
Guatemala, January 1994

THAT EVENING, I WANDER OVER TO ANNA'S SMALL APARTMENT IN Zona 2, still musing over the silent conversation between Mérida and Enríquez and wondering what unspoken cues have been given. I replay their last few comments and gestures over and over again in my mind, trying to get a grip on the nuances and cursing the fact that Guatemalans rarely speak of delicate matters in a clear or direct fashion. As I walk, my mood turns grumpy and I find myself missing Pat. It will be good for me to talk to Anna, for I trust her good sense and want to hear what she makes of it all. I have missed her, too, since we last saw each other at the Politécnica.

Anna is sweeping the small cement floor in her dining room when I arrive. At the same time she is squabbling with her adopted son, Jairo. Small and sturdy and completely Irish, she has a thick shock of short brown curls and a turned-up nose that gives her both a charming and combative look. She is sweeping with vigor and shouting affectionately, gesturing from time to time with the handle of her broom. Jairo is Guatemalan, but somehow he manages to look just like her, except for his deeper coloring. He is nearly twelve now, and also small, and sturdy, and combative, and he is standing just like she is, with his hands on his hips. His full rosy Mayan lips are pursed in a pout and he is sassing her back. Neither one gives way, but I can see that they are hard put not to break into laughter. I pour myself a cup of coffee from the stove and Jairo stops in midsentence to come over and give me a warm hug. Barefoot and shirtless, he tugs at my hair, utterly lacking in the self-consciousness of American adolescents. I marvel as he scoots out the door with a swiped cookie from the kitchen shelf, his shouts of laughter echoing outside as he finds his friends. He and Anna met long ago, when he was a street child asking for bread.

Anna immediately grins once he is safely out the door, shaking her head and laughing over his high spirits, which of course she greatly enjoys. We gravitate to the kitchen then and start making dinner together—for how many people, no one knows, as Anna's house will inevitably fill up with unannounced guests as the evening wears on. We scrape carrots and chop onions and set a big frying pan on the stove to heat up. A pot of water begins to boil and Anna tosses in a dash of salt and a box of pasta, stirring lightly and asking about the day. I tell her everything as I slice up bits of fruit for dessert, and later we sit down for quick sips of beer. She is amused by most of the story, guffawing aloud and throwing up her hands over my rude imitations of Mérida, telling me that I am very, very bad indeed, and then making far worse comments herself. I describe those last few moments with Enríquez, but she doesn't know what to make of it, either. She tells me to sleep on it, then pours more beer.

Rhett, an American labor rights worker, comes by and sits with us. We talk for a while about the unionists here and the foreign-owned *maquiladora* factories, and then Tina, the Irish journalist with the sharp wit and newborn daughter, arrives for a quick chat. Next comes Jairo with his neighbor, and then Andy, just back from a grueling forensic stint at a mass grave to the north. Soon everyone is chattering and eating and smoking and drinking. Anna puts on music. People break into groups and drift in and out of the house. Gloria and Sebastian come home too, have a bite to eat with us, and go quietly back to their room. Gloria is a tiny Mayan woman with long jet black hair and diagonally set eyes and is now in her ninth month of pregnancy, which leaves her exhausted. I listen to them chattering in Quiché for a while, Sebastian teasing and Gloria giggling. They are so very happy together that I have to struggle not to think about Everardo. It will soon be two years since he was captured. I know there is very little hope that he could still be alive.

Suddenly I feel very tired myself and I slip away to Anna's small sitting room and unfold a mat and blankets. It is long past dark and unsafe for me in the streets, so I will sleep here in this sane house with Anna's feisty, steady voice nearby. Hopefully I will have no dreams. Jairo comes in for a few stolen moments of television, curling up next to me and making me wish he was my own child. His sturdy gold-brown torso reminds me of Everardo despite myself, and I try to fight off the memories by listening to the soap opera with him. Together we make silly jokes about the characters and then, out of nowhere, he asks me about my work, listening very wisely and attentively as I speak. As always, he catches me off guard, shifting so abruptly into his adult persona. His dark eyes focus on my face, locking onto every word as I speak, his two smooth hands gripping my arm, now and then giving a supporting squeeze. From the beginning this street child has been on my side, on Everardo's side, and from the beginning he has understood everything. He asks for Everardo's picture and I let him hold it for a while as he studies the face and thinks about what I have said. Then he stretches and jumps up, a child again, and bounces out of the room to harass Anna a bit more and go on to bed.

I turn out the lights and curl up under the blankets, listening to the reassuring chatter in the dining room and feeling quite safe. The morning's conversation still tugs at the edges of my mind and I review for a few moments the events of the last few months. Where are we in all of this great carnival ride, anyway? We have an eyewitness; we have opened the grave; we have proved that the army took Everardo alive and that they lied about it all. The Inter-American Commission at OAS has entered protective orders on behalf of the prisoners. The U.S. Congress is not amused and, thanks to one senator, a very large packet of money has been quite seriously delayed. This has a domino effect, since many loans and grants from other countries depend on the arrival of the delayed U.S. funds. The heat is on, no doubt about it. And Enríquez wants something, but what? I finally drift off to sleep and dream that Everardo, dressed in his tidy uniform, is holding me gently in his arms, waiting for me to wake up and begin yet another day without him.

The Tower
Guatemala, January 1994

THE NEXT MORNING I DRESS QUICKLY AND HURRY OUT THE DOOR for an early meeting at the Pan American Hotel in the central plaza. I have a distinct love-hate relationship with this place, and I always approach its colonial doorway with mixed feelings of happiness and irritation, feelings shared, of course, by the hotel management with regard to my own controversial self. The interior is quiet and spacious, with a real fountain and sparkling water, beautiful flower arrangements, and the best coffee, fruit, and cinnamon rolls in town. Breakfast here is a delightful way to start the day, slow and delicious. The problem is that the waitresses wear coy Mayan peasant blouses and skirts and the waiters, quite sacrilegiously, are dressed in the clothing of the Cofradía, or Mayan priests. They themselves are charming enough, and often whisper discreet words of encouragement to me, even as the manager scowls his disapproval from the doorway. The rest of the room is filled with well-heeled foreigners and government officials in dark suits and light skins waiting to be attended to by the peons. This microcosm of Guatemala's contradictions never fails to both fascinate and irk me, and yet it always draws me back.

I walk slowly across the square, past the crowds of busy people heading for work in the nearby offices. A small group of demonstrators stands before the National Palace, holding up hand-painted banners and demanding the return of their lands. They are villagers, small and ragged and very thin, their faces stoic, and I stop to watch them for a few moments. It is cold this morning and a light drizzle is already beginning to fall, but they continue to stand there holding their banners, the women barefoot, small children strapped to their backs, the men gaunt. Somehow, despite everything, they continue to hope and to try. Their image moves me and I stand nearby for a few moments, watching and gathering strength from them. The National Palace looms omnipotent above us, ornate yet somehow military-looking with its pale green stone facade. Indeed, the second floor is filled with army offices and well-armed soldiers, and the turreted tower to the right houses the dreaded military intelligence offices. As with the Politécnica, I am reminded of the castle of the Wicked Witch of the West.

While I stand watching the tower, I suddenly remember yesterday's conversation with Enríquez, and everything seems to fall into place. What did he say? That Everardo might come looking for me in Texas ... that something else might have happened that we hadn't considered? These words had angered me yesterday, but suddenly I glimpse the edges of the message, the clue. I offered them a pardon if they would publicly present the prisoners to the courts, an act that would force them to admit they did indeed have secret prisons and torture specialists as a standard part of their official repertoire. They would have to humble themselves, confess, and receive pardon—and later settle for some international applause for their first steps toward reform. Frankly, they would rather die. For the first time I see the critical weakness in my offer. I forgot their pride, and worse yet, I forgot their masculinity. In Guatemala, this is no small error.

I wander into the hotel lobby and wait for my friend, still puzzling. What did they want, then? I sit down at a small table near the fountain and a waitress hurries up with a fresh white tablecloth and heavy polished silverware. I hardly notice, for yesterday's conversation is tugging more and more insistently at the corner of my mind. What did they want instead, then? If they did not want confession and pardon, what did they want? Did they want for Everardo to show up under some other circumstances, no matter how ridiculous, so that the problem would be solved yet no admissions made? Did they want him to "appear" in Texas looking for me, no explanations offered? It would be a preposterous scenario, but very much like the Guatemalan army. When hit by scandal, some pretext must be given to cover up the obvious, no matter how ridiculous the pretext, and no matter whether or not it is ever believed. The Emperor is not naked and that is that. Magic words must be spoken, the army absolved of all guilt, and anyone who wants to question anything aloud will have a tragic car crash or be slashed to death by a mugger. It's a fairly simple model, and usually quite effective.

Could this be what they want? The clues are so weak, far too weak to support my thoughts without anything more to go on. I need more hints, more information, which means I will have to go back and talk to them again. General Enríquez is leaving town on Sunday for a goodwill tour in Washington, ironically enough. Today is Friday, so I won't be able to see him before he leaves. That leaves Mérida, and I cringe at the thought of dealing with him again, especially alone. His office is right back in the square, up in that pale green stone tower I was just looking at. I could have another chat with him to test out my theory, I suppose.

My friend arrives, a quiet and cynical journalist who publishes what he can, and who periodically leaves the country for "health" reasons when he miscalculates. I tell him about the meeting and my new theory and he is intrigued, but shakes his head when I talk about going back to Mérida. I remind him that I have a lot of international attention these days, which is paramount to protection, and also suggest that if I just show up in the tower, I will have the element of surprise on my side. He nods drolly at this last point and notes that this is certainly true, that it will definitely be a surprise, as normally one is dragged into that office rather than appearing unannounced and banging on the door demanding entry. He rolls his dark eyes, making me laugh, but he refuses for a while to give me a smile. Instead he sips at his coffee thoughtfully. When he finishes, he tells me to give a call and let him know; then he tucks his notebooks and morning paper away in his small leather pack. He pats my hand as I leave, gesturing approval, and I suddenly wish he could go with me. Sadly, having coffee with me is dangerous enough, even for a journalist, and I must be content with his kindly friendship. Besides, if I am right, this conversation can take place only in the absence of witnesses.

I comb my hair in the scrubbed ladies' room and walk out the front door, past the ever-disapproving manager and back across the plaza to the stony green National Palace. My stomach lurches slightly as I climb up the wide front staircase and stand in line for the metal detector and security check of my bags. The downstairs reception area is filled with men in uniforms—police uniforms, army uniforms, palace guard uniforms, security agent uniforms, and, of course, the de facto *oreja*—"spy"—uniform of jeans, boots, bulky vest, and dark glasses. Guns are everywhere. The dark glasses always fill me with grim humor, as they are worn, as now, even in the dim and shadowy interiors of hallways and lounges.

The security man inquires discreetly as to which office I will be visiting and I tell him I am going to see Colonel Mérida. His brows knit slightly and he heads for a wall telephone as I march up the second stairwell and down the long tiled floor to the tower entryway, which consists of yet a third stairwell, a bit narrower and quite well guarded. A very young man in a costumelike uniform stops me there and asks for my papers and the purpose of my visit. I tell him I am Bámaca's wife and have come to see Colonel Mérida. He responds with a perplexed and very worried look and picks up his desk phone and calls upstairs. He explains in a low voice that I have arrived and that I am asking for a brief visit. He listens to a response and then nervously signals me to hand him my passport. He spells my name out letter by letter, and there is a long silence as he listens again to the voice from upstairs, nodding his head from time to time and watching me uneasily. As we stand there, I hear heavy boots striding across the hallway above. I watch uniformed military men hurry past me, some in pairs, preoccupied, others with armloads of papers, shooting me startled glances. Civilian government or not, I am clearly in their bastion. Moreover, I am trespassing.

Finally the young man signals me to go ahead upstairs, and I walk past him, up to the next floor and a small, rather bare sitting room. Once again, a uniformed man takes my passport, glancing quickly at the photo and then taking it inside for final approval. I sit on the worn sofa and wait, and after a few moments a man in a dark suit and a woman in a uniform skirt and blouse come out and sit across from me. The woman wears a large artificial smile, tense at the edges, as if we were at a strange party, and the man is simply tense—angry, in fact. He tells me that Mérida is out of town and cannot see me but that they are in charge in his absence and will take my message for him. While he is speaking, the ubiquitous cups of coffee arrive, and we take polite sips as we size each other up.

I am about to speak, but he starts first, clearing his throat loudly. He tells me that he has read my book, especially the last part, and has found it quite shocking and offensive. He also wonders loudly if the book does not violate a number of laws, since it is quite clear that I am a subversive. He is a small, angular man, thin in his cheap suit, and his whining, threatening tone brings back my own anger. I want to dangle him by the ankles out the tower window until he promises to produce Everardo, and I recognize, of course, that he would like to do the same thing, if not worse, to me. I cut him off and tell him I have not come here to discuss the book, which is completely legal in my own country, and that I have every right to marry anyone I choose, and to have my own opinions about the war. In the United States this is a matter of freedom of thought and expression. Isn't it the same here in Guatemala? I am coy—or rather, snide now—for we both know perfectly well that there is no such freedom here and that if I were Guatemalan I would be long since dead. We both also know that this cannot be openly admitted, a situation that forces him to smile weakly and nod in agreement, hating me. The woman gives a charming hostesslike smile and says nothing at all.

I take another sip of coffee and plunge in again, explaining in a more polite voice that I have already discussed my book with General Enríquez, the minister of defense, and have returned today to discuss a different matter, concerning my husband. The officer immediately responds that they do not have Everardo and that he is not a problem of theirs, other than that he is a subversive and needs to be captured and punished. My head begins to ache, for we are getting nowhere here, and I wonder if perhaps this meeting was a bad idea. I start again, pretending I didn't hear. I tell him that I have come to clarify a point made at my previous meeting with General Enríquez and Colonel Mérida, that I want to make sure there have been no unfortunate misunderstandings. I speak very slowly and a bit louder than necessary, trying to use the same tone of voice that they always use when trying to say something important without really saying it. It seems to work, for they both become quiet and lean forward expectantly, the woman looking as if she would like to take notes.

I explain that General Enríquez had mentioned the possibility of Everardo arriving in Texas to look for me, and that yesterday I had simply scoffed at this idea as impossible. However, after thinking it over, I did wish to reassure everyone that if I turned out to be mistaken I would be the first person to come forward and admit my errors. If Everardo did turn out to have grown a bit tired of the war after seventeen years in combat and came looking for me in Texas, then of course I would receive him with open arms, for after all, I loved him as a human being and not just as a combatant. Also, if he showed up alive and unharmed, and I turned out to be wrong about things, I would certainly correct everything publicly, especially in Washington, D.C., with the Congress. I tell them I am clarifying all of this so that they can rest assured that no "propaganda stunt" will continue as long as I get him back alive one way or another. I stop then and wait for their response. This is the test of my theory coming up now, and I hold my breath.

The two officers eye me over their coffee cups, then look swiftly at each other. Once again, the woman gives a charming but silent smile and the man does all the talking. His voice is much quieter now, and professional, though less than friendly. He tells me that he is quite pleased that I have come forward to clarify this matter and that I am quite right to offer to correct my mistakes. I interrupt and tell him that until I find Everardo alive, of course, I will be forced to continue my battle against the army with all my might. What else, after all, can a wife do? He ignores this sideswipe and leans back in his chair, relaxing his military posture. He tells me that he thinks my comments are quite intelligent and that he is glad to see that I am willing, under the proper circumstances, to change my ways, for just look at the terrible and unfair damage I have already done to the military institution.

But he is also pleased to see that I am an honorable woman, rather than a mere tool of the subversion. He looks toward his partner and waves his arm. After all, as they have said to themselves all along, wouldn't it be logical for Bámaca to go looking for me? Wouldn't it be normal for one to want to be with one's family members?

He is speaking in a slow "now hear this" tone of voice, and I have certainly heard him. I tell him I don't know if it is logical or not, but that if it happens I will publicly correct my position and even write a letter to Congress on the matter, thanking the army for their cooperation, and of course send them a courtesy copy. I lean back in my chair now, for I have tossed out my best offer. Will it be accepted? The man leans forward now and lifts the cheap coffeepot, looking directly into my eyes.

"You are a most intelligent young woman," he says in a precise, dead-level voice. "Won't you have another cup of coffee?"

I decline, for I now have what I came looking for. The two of them escort me to the top of the staircase and we shake hands formally, no pretense of any love lost between us. I start down the steps and he calls after me in a cold voice, noting that I am all alone, without the usual escort. The veiled threat is clear enough, and I know that he wants me to turn around, to show him some kind of fear. I almost hesitate in midstep and start to tell him, instinctively, that of course the entire international press corps is waiting for me outside. I don't though, for the threat makes me furious, thrown as it is like a small poison dart at my descending back, and I don't want to give him the satisfaction. I call gaily over my shoulder that I am indeed quite alone, as he points out, and that everything is just fine, thank you. Then I continue down the stairwell without looking back.

As I walk outside the bright sunlight strikes me full in the face, the rains long gone but the demonstrators with their ragged banners still standing stoically in the plaza. Behind them, on a small park bench, sits my journalist friend, pretending to write up his notes while he waits, unasked, for me to return from the tower. He sighs with visible relief when our eyes meet and we walk out of the square together, he with a quirked brow as I recount the events of the morning. We go over and over the strange conversation, and he questions me minutely on the gestures, tones, and manners of the G-2 officers, laughing at some parts, groaning at others. In the end, he shakes his head and tells me that he isn't sure what to make of it all but that it is very, very interesting indeed.

General Enríquez
Guatemala, January 1994

THE U.S. EMBASSY IS YET ANOTHER BUILDING IN GUATEMALA CITY that I do not like. It is indelicately large—far, far larger than anyone else's embassy down here—and embarrassingly expensive. Despite all this it isn't even pretty. Devoid of gardens and colonial charm, it sits like a giant, unimaginative stone box surrounded by security officers and protective gates. The words *Ugly American* are written all over it, in invisible ink perhaps, but everyone gets the message loud and clear. It is the one embassy in the City that no one ever goes to for political asylum, no matter how frightening the crisis. Asylum is never granted in that stone-hearted enclave, so why waste time on the impossible?

After my meeting in the tower, I drop by to touch base with Ambassador Marilyn MacAfee. I want to tell her about my strange visits with the military and gauge her reaction, even though I know it will be guarded. I want to watch her face and hands. Other than the fact that she works for the Department of State, a rather weighty problem to my jaded mind, I still have no concrete reason to distrust her, and I want to build an alliance of sorts. She has the power to help me, if she chooses to use it, and I have no spare bridges to burn. In fact, I have no bridges at all, and Everardo's life depends on my building a few. As I ring her secretary from the downstairs lobby, I remind myself to be wary but positive.

I am quickly ushered past the security post, through the special doors, and into an elevator. Upstairs, the ambassador receives me, as always, in her plush and ornate office with its glass table and Persian artifacts. As always, she is beautifully and expensively turned out, in perfect attire, her dyed blond hair impeccable, her hands weighted down with quality rings and bracelets. She greets me cheerily at the door with a kiss on the cheek, her manner that of a good sport and friend. I have not seen her since before the Politécnica and she laughs out loud at the memory, telling me in a congratulatory tone of voice that I have done something truly special. I ask if there is any news since the exhumation and she tells me no, that she has mentioned the matter several times to the Guatemalan army and that they simply responded that they do not have Everardo and never have. They also say that he must be dead, an intriguing contradiction. If they never had him, how would they know? I want to argue about this, but she cuts me off, telling me she understands my position but after all, what more can she do but keep on asking?

I tell her then about my strange meetings at the Casa Crema and with Mérida's cohorts in the tower and she listens with great interest, asking me what I make of it all. I tell her it seems as if they were sending out feelers on a possible compromise solution that would save face. She nods her head thoughtfully. Then I ask if she would visit General Enríquez on my behalf when he returns from Washington and follow up on the matter, see if anything can be clarified or hammered out. I add that I would have liked to speak with him again myself but that I know he is leaving the country on Sunday. It is already Friday night, far too late for a last-minute rendezvous with the likes of me, and I will not be here when he returns. Again she nods, but she tells her secretary to call over to the Casa Crema and see what can be done, promising to call me at Anna's if a second brief meeting can be arranged. We shake hands then, agreeing that it is an interesting turn of events and worth pursuing, and I hurry back outside to catch the bus to Zona 2. It is growing dark, and though I still travel without an escort, I can no longer trust the evening shadows. Too many people want me dead.

Back at Anna's, I find dinner on the stove and Jairo squabbling with his friend over a soccer game they are watching on the scratchy TV set. The electricity keeps shutting off, and they are frustrated, unsure as to which team is ahead. Anna herself is striding back and forth between the kitchen and tiny Gloria, who looks ready to give birth at any moment. I stir the soup and pour two glasses of wine, then stretch out in the leather sling chair in the empty living room. After a while Anna joins me, kicking off her shoes and sitting next to me on a painted footstool. She tells me about the cases at her office, the people killed in the recent land settlement, the changes in the resistance populations, and the unionist I have known for years who is now forced to leave the country. I close my eyes as déjà vu envelopes me. Nothing ever changes in Guatemala.

We drink the wine and I tell her about the visit to the tower, mimicking the thin officer with the whining voice, letting off steam. We are both cackling with laughter when the telephone rings, and we let Jairo answer, thinking it will be one of his new girlfriends responding to his blossoming charms. As it turns out, it is not a girlfriend at all. It is a staff person from the embassy calling at 8:00 P.M. to inform me that my meeting with General Enríquez has been arranged for tomorrow, Saturday, at ten in the morning at the Casa Crema. With this news, Anna and I stop laughing and sit up straight in our chairs, putting down our wineglasses and becoming deadly serious. She makes me repeat, word for word, the conversation in the tower, shaking her curly head and musing on what it could all mean. Something is happening, no doubt about it, but what? We switch to tea and puzzle for a while; then I go to bed early, trying not to think so much that I cannot sleep.

In the morning I fuss over my clothes again, a surefire sign of nerves, since I normally cannot even remember what I put on unless I look in the mirror. I select the dark silk blouse and black trousers donated by my aunt for the cause, thinking over my choices as if selecting weapons for a duel. Anna dashes about with Jairo but finds time to leave a hot mug of coffee for me outside my door. I drink it down like a war potion and pour myself some more. Someday, I promise myself, I will stop drinking coffee, but not today and probably not even this year. At least, thank God, I do not smoke.

I sail out the door, together with Jairo, the neighbor, Anna, Gloria, and the dog and we all run in different directions, calling good-bye and good luck and don't be late over our shoulders at one another. I take the bus again, jamming in between the schoolchildren off to weekend events and the housewives with babies and shopping bags, and we lurch off toward Zona 10. I am wide awake now and feeling both anxious and aggressive, as if approaching a crucial tennis match, or a court debate. A small bubble of hope is also forming. Whatever Enríquez has to say to me, I will leave with tiny nuggets of new information. How to analyze them, read them, use them—that will be the problem for tonight and tomorrow. For now, I just want the new data, the new readings. I want anything I can get.

We careen down the Avenida de la Reforma, and I jerk the bell as we approach the Politécnica. The bus comes to a halt, and as I descend the small steps, the driver mutters, *Suerte*—"good luck"—under his breath, his eyes meeting mine for just a fraction of a moment. He nods his head slightly, a twitch of a smile on his lips, and I smile back, grateful for this wink of recognition and support. Then I weave through the traffic, back to the black entry gate of the Casa Crema, and bang on the door with my fist.

This time there is no delay; the door pops open as if merely awaiting my knock. A tall young officer escorts me back to the masculine salon with its striped silk furniture, and he dutifully sets out the ritual cups of coffee, smiling as if I was a familiar and frequent guest. Then he bows and leaves, and General Enríquez enters, precisely on cue. He is in full uniform, striding briskly, his head thrown back and his arms slightly open in a welcoming gesture. He looks scrubbed, well slept, vigorous, and pleased to see me. Only his eyes belie the smile. They are narrowed slightly, watching me with great care, just as I am watching him. Already, the pulse at his temple is beginning its visible beat.

He walks up to me and I realize he intends to embrace me slightly. He is warily looking into my eyes to gauge my response. He wants a show of civilized behavior, and he cannot risk a sharp rebuff. Curious to see what he will do, I make no gesture of resistance, and he lightly places both arms about my shoulders, inviting me in a hearty voice to be seated. I choose the edge of the imposing sofa, and he hesitates for a moment, eyeing the cushion next to me, then chooses to pull the large wing chair up close to me instead. He hands me my coffee and we sit facing each other, close up, yet from separate positions.

Mentally we both clear our throats, wondering where to begin. He smiles broadly at me and I decide to make the first move, thanking him for meeting with me on such short notice, given his very busy schedule. He responds in kind, telling me that I am always welcome at the Casa Crema and that he will always be available for me. He has the greatest respect for me, he says warmly, and realizes that I am indeed an honorable woman. Moreover, this case is one of very high priority for the military institution to resolve. Indeed, it is of the highest priority. He pauses for a moment, then mischievously adds his thanks for my kind visit to his colleagues in the G-2 tower the day before. I look up and see a strange expression on his face—one of mixed consternation, slyness, and even reluctant amusement. There is another pause, and he smiles, closing his lips. It is my move now.

I plunge in again, forgetting that my direct manner is considered rude in Guatemala, and making him start slightly. I tell him that I asked for this visit for the same reason that I stopped by the G-2 tower yesterday; I want to avoid any possible misunderstandings. Enríquez relaxes and urges me onward with a gesture of his light-skinned hand, agreeing that misunderstandings are to be avoided at any cost. He has obviously been fully briefed, but he pretends to hang on my words, so for form's sake I continue. I remind him of his statement that perhaps Everardo would show up in Texas, trying to find me, and I admit that I was too hasty in rejecting this idea. If Everardo really did grow tired of the war and show up in Texas then I would certainly publicly admit that my claims against the army were wrong. I don't want anyone to think that I will keep attacking the army once the matter is properly resolved. I just want Everardo back. Nothing more, but nothing less. I begin to feel like a broken record.

Enríquez smiles broadly now and leans back in his chair. His voice comes out in a purr. Yes, yes, he has always recognized that I am a most honorable woman. Given this respect, he has been thinking a great deal about the entire matter. Perhaps Everardo will show up in Texas, but then again, perhaps he was wounded and simply got disconnected from his troops. Maybe he got a bit lost and disoriented and has been hiding out somewhere in the forest. Perhaps he is on a secret mission and just forgot to let me know. Whatever, the Guatemalan army, in order to clear its name, and also to help me out, can resolve this problem. In fact he, General Enríquez, has already given all of his intelligence networks a direct order to sweep the entire region and find that *subversivo* Everardo one way or the other. He reaches for his cup of coffee. My move.

My mind races after the new clues he has just scattered about. Perhaps Everardo is lost in the jungle, off on a mission, looking for me in Texas. All three silly scenarios have him alive, with the army looking for him. The military will gallantly rescue the damsel in distress instead of confessing to kidnapping, torture, secret prisons, and international fraud. Is this what they want? Am I reading him right? I tell him that if they find Everardo alive, I will write to Congress and tell them the matter has been resolved and that I am most grateful to the army for its assistance. The words stick in my throat, but I manage a crimped smile of sorts. Enríquez sits up and looks straight into my eyes, holding them for a moment. Then he fills my cup and leans forward.

You are a most intelligent young woman, he tells me in slow, clear Spanish, still looking into my eyes. Won't you have another cup of coffee? His tone is somewhat hoarse but has a bit of a wink in it, confirming that he knows that I know that he knows exactly what it is that we are talking about. His face is wreathed in a grandfatherly smile. Same traffic signals as yesterday in the tower, I note to myself, thinking back. His eyes are the color of shadows. I add that if Everardo is found alive, I will not object if he is legally detained as a prisoner of war, so long as he is humanely treated.

Enríquez continues to smile and nod, and I see him mentally jotting down this extra comment. He waits a moment or two to draw my full attention, then adds that he has been thinking it over very carefully. Who knows where they will find Everardo? Perhaps on his way to Texas? Or with the Zapatistas in Mexico? I cut in rudely and tell him Everardo has enough to fight for in Guatemala without running off to fight the Mexican government. I feel a jolt of anger. Nice try,

Enríquez, I think to myself. If you "find" Everardo fighting with the Zapatistas, this will cause problems for the URNG members living in Mexico. The army would like nothing better than to see them expelled. My anger grows as I examine this foul ball. I repeat icily that there is no way Everardo is in Mexico. He would never have left his own people. He is Mayan, and his ancestors were here long before ours were, I say, taking a jab at Enríquez's white skin and pale eyes. He looks quite unruffled, for I have forgotten that descent from the conquistadors is a matter of pride here. It is Mayan blood that is considered a taint, to be hidden at all costs. Hence the outrage over my shameless miscegenation.

Enríquez shrugs and pauses for a moment, then begins the game of cat and mouse again. Perhaps they will find Everardo with the CPRs, the resistance populations. These are the massacre survivors who long ago fled deep into the jungles to escape the army, which has been bombing them ever since. Human rights organizations are loudly protesting these attacks on civilian villages. The army has coolly responded that the men, women, and children out there are not really civilians at all, but *subversivos*, in fact. "Finding" Everardo with these people would thus be quite convenient. Enríquez is no longer smiling. He is watching me closely with those changeling eyes of his. I remind him that the CPRs are far to the north of where Everardo vanished, and in EGP territory instead of ORPA turf. Finding him there would not be credible, I point out bluntly. This time I pour the coffee and shove his cup toward him.

He says nothing, so I take the lead. Perhaps he was wounded and could not make it back to his troops, as Enríquez himself had suggested. I will not rule this out, I tell him. It is possible. Perhaps Everardo is simply hiding out in his home turf in the southwest. He would certainly know how to survive out there. If the army finds him, I will be very grateful. I cross my ankles and try for a demure smile. Let's get back on the track, I think to myself.

Enríquez looks a bit sullen but nods at me. Perhaps Everardo is indeed out there somewhere in the southwest. They will certainly do everything within their power to find him. He has already ordered the search. I repeat my gratitude, then remind him that of course I will continue to fight the army with all my strength until Everardo does turn up and I am proven wrong in my accusations. Enríquez looks yet more sullen. Finally we both nod and reach for our coffee cups, and for a moment there is an impulse to toast each other and our agreement. Instead we take a sip and stare, sizing each other up in this final round.

Enríquez wreaths his face in grandfatherly smiles once again. He looks forward, he says, to seeing this matter happily resolved. Indeed, when this long war is over, it will be very nice to travel to Texas someday. Perhaps he will stop by and visit Everardo and me there, have a drink with us and remember these hard days. He looks at me bemusedly for a bit. Love conquers all, he murmurs. She loves him even though he's a subversive, a villager, homely. . . . He does not mean this comment unkindly, but the racism outrages me nonetheless. I protest sharply that Everardo is a beautiful man. Enríquez looks at me and shakes his head. That's love, he murmurs, clearly baffled. That's love. Then he refocuses and says that perhaps, someday, he will attend our child's baptism up there in Texas. Over my dead body or yours, I wonder to myself.

His smile is quizzical now and we both rise to our feet, as the meeting has clearly drawn to an end. We have exchanged messages. Now it is time to think it over.

A few moments later, I am out in the sunlight again and strolling down the wide avenue toward Anna's home. My heart is in tumult. We certainly understood each other. I must think and rethink everything that was said, look at it from every possible angle, and turn it inside out. But it is the first signal, the first point of light, that maybe, just maybe, Everardo is still alive. Even this frail thread of hope makes me want to throw myself on my knees and weep for joy. Could he be alive?

When I reach Anna's house, it is filled with internationalists. They are sitting hunched about the table over morning coffee, talking about the latest news and planning an upcoming party. They break off their easy chatter as soon as I come in and they listen carefully to my description of the morning meeting. There is a deep quiet when I finish and they shake their heads and stare at one another. No one has ever come back alive before—no one. But could this be the first time? Could it be? We are all afraid to hope, yet the signals are far too clear to ignore. Perhaps, despite all odds, Everardo really is still alive. The thought leaves us awed and almost frightened.

That night as I pack for Washington, Gloria goes into labor. Before I leave for the airport, I am able to hold, for a few precious moments, this new Mayan child in my arms. He is deliciously beautiful, with silken black hair and diagonally set long-lashed eyes. I think about him on the bumpy ride home and wonder where that frail, tenuous new life will lead him.

Washington Again
USA, Spring 1994

YOU TAUGHT ME NOT TO HARBOR HOPES FOR THE FUTURE, EVERardo. You told me this would only leave me with a broken heart, and that it is best to live day to day, thankful for the small gifts that life might bring us. Never look to the future, for like the past, it will be bleak indeed. As always, you were quite right, Everardo. Yet now I cannot help myself, for hope is growing like a bright and tiny flame deep within me. At last we have a signal of some sort from General Enríquez. Exactly what it means, I am not sure, but it is far better than the grim silence of last year. It is the first faltering step toward dialogue and communications, the first pinpoint of light suggesting that maybe, just maybe, you are still alive.

I wake up each day in Washington in my own familiar bed, glad to be home again but also tense and frightened. The old fears as to what to do next, where to go, how to make this all work before they kill you are with me constantly. I have perhaps been given a second and merciful chance to save your life, our joint life, and this time I must not fail. I would not survive losing you twice. And so I work as if possessed by demons and suddenly my body seems to need nothing more than space at a spare desk and access to a telephone. Food and sleep become relatively optional, although every so often I crash and devour a box of chocolates or sleep for ten hours straight to make up for lost time. Otherwise, my dreams are haunted. Everardo, I will sleep when this is over and you are safe.

Enríquez arrives in town just a few days after I do, and I prepare for war. We are on my turf now, and I will not let him come here and sweet-talk his way to the money. I ransack my circle of friends and find out what his itinerary is going to be, then reach Capitol Hill just a skip and a jump ahead of him. I bring my updated files with me and go door-to-door to each and every office he plans to visit. I talk with the legislative aides, explain the case, and beg them for help. They are kind and concerned and immediately promise to raise the matter with the general and to insist on genuine action.

The aides are good to their word. By the time Enríquez arrives, he is taken to task again and again over the case everywhere he goes. He is unprepared for this buffeting and tries several different approaches, but none of them work very well. He blithely says he will see to the matter right away, and he is reminded that his cash flow depends on setting the human rights situation straight in Guatemala, including this case. They berate him for flouting the OAS protective orders. They wave aside his attempts to claim that the *compañeros* switched the body in the grave. Frustrated, he tells one aide that perhaps I am a tool of the subversive forces and that this is all a propaganda stunt. He is told in no uncertain terms not to lie to the United States Congress. The Guatemalan ambassador is horrified, the State Department escort is flustered, and I crow with glee when I hear the story. Give Everardo back, you donkeys, or I am going to shoot your pocketbook.

At the end of the week Enríquez appears at a reception for the human rights community that is held at the elegant official mansion of the ambassador. I wangle an invitation and arrive at the ornate front door with Pat and a crowd of friends from Amnesty International, the Human Rights Watch, and the Kennedy Center. I find the general himself in the crowded reception room, quite spit and polish in his medal-draped uniform, and surrounded by Guatemalan and U.S. military men murmuring last-minute words of advice into his ear. Our eyes meet from across the oak-paneled room and he looks both worried and resigned as he watches me approach. From the expression on his face he has been expecting me, and I notice that his neck and jowls are a bit more florid than usual. As he holds out his hand and forces a tense smile, I realize that he is slightly drunk as well. It is not noon yet, but he has evidently prepared for the worst by arming himself with a few martinis.

The morning is a bit surreal, for I pursue him about the room as he chats heartily with the guests, assuring them that he is very concerned about human rights, and that better days are coming. De León Carpio, a former human rights ombudsman, is now president of Guatemala, and so all will be well. Also, the peace talks will take care of everything. He is very grateful to everyone for their good advice and constructive criticism of past errors. They were quite right about many things, but that is all over with now. As he talks, he watches me uneasily, dodging around the hors d'oeuvres table, and announcing from time to time in a defensive voice that he has the greatest respect for me.

My friends soon fire off questions about Everardo and the army's continuing practice of holding secret prisoners of war. He sighs and repeats again and again that the military considers the Bámaca case to be of the highest priority. He assures them that he has no idea where Bámaca might be, but that he has ordered his intelligence units to sweep ORPA territory and find him. From across the room I see Pat's eyebrows rise swiftly, for I have told her about my long conversations in Guatemala. Neither one of us expected him to repeat himself here. Enríquez continues heatedly, saying that the only people gaining anything from Everardo's continued disappearance are those Marxist *subversivos* from the URNG. He, for one, certainly hopes the case will soon be resolved. More questions pour in and he becomes annoyed and says that if I would only tell him where I think my husband is, he would gladly fly me there in person in his own official helicopter. Too late he realizes his blunder, then deals glumly with the outraged protests. He moves on to another part of the room, hoping in vain for a better reception. I dog his every step.

After an hour or so he gives a gracious closing speech, repeating in a voice flat with irritation that he has the greatest respect for me and is certainly taking my case very seriously indeed, as is all of the army leadership. Of course, the army never had Bámaca as a prisoner, he repeats, but he has already ordered a very intensive search for him, and hopefully the case will be solved soon. He himself looks forward to the end of the war, when he can go to Texas to have a drink with Jennifer and Everardo and remember the old days. With that he clicks his heels and beats a hasty retreat. I start to follow, but his two military escorts hurry to block me, holding out copies of my book and clamoring sweetly for autographs.

My friends surround me now, outraged and curious and pouring out questions. "What the hell was that all about?" "Damned interesting, I've got to admit." "Congratulations, it looks like some kind of breakthrough is coming." "I thought he was making fun of you, or was something else going on?" Deb Hauger, a legislative aide from the Hill, presses forward to take my hand, her eyes sparkling. Enríquez just told her that he didn't know if Bámaca was still alive or not but thought he might be. Very significant, she tells me. Very significant. At this, I run to catch Enríquez at the door. I find him there alone, wearily buttoning his heavy overcoat. He turns as I approach and lays a hand on my shoulder, the grandfatherly look stripped from his tired face. "Now what?" I ask him bluntly. He will be in touch, he answers in a crisp, businesslike tone. He will be in touch soon through the embassy. As he vanishes into the snowy driveway, I struggle once more against the tide of hope that sweeps through me.

And so there it is again, Everardo, that feeler, the exploratory antenna I have been waiting for. But is it real? Enríquez clearly wants me to think you are alive. But are you? What other motives could he have up his sleeve? I can think of none though night after night I stay awake, turning the matter over and over in my mind, trying to look at it from every possible angle. Enríquez knows me well enough, and he knows that I will fight to the death if there is any chance at all of saving you. That's precisely why, until this, he has always insisted that you are dead. And now? Why is he building up my hopes?

I stay on in Washington for a few more days, then fly to Geneva, Switzerland, for the annual meeting of the UN's Human Rights Commission. I have been warned repeatedly not to expect too much, but I wish to leave no stone unturned. I give my brief presentation, ignoring the glares of the plainclothes Guatemalan agents, who manage to appear even here to keep an eye on things. Day by day I meet with the delegates from different nations, Sweden and Argentina and Spain and South Africa. I explain the case, give them my materials, and ask them to do something, to have Guatemala placed on the list of most serious human rights violators, a position it most richly deserves. The delegates are kindly enough and they sign my petition, but they explain to me again and again that the nation I must deal with is the United States, since Guatemala is under U.S. protection. For that reason, Cuba is going to be bashed and Guatemala is not, despite the fact that Cuba has ludicrously fewer violations.

This enrages me, and I meet with a young U.S. team member with cold blue eyes and steel-rimmed glasses. He explains that U.S. policy has already been set. I squawk and demand to see the boss, Geraldine Ferraro, knowing full well that a woman will always treat me better if it is at all possible. She hears me out and is sympathetic and at least takes the step of talking the case over in private with the Guatemalan team. Yet officially, it is just as the others warned me. Cuba is bashed; Guatemala is not. World politics first, human rights last.

Help comes unexpectedly from Monica Pinto, the UN special expert on Guatemala. A smart and tough redhead from Argentina, she is not afraid of the army in the least little bit. She issues a scathing report from the podium and includes the Bámaca case by name. I am moved to tears, the audience applauds wildly, and the Guatemalan civilian delegation, which inexplicably includes an army colonel, is shocked into silence.

Satisfied, I return to the United States and once again take up my speaking tours, crisscrossing the country and organizing telephone campaigns and petition drives. There is already a formidable network in place and I realize with some pleasure that the Guatemalan embassy must be taking quite a pounding and that the U.S. Congress must certainly be getting the message. I am also intrigued to see that the people who come to hear me speak are not just the usual suspects from the solidarity networks. Instead, they are housewives and young students, musicians and carpenters, and people from all walks of life. They share little more than a strong sense of decency and a willingness to speak out against injustice. Watching them, I realize that a genuine grassroots movement is beginning to grow and that people are angry about Guatemala. Perhaps, after all, this is not so impossible.

By late March, the URNG and the Guatemalan government sign a human rights accord as part of the ongoing negotiations. As a matter of law, it goes into effect immediately and all human rights violations are supposedly going to halt at once. I ask loudly if this means that Everardo and the other prisoners will soon be released, but my question is ignored. In Washington, there is a flurry of hope that the remaining issues on the agenda will soon be signed and that peace will come to Guatemala at last.

All too soon these hopes are shattered. Within weeks I have a staggering pile of grim clippings. The president of the Constitutional Court is shot to death in front of his wife and child as they return home from church. A congressman is shot and seriously wounded. Three Mayan members of the CUC civil rights group are shot to death as they gather wood. The CUC had been working to end the civil patrols in the area. A grenade is tossed into a private home; a journalist is shot four times; the archbishop deplores death threats against his human rights workers. In the Petén jungles of the northeast, thirty soldiers shoot a peasant to death in front of other townspeople and then threaten to massacre the entire village. A congressman's brother is found dead and there are serious signs of torture. Ninety-five percent of his body was burned. Unidentified men pour a flammable liquid on an eleven-year-old street child and set him afire. A couple and their baby are machine-gunned in their pickup truck, but the thousand dollars in their vehicle is not stolen. The bodies of three people tortured and shot to death are found in the Petén. A man is found dead in the Quiché with his hands tied, his body showing signs of torture. Eight unidentified bodies are found throughout the country within a week, all of them showing signs of torture. The victims include a pregnant woman whose face had been disfigured.*

I shake my head and fight back the fear. This is not working at all. The army thinks that all they have to do is sign a piece of paper and call it peace. Money will roll in from all over the world, their problems will be solved, and they can continue business as usual. There may be a few protests here and there over a bit of mess, but their funding will be safe and sound.

After all, the outside world has got to give peace a chance, doesn't it?

Unfortunately the State Department seems to be all too much in agreement with this. Its members are everywhere on Capitol Hill, telling Congress that peace is coming, that the civilian institutions are flourishing nicely, that more police are needed to fight common crime, and that NAFTA, the proposed new free trade pact for the entire region, is a great idea.

I go to visit Richard Nuccio at the State Department, for he is acting as the U.S. liaison in the peace talks now and is on reasonably good terms with Gaspar Ilom. I tell him of my concerns and ask him if he will negotiate for me with the army in a discreet fashion. If someone official, someone with some clout, could talk the matter over with them, promising confidentiality, then perhaps something could be worked out along the lines I have been developing with Enríquez. I beg him to try—to get the ball rolling for me at least. For a long time he ignores me, commenting blandly that soon the peace agreement will be signed and all will be well. I point out that a human rights agreement has just been signed and that the army killings are worse than ever. What good is a peace agreement if we are going to treat it as a meaningless piece of paper? Furthermore, Everardo will not live a day past the final agreement. Something has to be done now. Finally Gaspar intercedes for me and Nuccio promises to raise the matter. Later Nuccio tells me that he did indeed bring it up once and that the army was quite offended. He has now fulfilled his

*Guatemala Human Rights Commission/Washington *Update*, April–May 1995.

promise to Gaspar and he is not going to do anything else. Message received. I am in the way. The United States has business plans.

I meet with the others at the State Department too, anyone who will agree to see me. We have the same vapid and evasive conversations. The peace talks will fix it all. Guatemala is coming along very nicely. They are very concerned, of course, about my husband, but they have repeatedly mentioned it to the army, and the army says they don't have Everardo and never did. What more can be done? They have tried everything. I try to discuss various sanctions but they brush me off. Military aid was cut a few years ago and it didn't do any good. Besides, civilian institutions like the courts are coming along very nicely. There are marvelous changes in Guatemala. Watching them speak in their charming manner, with their charming smiles, I wonder for the hundredth time why it is that the embassy must always insist that the realities of Guatemala do not exist. Why do they always cover for these murderers? Why?

I return to Congress, where the House and Senate resolutions, with Everardo's name smack in the middle, are slowly but surely gathering signatures. I am convinced that this will help us more than anything else since the army's money is involved, and I go back to pacing up and down the hallways, talking with anyone who will listen. It has now been months since I last spoke with Enríquez and now the old fears are building in my mind again, driving me from bed early and propelling me from office to office until the last aide leaves for home.

Then the last straw breaks my back. I receive a copy of a letter sent by U.S. Ambassador Marilyn MacAfee to Representative Connie Morella. It is slightly over a page and requests certain modifications be made to the House resolution on Guatemala. I skim through the recommendations and stop dead at the line that asks for my case to be removed altogether. There is no request to remove the other human rights cases. Only ours, Everardo, only ours.

I want to scream aloud. MacAfee! You promised you would treat this case the same as all the others! You promised you would help! Why is it that when I have finally managed to buffer Everardo with a tiny bit of protection, you wish to take even this away? Do you want him dead? Why? You don't even know him. Why are you trying to keep me from saving his life?

Shutdown
Guatemala, June 1994

PAT AND I ARRIVE IN GUATEMALA TOGETHER AND HEAD FOR HOME sweet home, the Spring Hotel. As usual we are well matched, both of us mad as hell at Marilyn MacAfee and also very worried about the long silence from General Enríquez. What on earth is going on? We unpack our things and hang them up in the tiny closet, trying not to think about it.

Guatemala is tense indeed with the new rise of political killings. The army is in a panic at the thought of the UN team's imminent arrival to monitor human rights abuses. The team members will be traveling about the countryside to interview the victims and witnesses directly—quite a frightening thought. Overnight an antiforeigner campaign begins, and the old rumor that outsiders are stealing babies to sell for their organs is spreading like wildfire among the villagers. Graffiti suddenly covers the walls and army liaisons are spotted painting the graffiti. An American writer named June Weinstock is mobbed in a small town and accused of carrying baby organs in her backpack. She relinquishes the pack and nothing is found, but the mob goes wild anyway and beats her into a coma, finally leaving her for dead. A local official calls the nearby army base repeatedly to beg for help, but the military officer there denies assistance on the grounds that they should not intervene in civilian affairs, an excuse that provokes grim guffaws from the internationalists. The attack has been filmed and numerous army liaisons are identified in the crowd—both participating in the attack and urging it on. They are not picked up or questioned, though a number of unionists are arrested and beaten badly.

The U.S. embassy staffers insist there is no real evidence of army involvement and that this is merely a problem of cultural violence, a heart-of-darkness belief in witchcraft. When it is loudly protested that the villagers are quite nonviolent and that this wave of attacks happened overnight, the officials simply wave their hands and change the subject. All the same, a sharp tourist advisory is issued, and tourism comes to a near halt. The upper-class owners of the hotels and restaurants lose money and evidently have a few words with their military friends. The attacks stop overnight. Local officials go on television to convince the foreigners to please return, claiming that Guatemala is a kind and gentle culture after all.

Pat and I look at each other and shake our heads as our friends bring us up to date. Guatemala, I think to myself. It's good to be home, but I had better hang on to my hat.

Our first stop is the United States embassy, and I thank my lucky stars that Pat is with me. I want a witness and I want one who knows what is going on down here. I have long since come to utterly trust Pat's sound judgment and quiet discretion. Together we catch the bus and make the now-familiar journey to Zona 10 and through the embassy's various security checkpoints. We find Marilyn MacAfee upstairs in her elegant office. As always she is sumptuously dressed, now in a flowing skirt and blouse of raw silk, complete with a flowered scarf and heavy jewelry. She attempts the same cheery, good-sport manner as before, but even as she walks across the room to greet us, I sense that something is different, something is wrong. Today her manner is affected instead of natural, her eyes blinking a bit too much, her face pasty white and strained beneath her perfect makeup.

I begin by asking her once again what she has been able to learn about Everardo. As always, I receive the party line. They really don't know what has become of him, they have mentioned it repeatedly to the army, and the army insists that they don't have him. What more could they possibly do? The same wording, over and over again, from every official working on the case. I find it Orwellian and it frightens me. I ask what they have done other than merely to mention the matter, pointing out for the hundredth time that this is hardly likely to save his life, or the lives of any of the others. MacAfee seems to crumple at this and then becomes suddenly angry. Now Jennifer, she snaps in a scolding tone. Why do you insist on these matters? There is no evidence that any of these prisoners even exist. I remind her of Santiago's testimony, but she shakes her head with scorn. Santiago . . . well, who knows about his story? The words, *After all, he is a guerrilla,* hang unspoken yet painfully clear in the air.

I sit bolt upright, shocked, and ask if she thinks that any evidence exists that Everardo was taken alive. She blinks rapidly then turns her eyes from mine, looking downcast. There is a long pause before her reluctant answer. Yes, you have compelling evidence on that one. I ask why Santiago would risk his life telling the truth about Everardo and then invent thirty-five other prisoners? Moreover, everything he has told us so far has turned out to be the truth. Marilyn looks up, her face masked but clearly unhappy. Who knows? she says. Who knows? In any event, there is no reason at all to think that Everardo could still be alive. Terrible things happen in Guatemala; we must accept this.

Her words stop me cold. What is happening here? What has changed? I feel a fine sweat of fear breaking out at my temples. I ask MacAfee point-blank if there is more information, if anything is being withheld, if she knows that he is dead. She shakes her head no, then tells me again that one must be realistic. I remind her that for army intelligence, Everardo is the goose that laid the golden egg. He is a founder and a commander with seventeen years of experience in the mountains, and there is nothing he does not know. He knows every trail, every safe house, every code, every strategy. That is why Colonel Alpírez had a doctor standing by during the torture session in San Marcos. They wanted to be sure he survived. I also remind her of my conversations with Enríquez last January. Why on earth would he make such comments, even in public in Washington, D.C., if Everardo was already dead?

Once again, MacAfee tosses her head and purses her lips in a disparaging twist. Oh, now, perhaps those meetings didn't happen as you think. Colonel Keller was at the D.C. reception and he says you are putting words in the general's mouth. She looks at me point-blank and says , rather condescendingly, that as a woman she can understand how I might need to believe certain things but that I must be realistic.

I stare back at her and her eyes, glassy and almost tearful, dart in another direction. Her face is wreathed in disdain, but beneath this there is a strange blend of pain and discomfort. I receive her message loud and clear though. Now the official story is that I have gone daft from the tragedy and am hearing things. This comes as no surprise, for it is a standard embassy approach to problems. They say the same about Sister Dianna Ortiz and everyone else with inconvenient information about Guatemala. But why? I press her again for information about Everardo, but she shakes her head as if I were a tiresome child.

I change approaches then and ask why she tried to have Representative Connie Morella remove my case from the congressional resolution. She is shocked by this question and I sense an uneasy shifting in the staffers' chairs around us. Bull's-eye, I think grimly to myself. She sputters that perhaps such congressional measures are inappropriate at this time. I point out that she asked for only my case to be removed, none of the others. Why? She has always promised to treat my case the same as all the rest. I watch her carefully as I speak and notice that she is flushed and unsteady now, her eyes darting about. This woman does poorly indeed without a script. After a long pause, she replies rather lamely that she will have to review her files.

Downstairs, Pat and I break into furious chatter, comparing notes and swapping outraged comments on MacAfee's words and strange demeanor. We are particularly angry about her insinuation that Enríquez never really made any of his strange comments. After all, back in January, she found these interesting enough to make a Saturday-morning appointment for me with Enríquez on twenty-four hours' notice. Why the change? What has happened?

We head for Colonel Keller's office, determined to get to the bottom of all of this. He answers our knock and ushers us in cordially, offering us two straight-backed chairs. He is a small, trim man, matter-of-fact in style, and his office is neat as a pin. No nonsense here, I think to myself with relief. We exchange civilities for a few moments; then I ask to compare notes on the reception for Enríquez back in Washington. Keller nods crisply. Glad to help if he can. Fire away. I give him a rundown on the general's comments as I remember them: that he had the highest respect for me, that the case was of great priority for the army to resolve, that they did not have Everardo but that he had ordered an intensive sweep of the region to find him, and that he hoped someday to have a drink with us both in Texas. Keller nods. That's what the man said. Pat and I exchange glances. Goal. The ambassador is lying.

As we speak, the door flies open and Marilyn MacAfee hurries in, uninvited and flustered. Keller hurries to pull out a chair for her and she plops herself down, waiting to be filled in. Keller's face is serene, and he clearly has not a clue as to what is going on. I repeat my recollection of Enríquez's comments and turn to Keller, who again nods and confirms that we agree on what was said, his manner straightforward. Pat is poised on the edge of her seat, her eyes flashing an anger that matches my own. MacAfee's face is blank now, and she begins to mumble that perhaps I have mistaken Enríquez's meaning, that even though he said such things, I may be misinterpreting them. I remind her that she was not there with me in the Casa Crema during either meeting. She is a bit slumped in her chair now, and there is little more to say. As we rise to leave, I once again want to scream at her, shake her by the shoulders. Why? Why are you blocking me? Why?

Over dinner, Pat and I compare notes and boil over. We are both furious with MacAfee and we are both frightened. We think about the darting eyes, the glint of tears, the poorly concealed fabrications. What is happening? Does she know that Everardo is dead? Why won't she tell us? The question hangs between us, tormenting us both.

I decide that the only way to get some clues is to return to General Enríquez himself, and soon I am seated on his striped silk sofa, sipping coffee and glowering at him across the polished tabletop. Once again I sense a discreet change in the air. There is no Grandpa act today and I see uncertainty and tension on his round white face. The shift is subtle, but it frightens me. Watching him, I ask point-blank what has become of the search for Everardo and where we go from here.

Enríquez takes a long sip of coffee and sizes me up. Well, he tells me, his voice struggling to take on a tone of friendly concern, his men have carried out a very thorough search, just as he had ordered, but they found no trace of Everardo anywhere. He, Enríquez, is quite certain that his men would never lie to him about such a matter. So really, he doesn't know what to think. Perhaps Everardo is dead.

I feel the blood drain from my face. So is this the moment now, Everardo? Must I finally give you up? I brace myself, determined not to weep in front of this beast in a fancy uniform. Then I look up and see a shrewd, calculating look on Enríquez's face as he measures my reaction. Furious, I put my coffee cup down on the table with a small click of china on wood, tapping it to gain his full attention. I start to ask what has happened, but he cuts me off unexpectedly.

Then again, Enríquez says smoothly, perhaps Everardo is still alive. He gives me a bland and fatherly smile, enjoying the power he has over me now. Soon the United Nations human rights monitoring team, MINUGUA, will be here. Perhaps they will be able to solve the matter. With this, my patience snaps. The MINUGUA team is months overdue already and the army has killed quite a lot of people meanwhile. Enríquez starts to protest, but I talk right over him. The army captured Everardo a long time ago and everybody knows it. MINUGUA is not going to find anybody at all unless the army wants them to. Am I quite clear? Perhaps he should have another chat with Colonel Alpírez or Major Sosa Orellana. They know where Everardo is.

Now it is Enríquez's turn to interrupt. He sits bolt upright as I repeat the two names and leans across the table and grabs hold of my wrist. The physical contact startles me, but I make no effort to remove my hand, for I see that he is trying to tell me something. He speaks very slowly now in a low, deliberate voice. He is not saying that MINUGUA will find Bámaca, he explains, making dead level eye contact. He wishes to be very clear. He is saying that perhaps Bámaca is lost or is hiding out somewhere. Maybe if he sees a MINUGUA team nearby, he will have enough trust to turn himself in. I look back into the general's watchful face. Do you really think that this is possible? I ask bluntly. He answers me in the same slow, deliberate voice. Yes, it is possible, very possible indeed.

Pat and I stay up late into the night turning these strange conversations over and over again, trying to make sense out of the situation. She leaves for Washington the next morning, but I stay on for a last few meetings, desperate for more clues. I visit with the new head of intelligence, a Colonel Rivas, who looks as if he would like to saw me in half but is too polite to say so. I meet with a new general, who listens very carefully to my pleas for help. I offer to drop all charges against the army and to go into quiet exile with Everardo to any country of their choice—Paraguay, Taiwan, wherever. We could drop out of sight together, whatever the army wants. He listens carefully and promises to take it under advisement. I meet with the chief of police and he promises to investigate. I ask if he can investigate Alpírez or Sosa Orellana and he looks horrified, pointing to a ceiling light and indicating that his office is bugged. I meet with a member of the governmental peace team and he tells me it would probably be best for one's husband if one would be a little quieter, no?

I return to Marilyn MacAfee and again demand an explanation for her letter to Congress. Again she stammers a bit, then explains that, after all Everardo was a combatant. I ask her if that makes any difference in the eyes of the law when it comes to torture and she admits it does not. After a bit she tries to take on her old chipper persona, becoming jovial and cheery. Perhaps she should concede my point on this; she will certainly take it all under advisement. I don't answer, for I am far too angry. Concede my point? You have tried to strip away the only protective buffers I have been able to place between Everardo and his death by torture and you talk as if you were granting me a point in a game of golf. I close my lips tight and leave the embassy in a fury.

As the plane takes off, I feel the old pain pressing against the back of my lungs and making it hard to breathe. Once again I am leaving Guatemala without Everardo. Will it ever be different?

Battle Plans
Summer 1994

TIME IS UP. THIS MUCH I UNDERSTAND WELL ENOUGH, EVERARDO. The international community is pressing hard for a quick and final peace accord. Sick of this thirty-year war, they are looking the other way when it comes to human rights violations. The killings are still rising sharply, but nothing is said or done, for no one dares jeopardize the negotiations by insulting the military. The United States, meanwhile, is bent on a regional trade plan for all of Central America and they want the ever-lucrative Guatemala market included. That can't happen with an embarrassing war still going on, and suddenly a final peace accord is being touted as the snake-oil cure to all problems, even though the reality unfolding in Guatemala shows that it will solve nothing at all.

They are talking about signing by Christmas, and then Everardo will be dead, even if he has somehow managed to survive until now. When the war is over, they will no longer need him or his intelligence information. They will certainly not allow him to go free and talk about the abuses and tortures he suffered, or the killings he witnessed. Most importantly, they will not allow him to go free because they hate him, because he led a Mayan slave uprising and made fools of them for seventeen years. On the day they celebrate the cease-fire, it is all over for us both. They say we have until Christmas.

I have already decided what I will do. There are not many options left and I like none of them. I can stand by and weep like a grade-B movie heroine; I can walk endlessly about the halls of Congress, knowing that such an effort is far too slow at this point; or I can fight to the death as a matter of principle and the hell with the consequences. I choose the latter as the only approach I can live with. Everardo and I are a package deal and we are staying together.

I have decided on a hunger strike, but this one will not be for seven days. This one is inspired by Bobby Sands, an Irishman who died of hunger for his principles in a remote British jail cell thirteen years ago. This one will have no time limits, no fruit juice, no nothing. This time I will lay myself down in front of the National Palace in Guatemala City and wait until they bring me Everardo. I am not leaving without him again, and that is that. This time I will fast to the death if I must. Perhaps if I lie dying there, someone will stop to think about where he might be lying, close to death. If I suffer, maybe they will understand what he is suffering. Maybe if I make it all real enough, if I turn myself into a giant mirror, someone will take action to save his life. If they don't, then at least I will not have acquiesced. At least I will have fought.

I go to the library and begin to read through the medical articles that a friend has located for me. I read about the political prisoners in Ireland and South Africa and other parts of the world, sadly learning about them from these clinical pages that chronicle the slow weight loss, the organ damage, the blindness, the deaths. I had heard of these people long ago from vague press stories, but now as I read I really begin to understand them, to value them, for these were no easy passings. These were men and women of principle, who lived and died for their beliefs.

I begin to take notes on a yellow pad. Most of these people were able to survive for forty to fifty days. Some lived longer, some much less, depending on their body weights and initial health. I have a definite advantage here, for my heart and lungs are very strong and I am constructed like a small cement mixer, with plenty of natural stamina, no ulcers, and a lifetime of good nutrition to back me up. Body fat is evidently the key to longer survival, according to these articles, and I have plenty of that, although I will need much more. I jot down ice cream and red meat on my list of chores, wrinkling up my nose, for I like neither one. No matter, I will begin to gulp them down together with chocolates and vitamins, supplementing every meal with plenty of fats. Soon new jelly rolls will begin to form about my waist, outraging my feminine ego but making me feel safe and ready.

I read more and more. I must drink a staggering amount of water each day to make up for the fluid content of normal foods. Otherwise I could suffer serious organ damage and most likely kidney failure fairly rapidly. I must take some salt and potassium to keep my mind clear and to prevent heart malfunction and other disasters. A dash of sugar is necessary, too, not for the calories, but to prevent my system from becoming too acidic, a surefire route to organ collapse. All these things must be carefully balanced, an impossible feat in the middle of the central square. I think about it for a while and then remember Pedialyte, a solution of water, salts, and glucose that is given to babies to prevent death from dehydration. I check out a bottle in a drugstore, and sure enough, it has salts, potassium, and a wee bit of sugar. Basically Gatorade without the calories, I think to myself. It should do nicely and keep me clearheaded to boot.

Next I write up some plans. I draw up a list of all the groups across the country who have offered to help, then put down their addresses and telephone numbers. Then I draw up a basic fact sheet and model petition, together with a list of phone numbers for the White House comments line and other key offices. We will need a massive number of calls and letters to be made if this is going to work, and that means getting tightly organized. I know I can count on Pat and Alice for endless help, and now Sister Dianna Ortiz is hard at work in their office as well, making it a team to be reckoned with. I also write up a list of people who would probably volunteer to go to Guatemala as observers, to sit with me throughout the hunger strike, to write down license numbers, to call for help, to phone the embassy. As I write, I realize how many extraordinary people I have come to know during the last two years.

I type and sign a note making clear my position on medical care, explaining that while I am sound of mind, I have decided to undertake a serious hunger strike and must decline any and all medical care during that strike no matter what happens. I do not want to be dragged out of the square as soon as I grow weak on the grounds that this is what I would have wanted. Last of all, I draw up a power of attorney. If I lapse into a coma, someone must be legally able to sign things for me and to take care of my affairs. That will have to be someone strong enough to respect my wishes if things go badly. I talk it over with Pat and she agrees, miserable about the project but ever supportive.

Public attention is going to be a key ingredient if this is going to work at all. The goal is to humiliate the Guatemalan army into giving Everardo back alive, to fry them in the international limelight until they bend. I am pretty sure they could never withstand the political uproar of my going into convulsions and heart failure on the front steps of their National Palace. But they will survive quite nicely if they can censor it—easy enough in Guatemala. I am going to have to win coverage in the international press or both Everardo and I are lost. We may be lost anyway, but I want to stack the deck in our favor as much as possible.

I draw up a list of friendly press people with their telephone numbers and some notations about their areas of interest. Then I make a few random calls to public-relations firms that I have heard about in the past. Most are indifferent; most have clients in the U.S. government. I am too small a fish, far too weird, I have no money, and no one cares about Guatemala. Okay, Everardo, we are going to have to do this the hard way, but what else is new? I add press calls to the list of tasks for the support network.

Finally I fly back to Guatemala for one last visit, to take the pulse rate, as it were, of our situation. Is it really so dead that this hunger strike is the only road out? I have little hope as I arrive, and my predictions turn out to be quite correct. I visit Marilyn MacAfee one last time, but she is once again aloof and rather strange. In her eyes, she has done whatever she can, and it is clear that there is little more to be said between us.

Enríquez is no different. I call at his office in the National Palace as usual to make an appointment. I am told that they will call back right away. Days pass in silence. I return and they tell me he is out of town till the weekend. I offer to meet him over the weekend and they tell me this is impossible. I tell them we have met on weekends before and they answer that he will not be back for weeks. I go down the hallway, intending to speak to some of the other generals, as I have in the past. They tell me I must first speak with Enríquez and point back to the first office. He is in there right now. I stomp back down the hallway but am not allowed even to enter the waiting room. No, there must be some mistake, says the colonel as he pokes his head cautiously through the half-opened door. The general is not here today, nor do they expect him back for weeks. Perhaps the next time.

The patient quite clearly is dead. I fly back to Washington and begin my final preparations. I go to the local camping store and buy a flat foam pad to sleep on, a heavy poncho, and some large plastic bottles for drinking water. Then I pack a suitcase full of sturdy warm clothing. As I open my mail, a check plops out—an anonymous check that will cover all the expenses and still leave five thousand dollars, which hopefully will attract a press specialist to help out for one month. I can hardly believe my eyes.

The next day I meet with the Fentons, who head a small public-relations group that has been interested in Central America for many years. David and his wife, Beth, immediately understand what this case could mean in the long term and they quickly offer to help. They will do everything they can, although the lack of advance notice throws them into fits of worry. They chide me, explaining that normally months are spent in preparation for an event like this. I shake my head. If word was to get out in advance, I would never be allowed into Guatemala. Besides, time is up. I'll just have to take my chances.

And so I do, Everardo. My bags are packed, my papers are typed and delivered, my plans are worked out as best I can, and my mind is utterly made up. This may work out and it may not. But you and I are staying together.

Hunger Strike, the Beginning
Guatemala City, October 1994

IT IS A QUIET MORNING, EARLY YET, AND FEW PEOPLE ARE IN THE square when we arrive. The light is still a bit dim and the roar and smoke of the traffic is an hour or so away, giving us a margin of peace and quiet to work with. I have learned my lessons well from the Politécnica strike, and this time all our efforts flow smoothly, effortlessly. We lay down the four banners of bright yellow waterproof cloth in a neat square directly in front of the looming National Palace. These proclaim my message clearly enough in black inked letters. EVERARDO, I LOVE YOU, I WILL WAIT FOR YOU HERE UNTIL THE END. REAL PEACE YES, FAKE PEACE NO. GUATEMALAN ARMY, WHATEVER HAPPENED TO THE HUMAN RIGHTS ACCORD? GUATEMALAN

ARMY, WHY DO YOU VALUE PRIVATE PROPERTY SO MUCH AND HUMAN
LIFE SO LITTLE?

We anchor the banners in place with small cinder blocks and set
my foam pad in the center, together with a stack of my declarations
to hand out and several large bottles of drinking water. Three fold-up
chairs are set off to one side, several feet away, for the observers. They
must be close enough to see everything yet far enough to be clearly
nonparticipants. Now they sit down with a large bag filled with pon-
chos for the rain, some paperback books, emergency telephone lists,
and some tubes of sunscreen lotion. I sit in the center of the square
on the thin foam pad and put on my small headphones, listening to
the wild chords of Beethoven's "Ode to Joy."

Let us begin. And indeed we do, quickly and quietly and without
so much as a ripple, at least for now. As the music flows through my
mind I feel a tremendous sense of peace, for all is ready now; all is
done. The mad scramble of arrangements is past; the decisions are set.
I am here for better or for worse. I am here until it is over. I close my
eyes and drift for a bit. How I long for this to be over, Everardo. I feel
neither fear nor exhilaration, only a strange serenity, the freedom that
comes from crossing the final line and accepting the consequences.
There is nothing left for me to fear.

Slowly but surely a circle begins to form around me, quiet and supportive. Out of nowhere people begin to appear, housewives with
their children, women from the marketplace, a man carrying a briefcase, workers in their tattered clothing. As I look up I meet shy smiles,
dark eyes that search mine with pained understanding. As I pull off
my headphones I hear their words. Everardo, they want to see Everardo—his picture, that is—and I hasten to unwrap it and place it on
the front banner. They crowd about his image, nodding to one another and asking me about him. Where was he from? Which language
was his own? How long was he with the guerrillas? Do I think he is
still alive?

I stand up and give them my summary sheets and they take them
eagerly, mulling them over and pointing to different sections. Some of
them do not know letters, so they shyly ask me to read the print aloud
and I end up in a huddle with everyone, talking over the case and ex-

plaining everything. As I speak the circle begins to grow, and suddenly there is a huge crowd around me, asking for the handouts and pressing to see his picture. Small dark hands reach out from all directions, gesturing for the sheets of paper and pointing at Everardo's black-and-white image, so stark against the yellow fabric of the banner.

Then the press closes in. Men in dark suits with heavy camera equipment race down the staircase of the National Palace and head straight toward me. I look up at the stone towers looming above us all and see the guards now too, as they scurry back and forth across the parapets, their rifles slung across their shoulders. An officer with a stiff military hat pokes his head from a high-up window. Ah yes, we have been noticed indeed. The reporters muscle their way through the crowd and the crowd jostles them back, eager to see what is happening. Microphones appear an inch from my teeth and suddenly there are blinding camera lights everywhere and I am on the air, explaining that I am on a hunger strike to the death, that I am not leaving until Everardo is released to the courts. The cameras whirl as I explain yet again why I believe that he was taken alive, how he vanished in combat in 1992, how the army claimed he was buried in Retalhuleu. I speak about the eyewitness who escaped and who had seen Everardo alive and undergoing torture, how I opened the grave and found the body of a different young man, who had been tied up and beaten to death. The crowd nods at me, the swooping dark eyes meeting mine in a collective link of sorrowful comprehension. The cameras take them in too, then, and they abruptly turn away, frightened. It is quite dangerous to be out here with me, and they know it well enough. Yet they do not leave, and as the hours pass, the crowd continues to grow.

The observer team is hard at work. Susan Lee is back and hurries about, fussing over the banners and checking the ink work, bringing me water and running to make copies of the vanishing handouts. The Schriders are on their way from Quezaltenango, and the Texas team is in full swing with the phones and schedules. The international community pitches in too, filling in on the night shift and helping with supplies. The sun comes out and burns in a wild glare for a few hours, making me wilt and long for the shade, but tents here are forbidden. I could set one up anyway, but then the authorities would have an excuse to force me out of the square, so I must settle for a hat instead.

Marilyn MacAfee arrives with several security agents as escorts. She looks sad and worried and tells me that she has the greatest respect for me. I ask her to please take action for Everardo, but even as I say the words, I know it is no use. She speaks for a while about her own vision for Guatemala, of the need for evolution instead of revolution, of a place where the civilian institutions can slowly but surely come to rule. I point out that the army will never allow them to rule unless we do something, but she does not seem to hear me. She promises to send a patrol car regularly to check on my safety. And Everardo's safety? The words hang in the air between us, unspoken, as she takes her leave.

After a while the afternoon rains sweep in, for now it is the rainy season. A cooling wind arrives out of nowhere and the circle around me quickly breaks up, people hurrying for the shelter of the nearby buildings. I pull out my poncho and tuck Everardo's photograph into its wrappings in the nick of time. With a vague rumble, water bursts from the skies in a wild downpour, flooding across the plaza and splashing up from the pavement in sheets. Within minutes I am soaked to the skin, rather enjoying the cooling effect and the soothing sounds of the rain. I wrap my poncho close about me and sit on my waterproof foam pad, watching the men in the parapets who are busily watching me back. You up there, I think to myself, you had best get used to this, for we will be watching one another for a very long time to come.

When the rain is finally over dusk has fallen, and I begin to shiver. I take my bundle of extra clothing over to the nearby Pan American Hotel and change quickly in the ladies' lounge, wringing out my sweater in the sink and pulling out a heavy jacket. My head is beginning to throb and already I am very hungry. I have to remind myself that the first few days are always the hardest and that I must brace myself for what is yet to come. It is going to be a long time, a very long time indeed, before those men in the towers begin to budge. I am pretty sure my body will outlast their nerves, let alone the nerves of the international community. But it's going to be a close one at best and I had better learn to think about anything but food.

Back in the square people are circled once again about my banners, waiting for me to return and to explain to them what I am doing and why. We talk for a long time, even as the sun sets, and they help us light the candles we have brought. This time I am wiser and I have brought candles set in deep glass wells, and for a while they glitter warmly around us as we speak. In the safety of the shadows the others begin to comment more, telling me of their own vanished relatives, and their hatred and fear of the army. Finally they drift away, home to their children and their endless chores. I slide into a heavy blanket roll and try to read for a while with the help of a small flashlight, but soon I find that I am too exhausted to concentrate. I pull out my music again then and curl up, listening to the soft and fluttering tones of the Mayan marimba. When I awake the next morning, the earphones are still hanging loosely about my throat and Everardo's photograph, sheathed in protective plastic, is gripped closely in my hands.

Blowout
Guatemala City, October 1994

IT'S GROWING WHITE-HOT NOW, EVERARDO. THE CROWDS STAY DAY and night and the international press corps has arrived. Mike Wallace from *60 Minutes* will be here soon and *People* magazine has already published a story. The army officers in the tower are beginning to lose their cool. Day by day, journalists storm out of the palace offices, outraged by the comments they are hearing. Perhaps the body in the Retalhuleu grave really is Everardo's and I just got confused because all *indios* look alike. Perhaps I am not really married to Everardo at all, since really now, how could a white Harvard-educated lawyer take up with someone like him, so dark and with such thick lips? Meanwhile, the White House is getting more than a hundred calls a day from furious voters. We are definitely making ourselves heard.

I am hanging on, Everardo, but it isn't easy. It's been more than two weeks now and the hiking muscles have disappeared from my legs and my mind is full of wild electrical static. I cannot concentrate well enough to read much and conversations exhaust me, my throat and lungs turning to parched, scratchy surfaces as soon as I open my mouth. I can stand and walk about, and make the five-block trek each morning back to the Spring Hotel to shower and change my clothes. But it is getting harder and harder. I must stand quite slowly or I begin to see sparkling black stars, and once I am on my feet my heart accelerates, beating at a strange shallow speed that leaves me out of breath. I no longer crave food, for my body has retreated to a trance-like state of hibernation. Yet I am cold, Everardo. I am always so cold.

An explosion is not far away and we all know it. The dark-windowed cars are hovering nearby. But what will blow and when and how? We have no idea. This is a roller-coaster ride without a steering wheel or brakes, and all we can do is hang on for the ride. It's starting to get scary.

The army makes the first move, using its traditional approach to such problems—namely, a less-than-discreet death threat. As I toss and turn in my blankets late one evening, a shadowy car screeches to a halt just in front of us and stays there for a moment, a large gun barrel protruding from the window and aimed straight at us. My observers scream in horror and leap from their seats, but even as they run toward me, the car roars off and vanishes into the night. We do not see the license plates, but for the moment we are just glad that everyone is still alive. Mulling it over, I decide in the end that it is a good sign. If the army really wanted me dead, that driver would have pulled the trigger and blown my head off. When they decide to kill they do not miss, but they are afraid now of the international spotlight. This was just a little note of fatherly advice, hand-delivered.

I decide to send a reply. Until recently, General Enríquez has been scoffing at my hunger strike, convinced that no mere female could possibly last more than ten days or so and that all he needs to do is wait me out. He thinks any day now I will faint and go home. No need to make any rash moves with all the internationals watching. Clearly, he has not read his medical journals. Now he is rattled, and I have every intention of rattling him a wee bit more. I pick up a pad of paper and handwrite a threatening note to him, pointing out that I am obviously serious about all this, that I plan to stick it out to the death, hardly convenient for their public image, and that if we don't work things out amicably, I also plan to initiate criminal charges against Colonel Alpírez, Major Sosa Orellana, and everyone else named by Santiago.

It takes me a while to write the note, for the words slide in and out of my tired mind like so many flipping fish as I struggle to concentrate. Finally I finish, and march across the street and up the stone steps of the palace, demanding entry. There is quite a tussle at the doorway, for the guards do not want to let me in at first, and they stare nervously at one another, trying to come up with an adequate reason. I point out that the building is open to tourists, that I have committed no crime, and that I am completely unarmed. When they still resist, I demand their names and badge numbers and the names of their supervisors. They suddenly relent, motioning me through the metal detectors with a shrug of their shoulders. Wearily, I climb the polished marble staircase to the second floor and stagger down the ornate hallway to the Ministry of Defense, where I leave the letter.

Apparently it hits its mark, for the next day a tall, thin man with cropped-off hair and suspiciously military posture walks toward my post in the square. He is dressed in civilian clothes and smiles wanly, bending to speak in a low voice into my ear. General Enríquez would like to see me, but in private. Would I please go to the back of the palace and meet him there in ten minutes? Nobody must know where I have gone. It must be quite secret. I nod in agreement and he strides quickly out of the square. No sooner is he out of earshot than the Guatemalans in the circle around me hiss out advice. That was an *oreja,* an "ear," an army spy. Don't trust anything he says; he's with the military! Didn't he look ridiculous in those civilian clothes? Who does he think he's kidding? Their wisecracks make me laugh, but finally I convince them that I should indeed meet with Enríquez. We agree that I will return within an hour and that they will watch for me here to be sure that all goes well.

I stroll to the back of the palace and find the thin man waiting there. He watches as I approach to make sure that no one is following me, an intent and anxious look on his face. Satisfied, he motions me swiftly through a side door, then hurries me into a back elevator. For a moment, I am frightened, for I do not like being alone with him outside the public eye, and I am far too frail now to put up much of a fight if this is a trap. We arrive on the second floor without mishap though, and as the door slides open he leaps into the corridor first, looking both ways to be sure the coast is clear. Then he leads me into a small sitting room and gestures toward a chair.

As I take my seat, the colonel in charge of communications enters and sits with me, clucking his tongue and telling me that the general will be arriving shortly. His face is wreathed in smiles of kindly concern. I look so very pale and thin these days, he says. Can't he get me something, a Coke or perhaps a piece of cake? I remind him curtly that I am on a hunger strike because they won't give me Everardo back, but he pays no attention. Perhaps a bowl of soup, then? I must be terribly tired. Come on now, no one will ever know. As he smiles blandly, I wonder if the word *moron* has suddenly appeared in bright red letters on my forehead.

As we bicker General Enríquez enters the room, his face flushed with anger and his features posed in a rigid smile of welcome. As he shakes my hand, I notice that another military officer has entered with him, but he does not step forward and we are not introduced. Instead, I sit down face-to-face with the general and the colonel, the other man to one side, carefully keeping his face turned in profile. Very well, I think to myself. Whose move?

Enríquez clears his throat, a vicious expression in his small blue eyes. No more Mr. Grandpa here. Well, he says angrily, once he held me in the greatest of esteem, but now he is convinced that I am nothing more than a tool of the subversives and that this is all a propaganda stunt after all. Indeed, he thinks I have gone quite mad. All the same, he still has much affection for me and for that reason he is planning to have me forcibly hospitalized if this goes on much longer. Out of the goodness of his heart, he will see to it I am placed in the best hospital in all of Guatemala, whether I like it or not. At this, I cut in and tell him that perhaps for humanitarian reasons he should worry a bit more about Everardo's health. Moreover, forcing medical care on me against my will would be assault and battery and quite illegal. This catches him by surprise and he pauses, off balance for a moment.

I take advantage of this to start in again on my ideas for a reasonable solution. Perhaps it can all be worked out. If Everardo is still alive, we could both relinquish our passports and go to a different country together, someplace that the army chooses, a bit like the witness protection program. We could leave the hemisphere even, until all this blows over. We could sign a legal waiver of our rights to prosecute Alpírez and the others, and I could dismiss my case against them at the OAS. There are so many ways, so many things we could do.

Enríquez waves my comments aside, his eyes sparkling with repressed fury. The real solution here, he says snidely, lies in Everardo's hands. If he was any kind of real man, he would see how I am suffering and come out of hiding to rescue me. If he really cared, he would do something to put an end to this. As he speaks, a high-voltage wire snaps in my head. I remember Santiago's story of Everardo bound and blindfolded, his body hideously swollen, his arm and leg bandaged, and a killing rage sweeps over me. I leap to my feet and stagger to the door. For a moment, Enríquez does not notice, for he has been looking out the window and smiling as he speaks. The colonel frantically gestures for his attention, but it is too late. I am out the door already and stamping down the hallway, indifferent as to who the hell sees me or what they think.

The next to make a move turns out to be Uncle Sam, who apparently is getting a splitting headache from all of the telephone calls and journalists' questions. Out of nowhere comes the news that Richard Nuccio will soon be arriving from the State Department to see if he can work something out. I wince a bit at the name, for I have found the man to be cold and unhelpful so far. Like so many others at State, he seems to see this as a "can't make an omelette without breaking some eggs" kind of situation. I see it more as a matter of "why machine-gun the guests to make an omelette?" Clearly, we do not see eye to eye.

October twenty-seventh comes around and it is my birthday. I am forty-three now, Everardo. You were with me with I turned forty and I thought it was the best birthday of my life. Indeed, it was the happiest. Yet as I awaken today I feel a strange combination of pain and near euphoria, for though you are not here I have set myself free, flung myself past all barriers in this battle for you. I float now beyond the military's furious reach, and whatever it costs I cannot be stopped. It is right, Everardo. It is all so right. I awaken slowly in the dim light, weak and dizzy, ever cold, yet utterly at peace.

After a while the square comes to life. As I stand to tidy up my blanket roll and shake the rainwater from the glass candle wells, my Guatemalan friends approach. They bring a large bottle of clean drinking water tied with a red ribbon, offering it laughingly in lieu of a cake. Then they break into "Las Mañanitas," the local version of "Happy Birthday," and serenade me for several rounds, making me laugh while the accompanists clap their hands. Later I settle into my chair and listen to my taped music, Peruvian flutes, Handel's *Messiah*, closing my eyes. When I open them later on, it is broad daylight and wreath after wreath of flowers are beginning to arrive. Some bear notes from friends; others have small cards with messages of warm support but no names. Tropical blossoms arrive from the human rights groups and unions. A large and beautiful bouquet comes from Marilyn MacAfee.

Richard Nuccio arrives too, and he stops to see me in the square as he heads to the palace for a talk with the army. He looks a bit worried and as he kneels to speak, we are ambushed by what seems like a hundred Guatemalan journalists, their cameras flashing wildly, microphones sprouting out of thin air. Despite military silencing techniques, they seem to know that in this small aperture of international attention, they can safely write, and now they burst loose from their moorings. The situation is surreal and I have to laugh, for here I sit struggling to keep my body from floating off into outer space, and here kneels Mr. Nuccio while microphones that resemble odd, furry muffs dart between us. Meanwhile we are totally encircled by a mob of friends, escorts, cameramen, and furious army spies. A bit hard to talk if one wants privacy, which Nuccio certainly does. He tells me he is here to help and that he will be talking with the army. He'll meet with me later.

He is gone all day, and by midafternoon I start to wonder what is happening. At last an embassy messenger stops by and asks if I will meet with Nuccio that evening at the ambassador's residence; a car will be sent for me. I accept, a bit mystified. What the hell is being said inside those green stone walls, and why isn't anyone at least discussing my position with me first?

As the hours pass, I receive visit after visit from Guatemalan friends and well-wishers. The university students come by and take my hands and wish me the best. I worry for them, for already one visitor has been stopped and beaten as a warning to the others, and we all know that a crackdown is not far away. They shake their heads and brush aside my fears, though. A group of young Mayan women, their black hair wrapped in brilliant ribbons, approach as well, asking to see Everardo's photograph. The youngest one hands me her baby girl to hold. For a moment I am afraid I will drop her, since now I am always at the edge of a faint, so I lean back against my chair just in case. The child's eyes steady me though, for they are exquisitely beautiful, tilted up and long-lashed. She seems quite unafraid and gives me a wide toothless smile as I stroke her dark hair. I hold her close and wonder fleetingly what our own child would have looked like, Everardo, but then I push the thought from my mind. No time for sentimentality, for it can only make me weak. I hand the baby back and the mother looks intently at me, reading my thoughts, and she squeezes my hand before walking silently away.

People bring letters and poems and more and more flowers and candles. If I am asleep they wait for me and then bring their children forward one at a time, introducing me ceremoniously, telling me of their own missing loved ones, telling me that I must live so that I can speak for all of them. As they depart, they bend to leave coins in a neat pile near my pillow, for water, for more candles, for whatever it is I might need. As the next visitor steps forward and then the next, I realize what they are doing, pouring their hopes and energy into me, giving me their warmth and strength like some collective mind-to-mind transfusion. They are willing me to stay awake, to stay alive, to stay with them.

At last it is dusk and the promised embassy car stops by to pick me up. I climb in, hoping that I will be able to fight off the encroaching drowsiness before the discussion with Nuccio, for nowadays it is difficult indeed to keep my eyes open much past sundown. My body fights hard for the safer, slowed-down metabolism of a deep sleep and it is difficult to resist. Soon enough, though, we arrive at the ambassador's official mansion and I am ushered quickly to an elegant back room, complete with a small polished table and a plush sofa. I sink into the cushions, my back muscles grateful for the escape from the hard chair in the plaza. There is a party going on somewhere else in the house, and I hear the clink of plates and silverware, and watch the waiters bustle back and forth with loaded trays.

Some embassy staffers arrive in dark gray suits and they keep me company for a while, drinking glasses of water with me while we wait for Richard Nuccio. One of them will be working on labor matters here, and I ask if he has looked into the Finca la Exacta killings. He mumbles a bit and I tell him about the union leader who was taken away in a helicopter with a bullet through his belly, then found dead in the woods. According to his friends, the body looked as if he had been tossed from the aircraft. The man coughs for a moment and then asks if I know which helicopter that was, that there seems to be some confusion as to which helicopter. I stare at him, gathering my thoughts, wondering if it is worth the energy it would take to answer this man who does not want to understand.

As I think it over Nuccio arrives, walking briskly down the hall and giving me a firm handshake. He sits down next to me with an air of optimism and tells me he has good news. He has met with various military and governmental leaders, and there is a genuine willingness to call for an official investigation. He raises his eyebrow and it is clear enough that this news is expected to bring my hunger strike to an end. He is offering me a graceful way out.

I thank him and explain that the case has long since been quite thoroughly investigated and that I have long ago given everyone the proof. OAS has investigated and issued protective orders, and the UN special expert has firmly denounced the situation. This is not the time for an investigation, as if there was some real question as to what has happened. That would be a step backward. What needs to happen now is for Everardo to be turned over to the courts. Until that happens, I will not be eating. Time is up.

Nuccio looks shocked. But what if Everardo is dead? That to me seems simple enough, and I answer that if he is dead, then I want his body back and I want Alpírez and Sosa Orellana in prison. I personally believe that Everardo is alive, I tell him, because some villagers say they have seen him alive in recent months, and because he still has so much useful information. I also remind him of my discussions with Enríquez last winter. Nuccio scoffs and tells me that he has spoken with Enríquez and that those conversations were never negotiation sessions. Enríquez himself has told him this. He speaks to me in a chiding voice, as if addressing a truly silly child.

Now I feel anger at this man. You were not present at these talks in the first place, I tell him. Are you seriously going to believe General Enríquez, the same man who says perhaps Everardo ran off with some other woman? That maybe the body in the grave really is Everardo's, even though it's five centimeters too short, fifteen years too young, and has completely different dental patterns? The man who thinks a white woman could never really have married an *indio*? A leader of the worst human rights violator in the hemisphere? You believe his side of things? Nuccio looks at me coldly now. Yes, yes, he understands my point of view, but he has spoken with Enríquez about this and he believes the general is telling the truth about this particular matter.

And I am a hallucinating crackpot? I stare at him and realize what the strategy is here. Cook up some kind of official investigation; buy her off the hunger strike. The Guatemalan army will bog things down forever, no fault of the U.S. government of course. Soon it will all blow over and be forgotten. Jennifer was just a tragic and rather hysterical female who for emotional reasons could not let go, could not face reality. Everardo is simply one more of hundreds of thousands of dead here in Guatemala. Tragic war, this one. Best to turn to the future now. Crisis solved, case closed. Over my dead body, a voice roars in my head.

I tell him that I severely criticize his judgment call and that I will not be ending my hunger strike for a mere investigation. This would be a huge step backward and the army would use it as support for their claims that nobody really knows what happened to Bámaca. Moreover, an investigation in Guatemala is quite a joke and nothing will ever come of it. By the time the dust clears, Everardo will be dead. I will have no part of this. Why were all these arrangements made without even consulting me? I rise and put on my sweater. I was a fool to come here. Nuccio hurries down the hall with me, offering me lists of supporters who have been calling his office. He seems to see this as some kind of booby prize, a showing of friends and support in lieu of Everardo. I want to take the list from his hands, tear it to shreds, and throw it in his face.

As I storm outside, I almost walk over Ambassador Mulet, who has flown down from Washington for an emergency meeting about all this. His phone lines, too, are blowing off the hook. He starts visibly as I sweep past, but I do not stop to chat. Enough of this diplomacy nonsense. I climb into one of the official cars and we drift through the streets of the City, back toward the National Palace. As we drive, I remember Nuccio taking a call back in Washington as I sat nearby. I listened with surprise while he crooned affectionately to someone called "dear" and "honey" on the other end of the line. He was so openly loving to whoever it was, wife or lover, son or daughter. He clearly has someone he would fight to the death to protect or rescue. So why, then, can he not understand me?

Back at the square, people are still lingering, waiting for my return. I am weak and shaky now, so I wave and head straight for my makeshift bed, climbing into its comforting folds, my teeth chattering in the chill night wind. As my eyes begin to close, a young Mayan man approaches, his sculpted features soft in the lamplight. He quietly tucks a scrap of paper into my hands and touches my hair, then turns and swiftly walks out of the square. Curious, I unfold the paper and find a small poem he has written.

You are not alone in your struggle,
You have the suffering Mayan peoples
Supporting your courage, your love, your life,
Your hope for a new dawn.
Our minds and our hearts are with you.
Thousands of mothers, fathers, husbands, wives,
Sons and daughters are consumed in the tortured
Silence of their vanished families.
You are an example of sublime love.
You are an example of an unbreakable struggle.
Your cries resound from the borders of our lands.
Your cries are for those wracked with sobs for their loved ones.
Your cries are for a suffering people.
Your cries are for life in Guatemala.
Receive now the affection of the Mayan people, who call out
together to you that
We love you.
Signed, A Bird

I fall asleep with my shoes still laced to my feet.

The Explosion
Guatemala City, October 1994

THE ARMY CAN TAKE NO MORE AND BEGINS TO CHARGE LIKE A MAD-
dened bull. Enríquez roars about the hunger strike over national
radio, speaking so swiftly and furiously that I can barely make out the
words. The generals seize onto the investigation idea like drowning
swimmers, insisting that now at last their names will be cleared and I
will be exposed as a fraudulent subversive. They threaten to drag out

certain prisoners of war who will swear, after a wee bit of torture perhaps, that Everardo did indeed die in combat. This never quite materializes, since those who were with him at the Río Ixcucua battle have never been captured and remain safe and sound in the mountains. But the army threatens it anyway, knowing full well that I will receive the message. Get out of the square or someone is going to get hurt.

I am frailer and frailer as the days go by, but somehow my body has come to grips with the fact that it must follow the orders coming from my head. I can still stand and walk. I can still gather up my energies to speak with the crowds of friends and journalists. I can still fight like hell for Everardo, and I do so every single day. I ain't going to eat and no one can make me, and I ain't going to leave the square and no one can make me. The army is of a different opinion.

First a sturdy man in a vest approaches me in the square and I eye him with deep suspicion. He introduces himself as a forensic physician and explains that he has been ordered by the courts—upon military petition no doubt—to check on my health. The army has done its homework. True enough, they cannot force medical care upon me against my will, but they can legally act to prevent a suicide. This man is here to see if I am close enough to death to drag me out of the square and strap me down to a hospital bed without violating my right to free speech. This makes me burst out laughing despite myself. Why have they sent you, a forensic doctor? I am not dead yet, I say.

To my surprise, the man smiles back and seems kindly enough. He agrees that he cannot force me to submit to a checkup and shrugs good-naturedly. He has his marching orders and he has to give it a try. It is up to me. I rather like this doctor, for in his steady eyes I see that he, too, recognizes the implicit absurdity of it all. Why cause him trouble? After all, the man is under orders. I am pretty sure I can pass a physical, and I know for certain that I am not yet close to death. So I stand up cautiously, taking care not to move too quickly, for I know I will be dragged away the very first time I so much as faint. Then we wander about the square for a bit, looking for some place that the man can remove my shirt without causing a riot.

In the end we return to the Spring Hotel and he listens carefully to my heart, which seems to be developing a faint murmur, and to my lungs. Then he checks for any enlarged organs. He smiles to himself and comments that I am indeed a bionic woman and that I should keep drinking Pedialyte solution every day. I will be fine for a while to come yet. I smile back. The army will have to wait for a very long time if I have anything to say about it.

Asisclo Valladares appears off and on in the square, usually at dusk. He visits with the other protesters nearby and then wanders gingerly over toward me, asking if I remember him. I ask how I could forget him after that day in Retalhuleu, and he retreats, blushing beet red. But not for long. Soon he is calling for a Supreme Court hearing on whether or not to extend the original habeas corpus petitions into a full-fledged *averiguación*—"investigation." This makes me shake my head. I filed my habeas corpus petitions back in 1993, right after Santiago escaped. Some court officials went around to the local prisons and asked if Efraín Bámaca Velásquez were one of the inmates. The answer—what a surprise—was always no. The case was then closed. Now it will be reopened—to do what exactly? The courts have no power over the army at all, and I suspect that this will become but one more form of harassment. Oh well. I prepare my documents, for I will have to cooperate. Otherwise they will claim I am impeding the investigation. Meanwhile, I remain on my hunger strike.

More and more friends begin to arrive from the United States. The accompanist network sends two nurses, Kim and Liz, to stay with me. They set to work at once with hats to fight the sun and they check on my blood and urine. My blood sugar is down to forty-two and sinking fast. They are horrified, for much lower could lead to a coma. My kidneys are still strong, thanks to the interminable bottles of water I am drinking. My blood pressure is very low. When I stand, my heart beats far too fast. My left eyelid is drooping closed and will not obey my commands to remain open. I am doing well, all considered, but how much longer will I last?

My old Texas friends arrive in a delegation, making the rounds back and forth to the National Palace, the embassy, and the offices of different military spokesmen. Brother Joe Nangle and Marie Dennis arrive from Washington with cards and messages from my housemates. Then the Coalition Missing members arrive, and I awaken to see them rushing across the square to give me hugs and encouragement. Meredith reaches me first, then Josh and Trish and Peter, and then beautiful Dianna Ortiz. She sits down on the edge of my chair and puts a slender arm about my shoulders, bringing tears to my eyes, for I know what it costs her to return here, what memories haunt her in the night. Yet her presence gives me strength because she survived, Everardo. She survived and came back home. It is not impossible.

Abruptly, the friendly journalists are pulled off my case and a new crowd of thuglike men with press cards and dark glasses appears. From now on, they will be telling the story, they explain. The friendly ones return at night for visits and to warn me. These new guys are no ordinary staff writers. They have been sent, and I must be very careful indeed. Vicious editorial columns begin to appear. Perhaps I am doing this to sell my book, *Bridge of Courage*. I am doing it for the money. I am doing it to help the terrorists. I was never really married to that *indio*. Or the alternative, I am guilty of miscegenation. Imagine! How could I have been married to someone like that? It is impossible. Moreover, I am a foreigner. I have no right to tell Guatemala anything at all. I am making their country look bad.

On the streets, people pay no attention and continue to crowd around me day and night, bringing their children and telling me about their lost family members. My old friend Nineth from the GAM office, ever fearless, sends a group of women to sit nearby every single day in support of my battle for the disappeared. One of them, Sara, is some eight months pregnant, and only recently survived a serious stabbing by the death squads. Now she cheerfully sits in the sun with me for eight hours a day, hurrying back and forth to check on my health. Later she will give birth to a baby boy so beautiful he makes me weep.

A lawyer from the prosecutor's office arrives and says he wants to take some interrogatories as part of the investigation. He starts to pull out a sheaf of legal papers and set them down on the ground. I ask if we could meet in the quiet of his office. It is so noisy here, I do not have my documents copied, and it is hard to concentrate with so much going on. I don't want to make any mistakes, and I would like my lawyer to be present. He agrees, then complains to the press that I have refused to cooperate and that he will have to subpoena me.

Meanwhile, the Supreme Court sets its date for me to give my testimony. This does not worry me much, for I have given my statement a thousand times now and could do it again with my eyes closed. I will just have to rally enough energy to stay alert for several hours, easier said than done these days. In any event, I want the Supreme Court judges to actually hear some of this evidence. I know they can't save Everardo, but at least they will get some of this censored information. I jot down some notes, and send for more copies of de León Carpio's original letter, the autopsy report, my affidavit, and Santiago's testimony. I will be there, I think grimly to myself. Have no fear, I will make myself heard.

The crew for *60 Minutes* arrives—Debra De Lucca and several cameramen, who treat me with the utmost kindness and respect. They do background work and take lots of footage, hearing out the Guatemalans who come to visit and interviewing Sara and the women of the GAM. Mike Wallace arrives late one evening a few days later. I have watched him for years on television and worry that weakheaded as I am now I will not be able to withstand his sometimes-withering questioning. To my great surprise he is utterly patient and considerate, and he has already read every word of my affidavit. He is also fully familiar with every fact in this case, which wins him my prompt respect and trust. We spend several hours the next day filming in a shady hotel room, much to my relief, for here there is no smoke, no uproar, no crowd, no sun. Here I can actually think. I leave once with the nurses so that they can draw blood and check on my kidneys and glucose levels. When I return, I am weaker still.

We interview for a bit longer and he tells me that Marilyn MacAfee has denied him a meeting and that he wants to tell me something very important. He asks only that I reveal it to no one at all prior to his broadcast. I promise, ever hopeful of good news. He leans forward then and tells me gently that he knows from a confidential source that the embassy has a certain CIA report. This report confirms that Everardo was indeed captured alive by the army in 1992.

His statement hits me like a sandbag, and yet my tired mind is not even surprised. I think back to MacAfee's many statements, always identical, about how they have mentioned it and mentioned it, yet what more can they do? I remember the same statements, almost to the word, by Nuccio and Anne Patterson and so many other State staffers. I think of the numerous visits by embassy people to my square of banners in front of the National Palace as I have grown weaker and weaker. I think of their irrational calls for an investigation. So they have known all along. They have been watching me go through this hell, knowing all along and saying nothing. They know that the army took Everardo alive and they are covering for the army. And now? My heart lurches. Is it too late, Everardo, or do we still stand a chance, you and I?

For the first time, though, I feel a glimmer of hope. Within a week or so Mike Wallace will report the truth on *60 Minutes* and the citizens across the United States will all hear it, whether the embassy likes it or not. The truth is coming out if I can just hang on. Something is going to give, though God alone knows what. I have got to hang on; I have got to stay in the square.

And so I do. I stay in the square and the army mood grows nasty indeed. One day, a man with big muscles and closely cropped hair walks by with a billboard reading YANKEE GO HOME, and he stands between me and the palace, glaring. I glare back. Within an hour, another man joins him with a billboard reading COMMUNIST! GO BACK TO CUBA! I joke on the radio that perhaps the army should make up its mind where they want to send me, the United States or Cuba. The next day, there is a new tactic: A government official screeches that I have entered Guatemala without a visa, that they can find no record of a visa, and that they will therefore deport me. I have crossed the border illegally. The journalists career into the square and I show them my airplane ticket and the visa stamp in my passport. It is clear enough, La Aurora Airport, Guatemala Immigration Services. I am becoming irritable now. Why on earth would I hike across the mountains and swim the rivers to enter Guatemala illegally when a visa in the airport costs all of five dollars? Really now!

Next the army waits till I leave and then they send a veritable lynch mob of several hundred people screaming into the square after my two escorts, who are all alone and very new, and barely speak Spanish. The crowd accuses them of being URNG members, *subversivos*, and circles tightly about them. A friend calls a policeman over, but he is frightened and decides the mob is simply exercising its right to free expression. When I return the crowd has vanished, leaving the two women badly shaken. I call the embassy and they send a patrol car, but it seems that little can be done. I call over two loitering policemen and tell them what happened. They pretend they know nothing, so I mention that it would be very sad if another tourist warning had to go out as it did after June Weinstock was attacked. Just think how much money that cost Guatemala the last time around! Magically the crowd never returns.

I go to the Supreme Court and give my presentation, feeling strong and ready. I dress as carefully as I can, but my clothes are now billowing about me and I have difficulty climbing the stairs. Inside I brace though, and by the time I sit down, I am very ready. I hand over the copies of documents as I speak, and watch the circle of faces around me. These are judges watching me, upper-class people, well educated. Will they hear me out, or has this war divided the country so sharply along the lines of race and class that a fair hearing is impossible? They are cautious certainly, but as I fill out the facts and reason through the story with them, covering each and every possibility, they begin to nod ever so slightly. At least I have won their respect.

Asisclo knows it, too, and he wreaks his revenge. He has a government car drive up to Everardo's tiny village and bring back his terrified father and sister. I am not allowed to speak to them without an armed guard present and they are kept in strict official custody. They testify truthfully enough to the Supreme Court that they have not seen Everardo in more than twenty years and know nothing of his life or disappearance. Later they are taken to "appointments," no doubt with the army. I boil inwardly, because Everardo spent nearly twenty years protecting these people, staying far from his hometown, making sure that his family would never be identified or punished because of him. Message received. Back off gringa or we'll take his family. We can do it whenever we please. See how easy it is for us?

I am soon exhausted and dizzy, but the hearing takes most of the morning. I can sip only from the glass of water in front of me, instead of the usual quart bottles I must consume to stay alive. By early afternoon I am quite weak, like a badly wilted plant, but now I am due at the prosecutor's office for those damned interrogatories. I climb into a taxi and go straight to the address and am ushered upstairs quickly. There I am seated in a small closed office and Mr. Mechuko, the prosecutor, enters with his big stack of papers. My lawyer is nowhere in sight but Mechuko is in no mood to wait. I later find out that my lawyer arrived but was not allowed upstairs. We begin without her, a secretary coming to take down my sworn answers. Mechuko is part of this new investigation to help find Everardo and I am stuck with him, whether I like it or not. I like it not.

He does not disappoint my cynical expectations. He stands over me, breathing down my neck, glaring as if I was a criminal. He is a crude man, none too bright, and a bit too fat for his polyester suit. In my mind, I nickname him "Cheese Ball." He has some fifty-five questions, most of them repetitive because he has not done any proofreading, none of them geared to finding Everardo. "Was your husband a member of the subversive forces? Which subversive group? How long was he a member of that subversive group? How long was he a member of that subversive group? What? I already asked that? Okay, okay. So, did you know he was a member of the subversive forces when you married him? Are you a member of the subversive forces yourself?" He goes on and on and I answer through clenched teeth, hating him. Two hours pass and then another. My throat feels like sandpaper and my ears are ringing. They want me to faint in here. I know this. Then they will have an excuse to drag me to a hospital. I sit up straighter. I am not going to faint and they are not going to win.

Ramsés Cuestas, the chief national prosecutor, suddenly thrusts his head through the door. Tomorrow morning at 8:00 A.M., we will be exhuming two graves in Coatepeque that could be Bámaca's, he says. I start, horrified, then remember the strange man this morning in the courthouse hallway. He said that two guerrillas were killed near Coatepeque in 1992 and were buried in the city cemetery there. But after we talked, it was clear that those *compañeros* died more than a week before Everardo disappeared and that they looked nothing like him.

I tell Ramsés Cuestas about all this, but he is not interested. He is red in the face and looks like he would like to bite me. I ask him to give me at least a few days to get a lawyer and a forensic specialist so we can do this right. He barks that the exhumation is on for tomorrow. I can be there or not, as I choose. He leaves me to Mechuko again and the session drags on, long past five o'clock. How on earth will I ever find a lawyer now? Why are they railroading me? Don't they want a correct identification to be made? Finally we are finished and I stagger into the streets and back to the main square. My escorts have become frantic with worry and rush to meet me. I explain what is happening, and they divide up, some to find a friendly attorney, others to find a photographer, drivers, and hopefully at least one member from the Guatemalan forensic team. It is late, but with a little luck we will find someone. The army is pulling a fast one here, but what?

Eventually a small team is pulled together and by midnight I am installed in an office chair while my attorneys type frantically. We are filing a protest motion, demanding more time to prepare, to obtain a specialist to examine the body. I feel as if I am floating through outer space. It has been twenty-five days without food now and I have been running about and speaking all day long. Worse yet, I am now wet from the evening rains. Kim, the nurse, worriedly takes my pulse again and again. It is far too low, but no matter. Something is coming now, and that something is bad. What are they doing, Everardo? They know you did not die in Coatepeque, so why are they insisting on all this? Is it for show? Or is it something else, far worse? Is this a crude attempt to give me your body back? Have they brought your body in from some far-off place and reburied you there, for me to find tomorrow? I am afraid, Everardo. I am very much afraid.

At four in the morning we all pile into vehicles and head off toward Coatepeque. There is no time to lose, for this town is some five hours away, across bad roads, at the other side of the country. Kim comes with me, worried, for I am exhausted now and things are about to become much worse. The ride will be difficult and we are heading into the hot tropical region of the southwest, where my dehydration will become more severe. I climb into the back of the Schriders' truck, for there is a small mattress in the back. I hope that if I sleep for a few hours on the way that I will manage to avoid a cold or cough. I know without asking that even the smallest illness would bring me down now, and bring me down fast.

We reach Coatepeque on time and I awake slowly and painfully, shaking my head to try to clear my thoughts. My God, I feel a thousand years old and the day is only just beginning. I've got to brace; I've got to be lucid. This is important. Chuck Kyle from the U.S. embassy is waiting for us on the steps of the public ministry. He is a decent man, tall and sturdy and very Texan, and I am glad to see him. At least this man has always been straight with me, unlike the others. He comes forward now, looking tired out himself, and a local prosecutor stands sheepishly at his side. The exhumation has been postponed for my convenience. It will be rescheduled for next week. Will I please be sure to attend?

The others are just beginning to arrive, tumbling out of their cars and struggling to park. They shriek at the news, but there is little we can do. My lawyers go inside and bicker for a bit with the prosecutors, and then we go together to the court to read through the case files of the two dead men we will be exhuming. I sit down on a dingy sofa and flip through the thin folder of the first victim. A young man in olive green, with a gun—yes, a *compañero* all right. Too short and too young, though, and with a narrow face. Hardly you, Everardo, with your broad cheekbones and squared-off jawline. The second man is also of a different age and height and he has a small mouth. I hold up Everardo's photo and my lawyer shakes his head ruefully.

I read a statement into the court record. Neither of these descriptions fits my husband's appearance in any way, and for the following reasons. With this, I hope that the whole mess will be canceled, but no such luck. The prosecutors are still insisting that this exhumation could be very important. Why? They are terrifying me, Everardo. They are truly terrifying me now. But if you are out there in that grave, no matter what the ruse to bring you here, then I have to know. I will be here for this exhumation.

Finally it is time for the long trek back to the City, and the Schriders bundle me onto the mattress in their truck. A group of people gathers, watching as I smooth out the blankets and pointing at me.

For a moment, I do not catch their words, but then I hear the older woman at the front quite clearly. *Que Dios te bendiga,* she tells me. *Que Dios te bendiga.* She is saying, May God bless you.

When we get back I can barely move, and for the first time I consent to sleep in the hotel room, for I am fearful of becoming ill. I must hang on still. I must. Something is going to break soon and it had better not be me. I must will my body to hang on. The bed feels incredibly soft and dry after the long month in a sleeping bag, wrapped in sheets of black plastic to protect me from the rains. I barely have time to remove my filthy clothes before I collapse into the warm blankets and fall sound asleep.

The next morning it is hard to return to the square. But I must and I do. I am staggering now, for the last two days have taken too much out of me. Worse yet, it isn't over. I still have to return to additional court sessions, and now there are emergency meetings with my lawyers to boot. Moreover, we will return within days to Coatepeque for the exhumation. The international press corps is everywhere now and I am delighted to see them but almost too weak to make it through the interviews. My mind is filled with infuriating static and my lungs feel like a blacksmith's bellows. A friend has arrived recently with a donated cellular phone and I try to use it, but the army has blocked the number for the third time in a row, so I must walk about in search of a pay phone that works.

I check in with Washington and talk with Alice and Pat and Dianna. They have not left their office for days now, and they have taken to sleeping on the floor in case I need anything, in case an emergency arises. They have become a veritable mission control center, organizing the telephone campaigns, speaking with officials, working out strategies, and answering the endless calls of inquiry from the furious public.

There is no time to drink enough water and I begin to see stars every time I walk. I cannot faint or I lose this mad race. I must not let myself faint. I learn a trick and pretend to bend over to tie my shoelaces whenever I feel dizzy. This allows the blood to rush to my head and no one ever notices that anything was wrong in the first place. I begin to use it often. My upper lip is a bit more of a problem, for like my eyelid, it is beginning to disobey my commands. It is stiffening slightly, making my speech slur imperceptibly. I hear it though, and so does Peter Kerndt, a member of Coalition Missing who also happens to be a physician. I cannot fool him at all. He has spoken at length with Kim and Liz about my blood tests and glucose levels and he tells me that I have perhaps another ten days left before things start to go haywire. Ten days left to put up a good fight. Is it enough?

Bob Brown, one of the observers, suddenly arrives from the hotel, elated. A young man with short hair just walked in, asking for Jennifer. Bob offered to help and the man said he had news. I may be a soldier, he said, but I do have a conscience. I guarded Everardo myself not long ago in a military base. My head jerks up at this and the other escorts burst into cheers. This is not the first such report. There have been several others. A young woman whose boyfriend worked in the G-2 division came by once. She felt sorry when she saw me in the square, starving, and so she asked him, What about that guy Bámaca? Her boyfriend was very nervous and made her promise not to tell. Yes, Bámaca is alive, he said. He had seen him in a military post about six months ago. She didn't want to get her boyfriend in trouble, but she thought it only right to tell me. Then, of course, there were the villagers of El Tumbador, not far from Everardo's own village, who said they had seen him in army uniform, being dragged about by soldiers to check the different cars coming in from Mexico.

This new report cheers me but also drives me mad. Is Everardo alive still? So many people tell me yes. The war is still on, so his information is still valuable. There were those talks with Enríquez. Yet those talks broke off, and now they are irrationally dragging me to another exhumation. Why? They know the Coatepeque grave is not his. Or is it now? What game are they playing? I am sick with worry.

The *60 Minutes* program airs and is watched across the United States. It is also viewed on cable TV by much of upper-class Guatemala. It serves as the spark to a barrel of gunpowder, and all goes wild from then on. Supporters rush to the square in a frenzy of rage. The journalistic community lays siege to the embassy. The Spring Hotel gives up trying to use their telephones for anything else but us. The White House comment lines are close to meltdown. The army is momentarily struck dumb, but I know that soon, very soon, there will be an insane outburst of rage that will sweep me from this square like a murderous tidal wave.

I meet again with my lawyers. Then as I struggle back to the plaza, I see Jose Pertierra standing near my banners, cigar hanging from his mouth, kindly face sparkling with glee at all the uproar, and relief at seeing me alive and in one piece. For a moment I think I am hallucinating, and then I realize he is really there. I am overwhelmed with gratitude and relief. The eye of the hurricane is approaching and I need to talk over my strategies with someone. No one understands me better than Jose, and there is no one I trust more. As he throws his arms around me, a huge knot of tension at the base of my skull begins to dissolve, slowly but surely.

Jose has good news. Back at the White House, several top officials of the National Security Council are willing to meet with me now. Arrangements can be made to meet with Anthony Lake and Leon Fuerth, national security advisers to Clinton and Gore. This makes me smile, for before this hunger strike began, not even the lower rung of staffers there would meet with me. But a meeting is not enough now. It is simply not enough.

I gather together my closest friends—Jose, with his cigar and his partner, Jim Malone, and Darryl, my friend of eleven years, with his serene eyes and calm thinking. We have known each other ever since my earliest trips to the refugee camps in Mexico. I call over the nurses and Peter Kerndt as well, and we all mull over the choices. As I approach death, or a condition that the army can reasonably claim is approaching death, they can take me away whether I like it or not. They can force me into a hospital. I risk being given drugs to lighten up my mood a bit. Needless to say, I risk quite a lot once I am in their care. I have about ten days left, maybe a bit more, maybe a bit less. My body is proving to be startlingly strong, thanks largely to my startling stubbornness, but time is running out.

I have two choices. I can take advantage of the new situation and go back to D.C. and fight. There is a huge breakthrough now, thanks to *60 Minutes.* Now it is known beyond any doubt at all that Everardo was taken alive, we certainly have the White House's attention, the U.S. public is furious, and the State Department officials have egg on their face like never before. They have been pretty well mulched by Mike Wallace. If I stay, I lose this window, for I will end up hospitalized, perhaps for some time. I am risking kidney failure now, as well as other serious problems, and I would not arrive back home very quickly. By then the window will have closed.

Then again I have sworn I would never leave without Everardo, and Everardo is not here. I want to finish what I have started. But the army is not going to let me do that. They can stop me legally and they will, and they are not going to stand for much more. The thought of them making any of my decisions for me makes me boil, for I will never let them have control over me. I would rather be dead. Perhaps I should just toss away my Pedialyte solution right now. I know I would collapse within a day or two, that even now I am pushing the outer edges of the envelope. The medical folks shake their heads. If I stop the Pedialyte, I could end up with kidney failure or worse and I will be out of commission for a very long time. Cutting things short will not make the crash any less serious. My choices are to end up in a hospital for a very long time or to return to D.C. and try to use the new situation. I don't like either choice.

In the end, I postpone a bit. No way I am leaving now, no matter what, under this hammering by the army. That just makes me stubborn. Also, I want to see who is buried out there in Coatepeque. If I find Everardo there, then the strike is over in any event. If it is not Everardo? I pray fervently that it will not be, the thought terrifying me. But if it isn't him, then what do I do? What is best, Everardo? How do I save your life? As my exhausted mind lurches again and again through all of the options, I see no clear way out of all of this.

Soon it is day number twenty-nine and we are piling into the line of vehicles that will take us back to Coatepeque. A support delegation has arrived from the United States to help us—Anne Manuel, from the Human Rights Watch; Mr. Makau, an instructor from the Harvard Law School's human rights program; a second cousin named Bernard Harcourt, whom I now meet for the first time; and a tall, slender woman named Kathryn Porter, wife of Congressman John

Porter and a formidable human rights advocate herself. They are in a flurry over a published death list that appeared today. Eight people are on it and I am number one, described as an expert manipulator of the Marxist masses. I glance through it and find that I am in very honorable company. Karen Fischer, a relative of de León Carpio, is on the list for her work on the Carpio Nicolle murder case. She is described as a promiscuous drug addict. Helen Mack is on the list. So are a number of unionist and civic leaders. It is signed by the Patriotic Anti-Communist League.

We arrive that evening in Coatepeque and I go straight to bed, in the hopes of conserving my strength for tomorrow. I will have to stand in the sun for hours and examine those bodies myself. I will have to state clearly and reasonably why each skull is or is not Everardo's. I cannot faint. I must be lucid. I must be able to answer the avalanche of questions coming from the press. I don't know if I can do it, but I must. I simply must.

The next day Kim anxiously takes my blood pressure and presses a floppy sun hat onto my head. Her nurse's soul is in agony, for she knows why I am destroying myself, and yet her entire psyche is geared to saving life, to repairing harm to the human body. I drink down an entire bottle of Pedialyte solution and hope for the best, for already the sun is hot and blindingly bright. We arrive at the gates of the cemetery and are met with a gaggle of press cameras and waving microphones. I stop to make a brief statement, hoping that this will do until the exhumation is over. As I speak, my eyes wander across the painted crosses and small tombs that cover the hillside below me and I find it hard now to choke back the tears and speak clearly. Everardo, I am so tired. Please do not let it be you today. Please, not you.

We stumble down the marble steps and enter a muddy clearing filled with weeds. Here lie the unidentified dead in their unmarked graves. A man cordons off the area with yellow tape and I step inside and sit in a corner to wait, hoping for silence. The press ignores the perimeter and leaps in with me, cameras clicking within an inch of my face, leaving me dizzy.

Finally the forensic people take charge and gently ask the journalists to wait until later, promising that I will give a full interview as soon as the proceedings end. Doctor Haglund, dressed in a tweed jacket and professorial shirt and tie, approaches and shakes my hand. He knows Guatemala quite well and has come down to assist the forensic team. I am grateful to see him and immediately like his quiet, firm manner. We talk for a moment, and I review the files with him, explaining to him what I will need to know, describing Everardo's teeth, his height, pointing out his face and profile in the handful of snapshots I have gathered up. Haglund is a listener. He nods carefully, clarifies a few things, jots some notes. I tell him that if it is Everardo, I will need a few moments alone with the body. I will need to say good-bye to you, Everardo, before your hair is washed down the sink and your bones are pulled apart and left clean and clinical on that wooden bench over there. I have to say good-bye to you first and I cannot do it on camera. Haglund understands, and I know he will see to it.

I return to my corner and the grave diggers appear and begin their grim work. The hacking sounds that I so hate fill the air, and the clods begin to fly, landing on the earth with dull, rhythmic thuds. Jose comes and sits next to me and Kim hovers nearby. It is good to sit, for my pulse can settle into a reasonable beat now and the blood stays in my head. I am determined to move as little as possible. The grave diggers continue, but they have dug a bit too far to one side and have to consult with the cemetery records and the forensic team. They decide on a perpendicular trench and go back to digging. Soon some bones appear, including a human femur. No plastic bags were used here, and a local official mumbles apologetically that they run out rather frequently. The grave widens and soon two bodies appear. They have been thrown into the pit facedown. One of the men was rather tall and his legs have been bent at the knees to make him fit his grave.

Dr. Haglund leaps into the opening with the forensic team and they begin their work, meticulously dusting off each and every bone, making sure that nothing is missing, searching for bits of clothing, a bullet casing perhaps, anything else that will give us information about the dead. Soon the bones are lifted one by one out of the grave and laid out on a small wooden table to one side—legs, arms, ribs, now a head. Now another head. The team carries them one by one to the table and slowly the bodies begin to re-form on the wooden planks. Haglund washes the heads in a bucket so that I can clearly see the teeth.

It is time now for me to go and look. The photographers are poised and ready to record my expression as I examine the skulls. I will myself to stand up straight, to walk slowly over to the table, to remain clearheaded and free from fainting. As I walk, my heart races up to its strange light flutter, too fast and too shallow. I place my hands on the edge of the table and take a look. The first skull has a neat bullet hole in its base, for the man was given the coup de grace. I stare at the teeth, but this is not Everardo. The extractions are wrong, and the spacing is off. I look at the second head. The side of the skull has been blown off, perhaps by a shotgun blast at close range. The teeth? It is not Everardo. I point out the difference, relief sucking the air from my lungs as if from a punctured tire. Haglund takes notes. The forensic team works furiously on their report. I return to the shade, waiting for it to be over. Finally, the bodies are placed back in their pitiful space in the earth and I ask Jim Schrider, a former priest, to say a brief prayer for us all. We join hands then and bow our heads, giving respect to these ruined human beings as best we can.

The prosecutor is not happy. He thinks we have looked at the wrong place, that we should open up some more graves. We ignore him and walk out of the cemetery, leaving him sputtering to himself. It was not you, Everardo. At least for today, it was not you. I think it over as we walk slowly back to the waiting cars. They just wanted to frighten me, to wear me out. They thought if they stood me up in the sun for eight hours and made me look at these mutilated human beings that I would finally give out, pass out, and they could legally drag me away and end the hunger strike. It didn't happen. I have been tying my shoelaces all afternoon to keep the blood flowing to my head, to keep from fainting. It worked. I am still on my feet. They have lost this round yet again. But for how much longer?

We return to the City and I stay up all night thinking. Suddenly, the right decision seems clear enough. Everardo may still be alive, but if I am dead, I cannot fight for him. Even if I stay here, the army will eventually force me into a hospital for medical care. I might survive, but my strike will come to an ignominious end. In effect the army will win, and worse yet, I will be under their legal control. This I will never allow. The military is not going to call off my hunger strike for me. I am going to put them in jail. It is best to pack for home while I am still free and strong enough to keep on fighting. New doors are opening in Washington, and there is the new information from Mike Wallace. Maybe, just maybe, I can make things work now.

I get up early and begin writing a final statement and hunt down Jose to help with my grammar. It must be letter-perfect, for this will be my last rally. I stagger about all day, speaking with well-wishers, making copies, and arranging for a press conference in the square the next morning. I visit my lawyers and check on what I can say and what I cannot. I go over and over Santiago's report to make sure that my facts are right. That night I stay up late, reading and rereading the materials by the dim beam of my flashlight.

In the morning I manage to stand and walk the few blocks to the Spring Hotel for a shower and a change of clothes. I am terribly dizzy now, and strangely nauseous, but it doesn't matter. It is almost over. I think we have a chance, Everardo. I think we have a chance. I stand for a long time under the hot water, for my own body can no longer maintain its base temperature and I need to bring the warmth back to my arms and legs. Then I dress slowly and stumble off to meet Jose in the square. There is a message from Marilyn MacAfee at the desk as I leave. She would like to speak with me as soon as I am free. I glower at the note. Now what the hell could she possibly want at this stage of the game? I'll be there, though, I decide sullenly. You never know.

In the square a large crowd of journalists has gathered, and their cameras are set up, trained on my empty chair. I want to stand but they protest, for they cannot rearrange their tripods without a bit of work. I sit down on the large wooden armchair and pull out my statement. I have been carrying out my hunger strike in order to save my husband's life. I will end it today for many reasons. New information has come in and I have been invited to speak to high-level staffers at the White House. This I must do if I want to save Everardo. But I will return very promptly to petition the Guatemalan courts to press criminal charges against the following military officers for kidnapping, torture, and obstruction of justice. I name Col. Julio Roberto Alpírez, Major Sosa Orellana, G-2 specialist Simeon Cum Chuta, Major Soto, and all the others Santiago told me about so long ago. I name them all and include General Enríquez—for withholding evidence. When I finish, I look up at the cameras and find myself face-to-face with a circle of terrified journalists. They stare at me agape, as if I have clean lost my mind. Not only have I accused military officials of the highest level but I have also named them out loud in the central plaza. I ask if there are any questions. The journalists shake their heads and hurry out of the square.

I move my things into a small room at the Pan American Hotel, for Jose and I both expect trouble now, and our flight does not leave till tomorrow morning. We doubt that the iron gate at the Spring will be strong enough to withstand the fiery belch of army rage that my statement is likely to produce. Worse yet, trouble is already brewing in the streets over a recent increase in the bus fare, a historically sensitive issue that inevitably provokes wild and bloody riots. Tonight I will stay behind locked doors.

We stop for lunch, Jose for a quick sandwich and I for a glass of water mixed with a miraculous bit of mango juice. Today is day thirty-two and this is my first meal. Kim is anxious to bring me back slowly, for real food at this point could do me bodily harm. To my surprise, I have little interest in drinking more than a few sips, for it tastes sickeningly rich and sugary and feels heavy in the pit of my stomach. My body craves the light safety of plain water, but my mind overrules it. I drink very slowly, forcing the liquid down. Tomorrow I will try still more.

Next we hurry to the embassy for the meeting with Marilyn MacAfee. In the taxicab, I want to curl up and fall asleep, but I fight the urge, knowing that I must carry out this last task. We pass through the front security gate, then bicker with the staff about whether or not Jose may attend the meeting with me. We insist, since he is my lawyer, after all, and they finally give in and take us upstairs. Marilyn greets us at the door, looking pale and very serious. Her staffers trickle into the room with us to take notes and listen to what she says.

When we are all settled, she clears her throat and gets straight to the point. Yesterday she issued a démarche, or formal diplomatic statement, to the president of Guatemala. It stated that according to U.S. sources, Bámaca had been captured alive in 1992, he was slightly but not seriously wounded, his wounds were not life-threatening, and he was a prisoner for a while. There is no information to show that he was alive for long after that.

Jose and I stare at each other, our eyes popping, and we immediately burst into questions. What does it all mean, especially the part about having no information that he was alive for much longer? How long? What kind of concrete information exists? Who did what? MacAfee waves off the questions, looking tense and anxious. That is all she is able to tell us today. We protest loudly, but she will not budge, so finally we rise and head for the door.

Back at the hotel, there is a last good-bye dinner for all of the escorts, for they have grown to be close friends. They try to be merry, but it is difficult, for riots are breaking out in the streets over the fare increases and Maggie, an eighteen-year-old observer, has just seen people shot to death not far from here when the police opened fire on an unarmed crowd. She is back at the Spring with a friend, weeping inconsolably. We eat quietly and break up early, knowing well enough that no one can be out after dark tonight.

Upstairs, I pull off my clothes and collapse on the bed, turning on the television to watch the news. Outside I hear shouts and running feet and occasional gunfire. I flip through the channels and find what I am looking for. Scenes of the university flicker across the screen— the fleeing students, the SWAT patrols, and the crazed men with their cruel clubs and heavy boots. I remember them all too well and watch the scene in horror.

Later I will learn that a young law student, Alioto, died that night. I will remember him coming to the square to visit with the others, a shy and gentle young man. Now as he runs, he is shot through the thigh by the police. His friend tries to drag him to safety, but he is bleeding profusely from a ruptured artery. A medical student calls out to leave him with the other wounded people, that an ambulance is coming. That friend leaves him there and runs, thinking he will be safe and cared for. Instead, the police close off the campus and the ambulance is not allowed to enter. The medical student takes a bullet too, and is dragged away. Then Alioto is surrounded by police and kicked to death as a nearby journalist miraculously manages to photograph the horrible scene. They leave Alioto for dead, covered up by a police shield, but he manages to push it aside. Many hours later he is pronounced dead in a hospital, his skull fractured, his liver ruptured, his lungs collapsed. Later I will see the surviving film frames. I will see Alioto crawl from beneath the shield, surrounded by a pool of his own blood. He looks up at the cameraman and murmurs hoarsely through broken teeth. Please, *compas,* I cannot stand it.

Aftermath
USA, November 1994–March 1995

I THOUGHT I MADE THE RIGHT DECISION, EVERARDO. IT CERTAINLY seemed right at the time. With the U.S. embassy finally admitting that you really were captured alive, that you did not die in combat or run off with some other woman, I was confident that at last something would be done in Washington. I didn't expect this to be easy of course. To the contrary I expected matters to move at a rather slow and sullen pace. But I thought that something would be done, some steps taken to save your life. As it turned out, I was dead wrong.

As soon as I left the square, both governments began a frantic scramble to undo the damage, to clean up the mess, to turn things around and take away what I had won for you. It was clear when the reporters met us in the D.C. airport, telling us that the embassy was refusing to confirm the démarche. Even as I took my first few steps onto U.S. soil, it was clear that I had made a terrible mistake.

But at first I do not realize this, for I am immediately caught up in a frenzy of press interviews and emergency conferences with lawyer friends and human rights groups. Then comes a gaggle of phone negotiations back and forth with the White House to arrange the meeting with Anthony Lake, the President's national security adviser. Who may attend and who may accompany whom is no small matter, and the dates of birth and Social Security numbers for one and all must be sent in well in advance for clearance. I want Jose to accompany me, together with at least one or two other witnesses, but I am told that I must go alone or the meeting will be canceled. None of us like the sound of this. Why no witnesses, no advisers? But in the end we agree, for the White House refuses to budge. What else can we do?

And so I find myself entering the Old Executive Office Building by myself, and being ushered upstairs by Richard Feinberg, a thin and rather nervous man not much older than myself. He takes me to an elegant sitting room decorated in classic Early American style, with brilliantly polished wood tables and clean-lined chairs and sofas. Three men in dark suits introduce themselves and reach to shake my hand. They are Anthony Lake and Leon Fuerth, of the National Security Council and John Shattuck, who is head of the Human Rights Division of the State Department. As we sit down, I study their faces. I know a bit about Shattuck, for he taught previously at Harvard and had a good reputation. Since joining the State Department, though, he seems to have come unmoored, unable to do much about anything at all unless it falls within the party line. I mentally dismiss him as useless and concentrate on the others. Fuerth looks back at me and the expression of forced pleasantry on his face immediately tells me he doesn't much like me or what I've been doing. Lake, on the other hand, looks genuinely human. I decide to opt for his attention. Feinberg sits closely at his side.

After the initial round of courtesies about my health and perseverance, Lake repeats the message of MacAfee's démarche, confirming the official U.S. intelligence reports that Everardo was captured alive by the army in 1992 and that he had not been seriously wounded. He also repeats that there is no evidence to show that he was alive beyond the first few weeks of his captivity. The odd wording bothers me and I press him on this. But Lake assures me that there is no further information and that they have scraped the bottom of the barrel. If something new comes up, he will certainly let me know. I point out that Santiago saw Everardo alive many months after he was captured, and tell him about the other recent reports I received during my hunger strike. Lake shrugs and repeats that they are still looking, and will certainly let me know.

I tell him that I need to see all of the documents that are the basis of the démarche. I need to analyze them for myself and draw my own conclusions. I also need them for the court proceedings in Guatemala. He nods sympathetically and says he will see what he can do. I tell him I hope it won't be necessary to file a Freedom of Information Act request, since these take years to process and are rarely properly answered. If Everardo is alive, he does not have years to wait. If he is dead, I need to know, so that I can bury him and move on with my own life. I need for Mr. Lake to get me the papers himself. He nods and agrees that the Freedom of Information Act procedures are very inadequate, and he says that he has personal experience on that score. Again, he promises to help.

Next, we talk over the case itself and I give him and the others a careful summary of the facts. I include all the reports of the recent sightings of Everardo and explain why he is still of value to the Guatemalan army. Lake nods thoughtfully while the others take copious notes. Encouraged, I begin to discuss the different steps that could be taken. Some kind of strong signal must be sent to the Guatemalan army by the U.S. government. This will help Everardo and it will also help the peace process. If the human rights accord is treated as a joke, there will be no public trust in the rest of the accords. They must be enforced or they will become meaningless. There are many small sanctions that would send precisely such a signal. We could, for example, cut off all military educational funds. Why train people who do not respect the law? We should also immediately cancel plans to send the National Guard to Guatemala for the Fuertes Caminos program. Supposedly, this is a humanitarian project for building roads and schools with the army. But when the army builds roads, it is not for any humanitarian reasons; it is to better reach target populations. If we want to help with medical care or schools, why not send civilian doctors and engineers? Sending military people is a strong signal that we still consider the army to be our buddy. It's time to change the message. People are dying.

We talk over these different approaches for some time and Lake seems quite cordial and interested. Is it just a bedside manner, or will he really try to help me? I don't know, but I guess I will find out soon enough.

Next, I return to Guatemala to check on the investigation proceedings. The Supreme Court has appointed the human rights ombudsman to investigate the matter for thirty days. This quite appalls the ombudsman, who complains that the prosecutor is foisting off his dirty and dangerous work on him. I also need to find a lawyer to help me press for criminal charges against Alpírez and the others. Since the hunger strike it has not been possible to take so much as an hour off, and I am sick and exhausted before I even set foot on the plane. Yet there is not a moment to lose.

Guatemala, predictably, is radioactive-hot as I arrive and the army is breathing fire. The authorities are screeching that I am a subversive and will not be allowed into the country. As I pass through customs I hold my breath, but the immigration officer allows me in. Evidently they have not found a reasonable excuse to keep me out, and they do not want to look bad in the international glare. They are already in enough trouble and, after all, they themselves were protesting throughout my hunger strike that I should proceed through the court system, precisely what I am here to do now. The officer gives me fifteen days instead of the usual ninety. No more of these thirty-two-day uproars will be tolerated. As I settle into the hotel, I am served with legal papers. Asisclo Valladares has filed suit against me and now I am not allowed to leave the country. This makes me smile a bit. I am not allowed to enter, I am not allowed to stay, and I am not allowed to leave. Come on now, guys, make up your minds.

The lawsuit turns out to be quite a farce. Asisclo is literally suing me for threatening to seek criminal charges against the army. He is avoiding defamation claims, since I can defend those by simply showing that my statements were true, a matter the military does not wish to test in any court. Instead, he has filed under a remote civil statute that applies only to false claims of property rights. Local jurists cringe, for there is no way that this applies to my statements, and to my surprise, a quiet woman judge bravely dumps Asisclo out of court.

I also visit with the UN's new human rights monitoring team, MINUGUA. They have finally arrived. A slight, intelligent Brazilian woman named Leila Lima is assigned to my case. We hold a lengthy meeting on their jurisdictional rules, for they cannot review cases from the past, only current violations. Since Everardo disappeared years ago, the army's position is that MINUGUA is barred from investigating. I argue that it is an ongoing violation because Everardo may still be alive in a secret cell somewhere, undergoing torture. They nod and take notes and agree to help. Even the State Department says it will assume for purposes of the investigation that Everardo is still alive. Miracles never cease.

Meanwhile, the ombudsman's office is in a quandary over what on earth to report to the Supreme Court. Their thirty days are up. If they really tell the story right, someone will end up dead. If they don't, they will look ridiculous. The man assigned to write the report is very good, but he is developing a serious nervous tic. I ask for his opinion about the démarche and he is shocked, for he has heard nothing about it. I storm to the embassy and insist that the démarche be turned over to the ombudsman and the courts. After all, whose great idea was this investigation stuff, anyway? A verbal confirmation is finally sent, but by then the thirty days has already passed and it cannot be used. The final report sets out all of the rather obvious facts but concludes that it is "unclear" as to what on earth really happened.

Meanwhile, the army keeps up a blistering campaign against me in the press, claiming that I am trying to destroy the Guatemalan economy, that it is all a hoax, that I actually gained weight during my hunger strike, that I am just after money for my book, that I could never have loved or married that uncultured *indio* Bámaca. News of the démarche is strictly suppressed. Embassy staffers point out that I certainly don't have much support here, and I remind them of the constant flow of letters, poems, and flowers that I continue to receive on the streets. I also give them a copy of a support petition signed by more than twenty of the Guatemalan civil rights groups. They ignore all this and repeat that I have little popular backing. After all, Everardo was a guerrilla.

I return to the United States just a few days before Christmas. As usual, the bright lights and constant commercials drive me to despair. I just can't manage Christmas, Everardo. It reminds me too much of our last days together, of saying good-bye. This year it is worse than ever, for as I arrive in D.C., I hear that the National Guard will be sent as usual to Guatemala. Anthony Lake will not stop them, and General Enríquez is delighted. I listen to this news in silence, for I have grown used to these signs and signals. It is over, Everardo. The doors have closed again. They are going to do exactly nothing for you. The crisis has come and gone and we are both a thing of the past.

I go home and visit my tiny niece and nephew, watching them decorate the tree and unwrap their gifts. I hold them close and gather up as much strength from them as I can, for already my decision is quite clear. I was wrong to end my hunger strike in Guatemala. I should have stuck it out to the very end. Instead, I have charged like a bull at a red cape with nothing behind it. No matter. Now I know what I must do. I will give them a bit more time and then I will return to my hunger strike. I must make good on my word, pick up where I left off. Only this time, I will be sitting in front of the White House.

In January I reluctantly file my Freedom of Information Act requests with all of the different agencies that could conceivably have information about Everardo. It won't work, but I must put the authorities on legal notice, for I no longer trust them to tell me the truth. I am granted expedited or emergency processing, but then there is a long silence. I receive nothing.

Journalists begin to call, warning me about strange statements being made by various U.S. officials. Was Everardo involved in the murder of a U.S. ambassador and two marines? The question startles me, for those killings occurred in 1968, when Everardo was eleven years old and ORPA did not yet exist. Is it true that the URNG kills all of its prisoners of war? I blow my stack and send them the list of released prisoners I long ago gave the embassy, and suggest they contact Bishop Ramazzini for a personal account. Is it true that the guerrillas are carrying out a wave of terror against local officials? I refer them to Amnesty International and the Human Rights Watch and suggest they have a chat with the UN team. The Guatemalan guerrillas have never carried out such actions. They are not the Shining Path or the Khmer Rouge. It is no more true that all guerrilla groups behave alike than that all Hispanics look alike. The last call is the strangest, for a State Department officer has said he is unsure as to whether Everardo and I have even met each other. At this, I throw up my hands. Where did all his letters come from, then? Who on earth would starve to death for a total stranger?

Grimly, I set about planning my resumption of the hunger strike, setting the date for March 12, 1995, the third anniversary of Everardo's capture. I hold meeting after meeting with my despairing friends, all of whom are appalled by the idea of a return to the strike. My body cannot possibly take another round of abuse, they say. I am forty-three years old and the thirty-two days of starvation in Guatemala is far too close. They have a point, for my hair is falling out in handfuls and I am constantly exhausted. And yet I know that I can last for quite a long while again, that I can last because I have to. They groan and point out that there is now a right-wing Congress in power, headed by Newt Gingrich. I tell them that I don't care, that the only alternative is to let Everardo slide through my hands. They worry that the press and the public may not take me seriously this time around. I answer that it doesn't matter, that they will take me seriously if I end up in a coma. The U.S government is going to act only if they think they will be blamed for my death. Nothing else works. This provokes a chorus of protests, but I no longer care. It may work and it may not, but I will never just give up on Everardo. It is not a matter of strategy now; it is a matter of principle.

Robert White, former ambassador to El Salvador, comes forward and offers to help. He will pull what strings he can, see what he can find out. Meanwhile, I should inform the State Department of my plan to return to the hunger strike. With my permission, he gives them a call, and within hours I receive a message that Anne Patterson, a State Department official, wishes to see me at once. As I pack up my papers, I get yet another tip from a friendly journalist. A second démarche has been given, did I know? I am startled, for I have heard nothing. He is surprised too. Did I not know? The embassy has told de León Carpio that perhaps Alpírez and some of the others should be questioned again about the Bámaca case.

As I head for the State Department, I have quite a few misgivings. I have spoken with these people as well as with Marilyn MacAfee since my hunger strike, but all I get is the same eerie and irrational message. Yes, Everardo was taken alive by the army. Yes, he was lightly but not seriously wounded. There is no evidence to show that he is still alive. I pounce on this again and again. Is there any evidence to show that he is dead? A body, a grave, a credible witness or report, anything at all? Are they holding anything back? They shake their heads no. But then again, a very intensive investigation has been carried out and no one has found him alive. I must be realistic, they say.

I find myself in a small office in the State Department, feeling cynical and sitting face-to-face with Anne Patterson, Richard Nuccio, and other staffers. Nuccio and I are hardly on good terms since our meeting in Guatemala, but we both try to pretend that nothing is wrong. Patterson and Nuccio begin by expressing their regrets about my decision to resume the hunger strike, and I explain my reasons. I also ask why I have received none of my files under the Freedom of Information Act, and what new information they have received.

They confirm, a bit uneasily, that the ambassador has suggested that Alpírez and a few others should be reinterviewed, but they will not tell me why or what else was said. Instead, they brush my questions aside and tell me that really, they don't believe Everardo survived more than a few weeks as a prisoner. This makes no sense to me, and I remind them that Santiago saw Everardo alive and undergoing torture several months after his capture. At this Anne Patterson shakes her head and smiles coolly, telling me that the Red Cross interviewed Santiago long ago and did not find him credible. Angry, I point out that so far everything Santiago has ever said has turned out to be exactly right, and that perhaps the Red Cross opinion should be reevaluated. Moreover, the UN and the OAS have found him to be extremely credible. To my surprise, Nuccio nods and adds that he has also met with Santiago and found him to be quite believable.

What is going on here? Why are they trying to force an obviously incorrect story on me? To get me out of their way?

I start up with my questions again. What have they found out about Everardo? Why do they think he did not survive? Have they anything concrete, like a grave or a body or a witness or anything else? They shake their heads. They do not really know what happened to Everardo. Patterson points out that it has been three years and that terrible things happen in Guatemala. One can certainly draw reasonable conclusions. A very intensive investigation has been carried out, terribly expensive, but no evidence has been found to suggest that Everardo is still alive. Once again, I hear their oddly evasive yet carefully chosen wording. Once again, I sense a none-too-discreet nudge to give up on him, to assume that he is dead and leave the past behind me. This I will never do, Everardo, for I made that mistake once before. I assumed you were dead and I lost nearly a year in the fight to save your life. I explain this to Nuccio and Patterson, but they do not react.

Once again, they tell me there is simply no evidence to suggest that he is still alive. I tell them about the different reports I received during the hunger strike. Nuccio becomes angry and says he considers these to be some kind of cruel joke, but when I ask why, he simply stammers and gives no reason. Patterson tells me that the embassy itself has received no such reports and therefore cannot take them into consideration. I point out that few people would trust the embassy enough to go there with information. They both agree that they will officially presume Everardo to be alive for the sake of the investigation.

I have had about enough of the double talk and demand my files. Why have I not yet received anything? I have filed my Freedom of Information Act request and been granted emergency processing. Yet I have received nothing at all. They point out that these matters take time. I remind them that a life is at stake and they nod politely.

Next I urge them to take some kind of action, any action at all, to save Everardo's life. I tell them that it was a big mistake to send down the National Guard, but once again they seem indifferent. Nuccio tells me that sanctions would be impossible because they would hurt

the peace talks. The U.S. would seem nonneutral if they were to punish the army and not the guerrillas. This shocks a hoarse laugh from
my throat. We are already funding one side and not the other. If we
want to be perfectly neutral, when will we be sending a few million
dollars to the URNG? Patterson and Nuccio scowl at this bit of sass.
I add that true neutrality would mean sanctions according to the
crimes committed. The army commits atrocities on a daily basis and
the guerrillas do not. Nuccio answers that proportionality is not an
issue. I ask why not. He becomes openly furious then and tells me
that the guerrillas commit many human rights abuses, too, that they
are involved in a series of kidnappings, and that the State Department
has clear evidence. I tell him he is wrong, and he chides me for my
naïveté. This makes me grind my teeth. Listen, buster, I think to myself, you leave that cushy office of yours and walk every back trail in
Guatemala, you love those people and watch their agony on a daily
basis for ten long years, the way I have, and then you and I can talk
as equals about this country. But not before.

I say nothing, for this meeting has become an Orwellian nightmare.
As I rise to put on my coat, Anne Patterson smiles as if we have just
finished a lovely cup of tea together. Her eyes are like stone walls. I
walk home alone through the snow, mulling over the conversation.
Why the same evasive language over and over again? Why do I have
no papers from them yet? I am frightened, Everardo. Do they know
you are dead? If they do, why won't they tell me? What are they hiding? If they don't know anything, why do they push me so? Because I
am in the way of the peace talks? An inconvenience? My old nightmares return to haunt me and night after night I awaken to the sound
of your screams.

I fly to Guatemala but fare no better there. Marilyn MacAfee gives
the same official story. She has recommended that Alpírez be interviewed again, but she wouldn't really call it a démarche exactly. No,
there is nothing concrete, but really now, she doesn't think Everardo
is still alive, although she doesn't know what happened to him. I become furious and push her to the wall on this, asking if she has anything concrete at all, a body, a grave, a credible report, anything but
her personal opinion. She becomes very quiet then and hesitates, sink-

ing down into her chair. Then she shakes her head and says in a tiny squeak of a voice, "No." Her eyes dart away from me, moving toward the corner of the room. So why then does she think he did not survive? I can almost speak her lines for her by now. There has been a very intensive investigation and there is no evidence that he survived. One must be realistic, but the State Department will assume he is alive for purposes of the investigation. She becomes irritable and says she doesn't know what happened to him, and that I must speak with Washington about all this. She is not a lawyer and this is not fair. Not fair? I want to scream at her. Not fair?

Desperate, I stop by the MINUGUA office to speak with Leila Lima. She reassures me that there is nothing new. She has just been briefed by the embassy and Alpírez is to be questioned again. The ambassador thinks Everardo is dead, but there is no evidence one way or the other. After all, if there was, MINUGUA could not take the case. I leave feeling reassured. Surely the United States would not lie to the United Nations?

Back in Washington, I begin a whirlwind of activities to prepare for the coming strike. Alice and Dianna and Pat are already working around the clock, and my old network rallies. As they pull together and plan to send friends and supporters from across the country to a kickoff event in the park, I find myself very moved indeed. Where would I be without all of these incredible people? I know the answer well enough. I would be dead long ago—or worse yet, forgotten, all my efforts to find Everardo come to nothing.

As March twelfth approaches, my friends fly into a rage. Nuccio has met with several of the human rights groups and one by one the members have been calling to report what he is saying. He closed the door and said he wished to discuss a certain matter off the record, quite strictly off the record. He then proceeded to hem and haw and explain in so many words that my case was bad for the peace talks and that perhaps it was irresponsible to back me. When they tried to pin him to this position, he claimed to be misunderstood. One friend compares it to a wrestling match with Jell-O. Journalists continue to call, asking if the guerrillas are really involved in the latest string of atrocities. My nightmares are growing worse.

Friday, the tenth of March, arrives, and there are two days left before I begin the strike. Richard Feinberg calls abruptly from the National Security Council and asks me to stop by his office. I hardly expect anything good from him, for we have met already this spring and he gives me the same party line as everyone else. He also fails to give me any of my damned papers. Today, though, he seems flushed and hopeful. As I sit down on the plush sofa, he tells me that something has happened: The U.S. government has decided to cancel educational funds to the Guatemalan army, and next year the National Guard will not return to Guatemala. What about this year? I ask. Why can't they be withdrawn now? Why were they sent in the first place? He frowns. This will not be possible. Moreover, he wants to be quite clear about one thing. The U.S. government will not be doing anything further in this regard. There has been much soul searching and this is it. There are no more arrows in the quiver. We'll see about that, I think grimly to myself. He seems to read my mind and shifts nervously about in his chair.

For a moment, I feel rather sorry for him. It is so clear that he has been sent with his marching orders, sent to deal with the witch herself, to be firm with her. He is not very good at being firm, and he looks quite miserable. I ask him where the hell my documents are and he tells me they are still being processed, that I will get them very soon. I point out that my hunger strike starts in two days, and he winces. Then he tells me carefully that it is their "considered assessment" that Everardo is dead. I hear his tone and jump all over him. What do they know? What are they hiding from me? He shakes his head anxiously. I begin to choke with rage and despair. Look, I tell him. This is completely unethical. If you have no evidence that he is dead, you have no right to try to slow me down. I am fighting for his life. Why are you blocking me? If you know he is dead, you have got to tell me. I am forty-three years old and the last hunger strike is far too recent. I am risking kidney failure, blindness, cardiac arrest. If you know he is dead, you must tell me. But Feinberg tells me nothing but that I will receive my papers soon.

As I leave the office, I run into Bob White on the streets. He has traveled to Guatemala for me but could learn nothing more. Now he has just had a terrific fight with Richard Nuccio and he is boiling mad. He hands me a copy of Marilyn MacAfee's speech in Guatemala about the cutoff of military educational funds. It is long and flowery and talks much about impunity and the many other cases. About mine, there is but one line: "and that is why questions continue to swirl about the Bámaca case. What happened there?" I sigh with relief. At least there is still an open question as to whether or not he is still alive. Or is there?

A few days later, MINUGUA's first report comes in on the human rights situation in Guatemala. I read it anxiously. Could I possibly have been wrong about the kidnappings? Is something going on that I didn't know about? I scan the voluminous pages quickly. There is an endless list of abuses by the security forces, kidnappings, torture, murder, intimidations of court officials. The guerrillas are cited for property damages. Killings and kidnappings and terror? None at all. I breathe a sigh of relief. We are ready to roll, Everardo. We are ready to roll.

Torricelli
Washington, March 1995

MARCH TWELFTH, EVERARDO—IT FEELS LIKE DOOMSDAY TO ME. I get out of bed slowly, for even now I am exhausted from all the last-minute preparations. The hunger strike hasn't even started yet, though it will in a few hours. Now I must iron a clean shirt, pull some thoughts together for the rally later on, and gulp down some cold cereal. A huge mug of steaming black coffee finishes off my nerves, and I am grateful when my gentle friends at the house form a circle around me and pray for us both. As always, they pray for you and for me simultaneously, Everardo, for they have always understood that we are a package deal and that my life goes with yours.

I stop at the Guatemalan Human Rights Commission and find Alice and Pat and Dianna already hard at work, answering what seems to be a thousand telephone calls, making copies of our leaflets, and arranging for rides, meetings, and places for out-of-town supporters to stay. Friends are coming in from all over the Eastern Seaboard to attend the rally today, and they will stay on to visit congressional offices and demand help and information. My parents and sister arrive. More than forty longtime friends, many of them Guatemalan, have driven in from Chicago and are sleeping on floors across the city. Nineth is here from Guatemala, together with Amílcar Mendez, a young survivor of the Río Negro massacre, and a law student who was with Alioto on that terrible night. March twelfth is doomsday for so many of us, Everardo. It is painfully close to the anniversary of the massacre, and it is not far from Holy Week, when Nineth lost her dearest friend, Rosario, to the death squads. It is also close, so close to the Huelga de Dolores, a student political spoof that always leaves someone battered and dead in the streets, yet continues year after year in defiance. I sit down and drink more coffee, talking with the Guatemalans and suddenly feeling calmer. We are all here as a team, and we are together until the end.

By early afternoon, all is ready at last and we head off together toward the park. As I walk out the door I try to steel myself, for I know the weeks ahead will not be easy. I am not physically strong enough to do this, for the other strike ended only four months ago and my body is still raw. Congress has undergone a right-wing takeover, Jesse Helms and Newt Gingrich taking the lead. Listening to the long and rather rabid speeches on the radio, my heart sinks, for there seems to be no awareness at all that the Berlin Wall has fallen or that the Soviet Union no longer exists. This certainly bodes ill for us, Everardo, but no matter. They can't take you from me without the battle of their lives.

The sun comes out and the rally goes without a hitch, lifting my spirits tremendously. My mother has drawn a sketch of Everardo based on the photos and my own description of him, and the end result is uncanny. Dianna has it printed onto bright yellow T-shirts, and the crowd spontaneously dons them now to show support, turning the park into a sea of brilliant yellow. The Salvadoran community backs us, too, and a Salvadoran band strikes up the free-spirited rhythmic sounds of Central America. Soon people begin to dance and clap, giving us quite rightly a mood of hope and life, a demand for hope and life.

Next the talks begin, Nineth and Amílcar speaking so passionately of Guatemala and their long-dead friends and loved ones that they bring tears to my eyes, yet also give me strength. As I watch them, I marvel for the hundredth time at their ability to survive, to remain human, to fight on. I remember Nineth as she was ten years ago, so young and agonized, weeping convulsively over Rosario and the baby, living in terror of the cars with the black glass windows. I listen to Amílcar and remember his lonely walks through the cornfields to find, again and again, the battered bodies of his friends and colleagues. Now they are here to speak for us all.

After Amílcar comes the young villager from Río Negro. Dianna Ortiz translates for him, and as he speaks, they both turn pale and their eyes fill with tears. He tells how his mother and father were taken away and murdered long ago, leaving him alone with his brothers and sisters, the neighbors struggling to keep them alive. He was eleven years old then. A few months later, the army came with the civil patrollers from another village and they forced all the women and children to a remote mountain slope, promising that they would soon return home. Instead, they murdered the women one by one while the children were forced to lie facedown in the cold mud. The boy turned to one side and saw them garroting an old grandmother a few inches from his eyes.

Later he had a chance to run and did so, only to stumble across some soldiers raping one of the younger women. Confused and shocked, he crawled back to the group, where the men were now smashing the smaller children's heads against the rocks, then heaving them onto bloodied piles of bodies. As his own turn approached, a civil patroller took him aside, saying that he would take him home as a servant for his wife. The boy tried to bring his baby brother with them, but the man said no, there was no time to care for the smaller ones. The boy pleaded, but the man slipped a noose around the little one's neck and hurled him against a boulder. Then he took the older child home with him and kept him as a near slave for many years, abusing and beating him, until a relative was finally able to obtain his freedom. More than eighty people died that day, and the army is still threatening the survivors.

By the end of the afternoon we are throwing our arms about one another and singing the protest song of Central and South America, "We Are Still Singing, We Are Still Hoping," and "All I Ask of God Is Strength." The music gives me the final sense of peace that I need now, for the words are inexpressibly sad yet also fiercely defiant. As the rally finally breaks up, I walk across the park and sit down cross-legged in front of the White House. Tomorrow I will have my banners and pamphlets and books to read. Today I have only your photograph, Everardo, but that is quite enough. I need nothing more.

I return day after day to my small post there, dragging a large bottle of water with me and gulping down a tall glass of the hated Pedialyte every morning. Mentally I am serene and clear enough, for the difficult decisions are long since behind me. My outraged body is another story altogether, and it begins to disintegrate with terrifying speed. Within four days my upper lip begins to stiffen, imperceptible to the others, but a grim warning for me. By the end of the week my heart pounds when I stand, my veins sink, my blood pressure is low, and I feel that I could not possibly walk a city block. I do, though. I speak all day long with the journalists and visitors who come by and I spend several hours a day hiking up and down the halls of Congress, begging for help. Soon my head is reeling and I am cold even in the sun. I know I will never make it for twenty days, Everardo. I am trying, but I can't hang on.

My friends are already frantically at work, but the administration refuses to budge any further. They urge me to find a graceful way out, to bring this to a clean end. After all, I have made my point quite clearly. I should write the closing chapter of this play while I still can. But I have already chosen the closing chapter. For me, it will be the dizzying spread of those sparkling black stars before my eyes, a profound loss of consciousness that will sweep me off to some silent place where I can rest at last. Perhaps I will die, or perhaps I will awaken in a hospital with permanent injuries. I no longer care at all. In fact I almost yearn for my stubborn body to break down and finally set me free. I so long for this to be over.

Congress is paying close attention and they do not like what they are seeing. I receive a great deal of sympathy and respect during my visits to the various offices, as well as a lot of advice. Calls begin to fly back and forth between the different branches of the government and eyebrows are beginning to rise. Nobody likes this and they want something done, and fast. They are going to look into matters right away. I can feel things heating up and it gives me hope, but I also know that I cannot hang on much longer and I am frightened. I drink more Pedialyte solution, but it does not help and by the end of the week I have lost more than ten pounds—a sure sign of trouble.

On the tenth day I receive a call from Scott Wilson, the kindly aide in Congressman Torricelli's office. He has already told me that Torricelli is very upset about the case and that he wants to speak with me in person. Now he says that I should come in immediately. Would tomorrow morning be all right? I tell him yes, then spend the rest of the afternoon wondering what we will be discussing. There has been talk of introducing a human rights bill on Guatemala. Perhaps he would like my insights on this. Who knows? I spend a long time in a hot bath that night, trying to bring my body temperature back to normal. I have got to hang on. I have got to hang on.

The next morning I feel as if I am floating away, but I pull on my clothes and pile some of my fact summaries and documents into a folder. Perhaps he will want some of these. I place Everardo's photograph on the top, stopping to look at his face, for even now those dark and ancient eyes hold me so. Then I pull the flap closed and hurry outside to find a taxi heading downtown.

In Torricelli's office the air is rather electric and I know immediately that something is about to happen, although I cannot imagine what. The wheels of my mind are too exhausted to turn very quickly, so I sit down on the sofa and wait for someone to fill me in. Scott arrives, and then an aide named Jamey, and then the congressman himself. Torricelli is young and brisk with bright dark eyes and a feisty lift to his chin. He sits down across from me and inquires about my health, and then gets straight to the point. He has been looking into my case and he would first of all like to know just exactly what the U.S. officials have been telling me.

I sit up straight and give him a summary, explaining how the initial story was that they had mentioned it and mentioned it to the army, but that the army had denied taking Everardo prisoner and after all what else could they do? He flushes red as I say this, and I continue. After thirty-two days on my hunger strike in Guatemala, *60 Minutes* reported that the State Department had CIA confirmation that he had indeed been captured alive. After that came the démarche, the formal embassy statement that there was intelligence information that Everardo had been taken prisoner. Now everyone insists that there is no evidence that he is still alive. When I ask if there is any real evidence that he is dead, they say no. Yet they pressure me so to assume he is. I have asked again and again what information they have, but they will tell me nothing and I have received no papers. They just repeat that it has been three years and I should be more realistic.

I start to speak again, but Torricelli is openly angry now. He cuts me off in midsentence and says that he has received information from more than one confidential source and that he is now going to share it with me. Everardo was indeed captured by the army and he was killed in 1992, upon orders of Col. Julio Roberto Alpírez. Alpírez was a CIA asset, or paid informant, and he was also implicated in the death of Michael DeVine, an innkeeper and U.S. citizen who was murdered by the army in 1990.

Torricelli is still speaking. I know this because I can see his lips moving, and yet I hear nothing at all. I cannot hear his voice because my ears are filled with the terrible roar of a bullet as it smashes through flesh and bone—your flesh and bone, Everardo—and stops your fierce, clean heart forever. It echoes through my own mind just as it did years ago in Mexico when I sat listening to Emilio. Now I hear it again, that mortal roar of a bullet as it takes you from me and sets you free to roam the wild volcanoes for all eternity.

I am dead, Everardo. I am dead.

End of the Road
United States, 1996

AND SO, EVERARDO, YOU ARE DEAD BUT FREE FOREVER AND I AM left behind here all alone. In a few short months it will be Christmas season yet again, with all of its bright lights and glitter, and once again I must come face-to-face with the fact that you are never coming home. I will face it, Everardo, just as I have everything else, willing or not. I have long since learned that there is no other way to deal with this quirky life. Soon it will be five years since we last sat together on our small sofa in Mexico City, holding hands and writing names on musical Christmas cards and trying to figure out some sort of joined future for ourselves. We knew only too well what the odds were of ever living happily ever after, of your even living much longer at all. But we gave it our best, and what we had together, I will never forget. You, Everardo, I will never forget.

Bit by bit, I am piecing together what happened. The papers from the CIA and the Defense Department and the embassy and the President's investigation have arrived in folders and crates and hand-delivered envelopes, some voluntarily, some because of the public uproar, and still others because I took the CIA to court. Some of the papers are worthless—copies of the hundreds of desperate letters from my friends demanding that something be done, and the chilly official form letters sent in reply. Others are evasive or vague or have so many paragraphs blacked out, they are barely intelligible. But some, Everardo, are crystal clear with their grim information.

You suffered, Everardo. That is almost unbearably clear. The soldiers took you alive at the Río Ixcucua and somehow dragged you to the Santa Ana Berlín base, where they joyfully confirmed your identity. For seventeen long years they had hunted you with all their murderous fury, and now they had you in their hands at last. They gave you no swift death. Instead they took a poor soldier named Valentin to the riverbed and killed him there, then told the press they had found your body. When I showed up with the others to open the grave, they sent Asisclo Valladares to drive us out and sent the judge so many death threats that for a while they felt safe from any further interference. And then they turned on you.

At first they wanted you alive, but broken. They chained you to a bed and screamed and threatened and sent the other prisoners in to tell you that it was all over, that it was better to talk and be done with it. You never spoke. Santiago saw you sitting there on your cot, staring back at them with your fiery old-man's eyes, answering them with total silence. For a while they tried a good cop/bad cop routine, comically thinking they could trick you into a false trust and that you would speak at last out of loneliness. Colonel Alpírez has a former mistress, now in hiding, who says that he was in charge of "befriending" you, and that you were courteous and kind and gave him a cassette of music but never a word of information. Worse yet, to their way of thinking, you sometimes fooled them, telling them what they wanted to hear, and what the CIA wanted to hear. You said the food came from Mexico and the guns came from Communist Cuba. I laughed through my tears when I read that. You knew what they wanted to hear and it bought you some time.

When they couldn't trick you they turned to their usual methods of force. They tortured you, though at first they did it carefully. Santiago saw you bound to a table, your entire body swollen several times its normal size. The government files refer to more than one physician who administered drugs to "facilitate" your interrogation. The files also tell about so much else. They tell of the pits at the army base near Retalhuleu, filled with cold water, where prisoners were kept as part of their torture. To keep from drowning, they had to hang on to the cagelike bars above their heads. The papers tell of the well in the southwest where your friends were thrown after they were tortured and shot without trial. They tell of other *compas* tossed from helicopters into the ocean. They tell more than I want to know about.

And you, Everardo, you knew they were going after your very mind, for it contained all the information that they could ever hope for. If they could capture your mind, they could crush the URNG for good. You knew this too, and even in your drugged state, you never gave anyone away. Again and again you tried to escape, but they always caught you and dragged you back. Were you trying to force them to shoot you? Were you hoping for a quick bullet to free you from their hands? It didn't work. They placed you in a full body cast, an image that even now drives me to madness. That way they could continue with you at their convenience.

Still you never gave them what they wanted. Over and over again you gave bad information, sending them out on wild-goose chases for old weapons caches that were useless. They began to drag you with them as a guide, but even then you led them astray. There are several reports that you pulled them into a dangerous ambush that left the platoon leader seriously wounded. That sounds like your silent, thinking defiance, Everardo. That sounds just like you. Were you still searching for that one clean bullet to set you free at last? I think so. Knowing you, I think so.

Where and when and how you died, I still don't know for certain. I think they killed you after the ambush. I think you died in the fall of 1992. I think you are buried in Las Cabañas, the remote base that lies between Santa Ana Berlín and San Marcos. I think so, but I do not know for sure. There are other reports that say you were tossed from a helicopter, or perhaps thrown into the volcano, or maybe burned to ashes and scattered across a distant sugarcane field. Someday I will know the full truth. Someday. That much I have promised us both.

When we first met you thought I was a CIA agent, Everardo. This made me laugh, and it also rankled a bit. But your fears were all too reasonable. I see from the files that the CIA knew you were a prisoner almost as soon as you were captured. Within six days of the skirmish at the Río Ixcucua, they were notifying the White House as well as the State Department and several other agencies that you had been caught, that you were a very important prisoner, and that the army would be falsifying your death to better take advantage of your situation. They knew what would become of you. They never called the Red Cross and they never called the United Nations. So much for the Geneva Convention. They knew you were in the hands of their man Alpírez and they paid him $44,000 in July, the same month Santiago saw him bending over your bound, deformed body in the San Marcos infirmary. Funny, the coincidence. As it turns out, more than one of the officers in charge of your torture and murder were paid CIA "assets." The reports of your death began to come in as early as 1993. They knew all along, Everardo. They knew everything all along. Yet when I showed up begging for help, nobody ever said a word about you. Not until Mike Wallace blew the roof off with his *60 Minutes* program. Not until I was near physical collapse. Even then, it took another year and a half, plus a federal lawsuit, to get even these bits and pieces of information from them.

Throughout all of your ordeal you never spoke, Everardo. You knew every safe house, every arsenal, every contact, every code. You knew the military strategy for the entire war. You could have drawn a map to the private homes of the entire *comandancia* in Mexico City. Yet nothing under your command ever went down. The security rules required Gaspar to move the very night you vanished, for it is understood all too well that no one can hold out for long against the army's well-trained butchers. But he refused to move, Everardo; he refused to move. He knew you as no one else did, and he stayed at home, grieving, to show you honor.

As for me, I have tried to honor you by demanding the truth, by insisting that you matter. However much those bits and pieces of grim information cut me to the bone, I want them, each and every one of them, because you matter. I will not let them toss you aside into the shadows as if you were a mere detail of forgotten history. I will find out the truth about you, and all of it.

Torricelli's announcement set off a political firestorm that left both Washington, D.C., and Guatemala looking like the last days of Pompeii. President Clinton demanded an investigation, the Senate Intelligence Committee ordered hearings, and the press went wild, together with the U.S. public. General Enríquez fell into a rage and suggested that Torricelli be sued for slander. The military roared that I was a subversive and should be arrested at once should I try to return. U.S. officials stammered that they had told me all along that Everardo was dead but that I had been psychologically unable to accept this.

Meanwhile the repression rages on in Guatemala, Everardo. I have tried again and again to open the mass graveyard at Las Cabañas. At first I tried through the prosecutor's office, but Dr. Arango was shot at and placed under twenty-four-hour-a-day death threats, together with his young son, until he finally gave up and resigned. The new prosecutor has moved nothing at all, and she sits terrified and alone in her office. I carried out a vigil for all of you who may lie buried out there in that ragged field behind the base, and the army sent in two busloads of military men to mob me. They were seen changing into civilian clothes by the locals and identified by the human rights representative who came rushing to help. They stayed for a long time out there, surrounding me and screaming that I could never have loved you, that you were dark-skinned and ugly, with thick lips, that I would never have contaminated my blue blood with the likes of you, that you do not deserve a proper burial. As I listened I stayed silent, Everardo, for I knew they were there to provoke a fight and to kill one of the students sitting next to me. I said nothing, but as I listened, I realized I was fully capable of murdering another human being. I have it in me to use a gun or a knife. You would not like that change in me, I know, but it is there now, perhaps forever.

There are the regular death threats always, Everardo, and the threats to have me arrested, to sue me, to have me barred from the country. So far they have not dared lay hands on me, although perhaps someday they will. They are still not sure whether I am more trouble alive or martyred. After my testimony to the Senate Intelligence Committee, the FBI visited to tell me the military leadership was planning to hire a hit man to kill me. Alice's metal security door was pulled off its hinges and left in the street one night, though nothing but the office answering machine was stolen. Jose Pertierra's car was firebombed in the driveway at his home in Washington, D.C., at five in the morning. Twenty-four hours later, the Assisi house where I live was shot at. In the press, the public officials rant and rail against me.

Yet despite it all the people in the streets, your people, Everardo, continue to ignore the risks and rush to my side, giving me small gifts, embracing me and telling me of new babies named in my honor. They treat me like a rather scandalous version of Robin Hood and laugh at my outrageous antics, but they also give me their unstinting love. They love me for bashing the monster in the Politécnica. My doctor congratulates me as he writes out a prescription, the customs man at the airport welcomes me "home" and tells me I am loved, the soccer team members ask for my autograph, and the village women smile and hand me their babies. Someday I will go home for good, Everardo, back to the jungles, or perhaps to the mountains near your hometown. Someday I will teach reading and writing there and grow old with the people who remind me so much of you. But not yet. It is early yet.

The U.S. government says things will change. They will begin to screen their assets for human rights violations. They admit the reports to Congress were deceptive with regard to the real situation in Guatemala. They admit they were perhaps less than forthcoming in sharing information with family members. All this will change. But they will not take any responsibility for any specific cases, such as your death or Dianna Oritz's torture. We are lurching forward out of the Cold War, two steps forward, one step back.

But for you and for me, Everardo, it is all too late. You are dead and I am mutilated. There are days when it all catches up with me and I wish that I were dead too, dead and safe from all this uproar and struggle. I am tired, Everardo, so very tired, and I am not sure what is left to live for. Yet I hang on to the tattered remains of my life with grim and total obstinacy. The others will never have the satisfaction of hearing me surrender, of watching me break, of celebrating my death. I will hunt your killers down and place them in their prison cells, Everardo, or stand upon their tombs. I will find your body yet and bury you with honor in some green and quiet space. I will have the truth about you, all of it. I will fight to stay alive because there is work yet to be done.

And yet the softer side of me that you once knew is gone, or at least shocked into numbness. That part of me that could be young, a woman in love, that could think to marry and raise children and keep a family together, that part of me is burned to ashes. They tell me that time heals all wounds, and I hope that this is true, but I do not think so. Even after all these years, when someone says the word *love,* I can only see your face. The pain never goes away, Everardo. It never goes away.

Despite it all, though, there is something still alive deep within me. I can still laugh and swing a baby in the air and thrill to the perfect chords of Mozart or Handel. I am still moved by the wild greenery of your volcano when I see it far off in the distance. When your own people, the Mayans, crowd around me with their perfect tilting eyes and rich, easy laughter, I still feel the old fierce love for them that has been there since the very beginning. And somewhere in my innermost core, there is a wild and fiery will to resist, Everardo, to join hands with the other survivors and finish what you began. You knew that it would be this way; you foresaw it all and you prepared me well. Now it is your own pure will that burns within me, impossible to extinguish or deflect. Like the Hiroshima victim laser-etched forever into the marble steps where he stood so long ago, you have left your imprint upon my very soul.

And so I live on, Everardo. I have learned not to whirl about in the street when I sense you just there, at my shoulder, only a step behind. I have learned not to rush hopefully after strangers who seem, in the shadows, to look a bit like you. I no longer reach out in my dreams at night in the hopes that you are there in the darkness, home at last. I understand that you are dead. I have also learned that you will be with me forever. It is enough for me now. Stay with me, Everardo, and I will stand up straight and carry on.

POSTSCRIPT

NOW WHAT? THIS IS PERHAPS THE QUESTION I AM MOST COMMONLY asked by friends, family, and well-wishers. The answer is not simple. There is nothing we can do to bring Everardo or the other 200,000 Guatemalans back to life or ease their suffering. What's done is done. But we can and must take steps to protect the next generation, to guarantee much-needed reforms both in Guatemala and the United States. As with so many others around the world, we are left with the simple words *never again.*

Unfortunately, this is easier said than done. Yet it is possible if we fight for it. I returned to the United Nations Human Rights Commission in Geneva, Switzerland, in March 1996 with the CIA files under my arm. I denounced the Guatemalan army for kidnapping, torture, murder, and obstruction of justice. I also denounced the United States government for routinely paying for information that everyone well knew was being extracted through the cruelest of tortures, thus condoning and abetting serious criminal activities as well as violations of international treaties such as the Geneva Convention. I also denounced their failure to inform families, whether U.S. or Guatemalan, of the fates of their vanished loved ones. This leaves the relatives in permanent agony, and it shelters the military from any legal consequences for their crimes. In short, we have been obstructing justice, strengthening an official impunity that has led to hundreds of thousands of abuses, and if unchecked, will lead to hundreds of thousands more. There are enough dead in Guatemala.

The Inter-American Commission of the OAS has finished its investigation of the case. After Jose Pertierra's car was fire-bombed in Washington, they issued strong protective orders to the Guatemalan government, requiring protection of myself and all of my attorneys, especially my Guatemalan lawyers. Any day now, they will also announce whether or not they will take the rare step of sending my case to the Inter-American Court in Costa Rica for a full international trial of the Guatemalan army, a notion that has the military in hysterics.

After Congressman Torricelli's declarations, the Guatemalan government had little choice but to open a criminal investigation against Alpírez and the other high-level officers implicated in the case. Under Guatemalan law, the case is before a military court with military judges, and the outcome is more than predictable. It was first suggested that Alpírez should sue Torricelli for slander. Next, the charges were thrown out of court for "insufficient evidence"—before Santiago or I was ever even interviewed. There was much public uproar, and finally Dr. Arango was made special prosecutor. He managed to have the charges reinstated and then traveled to Washington, D.C., to take Santiago's utterly flawless testimony. He also interviewed a G-2 deserter who identified the body in the Retalhuleu grave as that of his best friend, a young soldier murdered and left on the riverbanks as a decoy. Next, Arango attempted to open the graves under the Las Cabañas military base, where Everardo is reportedly buried. Despite his authority and numerous court orders, we were all turned away again and again by the army. Arango was placed under constant threats together with his son, shot at, and finally driven out of office. A close friend on a similar case was shot and killed. His successor knows better than to push this case, and it remains in semiparalysis. The military court, meanwhile, has entered a decree that Everardo is indeed buried in Retalhuleu, just as the army always claimed.

Under Guatemalan law, I can act as a virtual equivalent of special prosecutor because I am Everardo's wife. Under international law, as well as U.S. and Guatemalan law, if my marriage was valid in Texas, it is automatically valid in Guatemala. The army's first step was to pay two Houston lawyers to file suit against me to try to have my marriage declared invalid, even though neither one had ever met me or Everardo, and even though they had no legal interests at stake. When that failed, my old friend Asisclo Valladares systematically began to block the registration of my marriage in the Guatemalan courts, using preposterous legal arguments, and often simple slander and fabrication. As I write, we are now before the Supreme Court on the matter.

Intriguingly, the CIA files answer many questions about Asisclo's conduct. A State Department memo reports Ramiro de León Carpio's initial comments on the failed exhumation of 1992. He states that Asisclo apparently arrived by helicopter, and that the real reason for calling off the exhumation was pressure by the army, the legal technicalities being just an excuse. Another document notes a conversation between the Guatemalan attorney general and Alpírez just after the Torricelli declarations. Alpírez had just testified to the prosecutor that he knew nothing of Bámaca, but then he told Asisclo of Bámaca's secret detention in Santa Ana Berlín, how Bámaca led a patrol into an ambush, and how they then decided to have him killed. Asisclo never reported any of this to the proper authorities, thus leaving himself open to criminal charges. In public, he has stated that he knows nothing about this document.

The files also show that Ramiro de León Carpio was on the verge of publicly denouncing Bámaca's murder by the army at last. The fact that he never dared to do so shows all too well how iron a grip the army still has on the Guatemalan presidencies.

The United Nations team, or MINUGUA, has been doing an excellent job of debunking army and U.S. mythology about the war. Gone are the days when the military leadership can blithely claim that a given massacre was carried out by the guerrillas, or stage false atrocities to be blamed on the left. Gone are the days of claiming that both sides carry out terrible abuses and are equally to blame. The U.N. investigates thoroughly and reports to the international community. They find that the security forces have a virtual monopoly on official acts of terror against civilians, including threats, rape, torture, kidnapping, and murder. The same goes for intimidation and reprisals against public officials, especially judges and court staffers. The security forces carry out all of these abuses with alarming regularity and predictability. URNG violations are quite rare. It is quite a simple matter, yet so key. We cannot create a better future until history is set straight.

MINUGUA, together with all of the other human rights organizations, has also repeatedly decried the attacks on the judicial system and the blatant obstruction of justice by the military. Judges and lawyers have been threatened and frequently killed, evidence continues to vanish, and court officials are terrorized. To date, not one high-level military officer has been sentenced for any of the crimes that have been committed. So much for the U.S. embassy's position that the "civilian institutions are coming along beautifully." Today that phrase is rarely heard indeed.

Meanwhile, I have filed suit against the CIA to force them to release documents to me under the Freedom of Information Act. I have also filed a civil rights suit against members of the CIA, State Department, and National Security Council. The files show that the CIA reported to the White House and State Department that Everardo was a secret prisoner as of the very first week of his capture. They also predicted that his death would be faked in order to take advantage of his information. No international human rights organization was notified, not even the Red Cross or the United Nations. Everardo was then in the hands of more than one CIA asset, including Alpírez. Both Sosa Orellana and Alpírez were School of the Americas graduates. In July of 1992, Santiago saw Alpírez bending over Everardo's torture table. That same month, Alpírez received $44,000 from the CIA. I say the CIA was paying for information they knew was being wrung from Everardo through torture and eventually murder. They say the money was for something else. My answer? Tell it to the judge.

The State Department and other officials don't have much to say as to why they waited until I was half-dead on my hunger strike and Mike Wallace had already exposed them on international television screens before they mentioned their internal memos about Everardo's captivity. By then, I had gone through the grisly exhumation process, risked having my head blown off for some time, carried out my first strike in front of the Politécnica and was thirty-two days into my hunger strike in front of the National Palace. Why didn't the démarche come a little sooner? I was once told that they didn't realize that the "Everardo" of the 1992 memo was in fact Efraín Bámaca. Yet their internal memos from March 1993, when I first made contact, refer to both names. The Intelligence Oversight Board states that no attempt was made to find any information until the 60 Minutes broadcast.

Even then, I was told only half the truth. I was told he was indeed taken prisoner, but the numerous and highly concrete reports of his death were never revealed to me until Mr. Torricelli stepped forward. A memo from the Defense Intelligence Agency, dated September 1993, states that Bámaca was not killed in combat, but was captured, interrogated many times, and then killed. In September 1993, I was sitting in front of the Politécnica on my first strike. On its face, the memo says that it was disseminated to the secretary of state and the U.S. embassy. I am told now that maybe it wasn't properly sent. There are numerous other reports of Everardo's death, as well. I am told that perhaps someone failed to enter both of Everardo's names in the computer, or that they spelled Everardo wrong and that this caused some delays. Yet again, their own internal memos as of 1993 show both names spelled correctly. Worse yet, a memo between staffers just after my long hunger strike shows a grim intent. The first memo worriedly reports that Mike Wallace has claimed that they know that Bámaca is dead and have failed to inform me. He wants to know what they know and how long they have known it. The reply memo states, "Good brief . . . I mean good grief! I spoke quickly about AFW re this, recommending that we stick to the guidance: 1) We do not know whether Bámaca is dead or alive; 2) We have no evidence that he was alive any more time than a few weeks after his capture; and 3) We have always acted on the assumption that he could be alive . . ."

Evidently, the CIA relationship with Alpírez and others in this case was simply too embarrassing. It seemed easier to pressure me to assume that Everardo was dead than to tell me the truth. Meanwhile, the State Department officials themselves continue to claim that they informed me of everything quite clearly. Once again, I say, Tell it to the judge.

The Intelligence Oversight Board has disclosed more files to other members of Coalition Missing members. We all have bits and pieces now of the truth, but we are missing the most crucial parts. Sister Dianna Ortiz still has no answers to her own horrifying experience.

As for the Guatemalans, they have nothing. Why don't they count? Because they are not white? Perhaps our most crucial goal as U.S. citizens must be to demand the declassification of all U.S. files on Guatemalan human rights cases. The Guatemalan people have the right to know what became of their family members. The Guatemalan justice system must receive all of the relevant information in order to bring an end to the official impunity that has caused so many brutal deaths. Only when impunity ends will a true peace be possible. Perhaps equally important, we as United States citizens need this information ourselves. We need to learn the truth about the role our own government has played in Guatemala. If we permit a secret branch of the government to exist, then we have relinquished our right to true democracy. We must insist on the truth and the whole truth and nothing but the truth in order to set our own house straight, to insist that our government answer to us.

To quote a favorite phrase of the CIA's, "The truth shall set ye free."

Note of Thanks to Mr. Richard Nuccio

Nearly two years have passed since my meeting with Representative Robert Torricelli. As this book goes to press, I learn that it was Richard Nuccio who, after months of soul searching, finally came forward and told Representative Torricelli the truth about Everardo. This act of courage and honesty has not gone unpunished by U.S. officials. Mr. Nuccio has been stripped of his security clearance and is being hounded from office. I can only say, Richard Nuccio, that you did the right thing and that it probably saved my life. You have my respect and thanks.

————————

All proceeds from this book support the efforts of the Everardo Foundation, a non-profit organization established in memory of Comandante Everardo. The Foundation is devoted to the promotion of human rights, rural health and education, racial equality, and the preservation of Mayan culture in Guatemala. Representatives may be contacted at 1010 Vermont Ave. N.W. #620, Washington D.C. 20005.

9 780446 520362